DICK HYMAN: PIANO PRO

A Browser's Miscellany On Music And Musicians

TABLE OF CONTENTS

Part III
HERE'S HOW! . . .

Part IV
ORIGINALS AND ARRANGEMENTS . . .

Two Little Stride Arrangements

From The Movies

FOREWORD

Dick Hyman is truly one of a kind. Over the years he has played jazz in every conceivable setting; has been a part of the pop studio world; has written scores for movies, several for Woody Allen; and has established himself as arguably the most versatile pianist now active, and a superb organist to boot.

I have been privileged to know him virtually throughout his career. I remember first hearing him at Wells Music Bar in Harlem, duetting with organist Charles Stewart — his first professional job. During the 1950s we worked together on many projects, on some of which he sublimated my compositions with his brilliant arrangements. By the 1960s I had moved to California, but we have never lost touch. Meanwhile he has shown another aspect of his multiple talents, as a writer whose essays in Keyboard Magazine reflected his encyclopedic knowledge of music, his ability to tell an anecdote with a wry sense of humor.

Whether or not you can read music, this book will be a delight if only for the recollections, the analyses, the mirror it holds up to Richard Roven Hyman as an extraordinary and admirable human being.

Leonard Feather

PREFACE

Most of the material herein appeared in a different form in *Keyboard* in separate issues of the 1980s. Much has been revised and added. The author thanks Jim Aikin of that magazine for his cooperation. *Thinking About Art Tatum* will be included in a new, as yet untitled book on Tatum edited by Arnold Laubich, Felicity Howlett, and Barry Kornfeld, and the author thanks them as well. Various original music co-published with WB Music, Polychrome Music, Next Decade Entertainment, Kendor Music, and Stone Ear Music appears, and I am grateful for their permission respectively. Thanks also to Jean Guarnieri and to Mort Goode for their generosity.

Going over one's earlier thoughts is a humbling exercise in self-discovery: what once seemed adequate expression cries out for amplification, correction, and adjustment. Music has changed, technology has altered the way we do things, colleagues have passed on, one's writing skills demand a bit more polished prose now, and before you realize what you've gotten yourself into, you are writing a new book.

The subtext remains intact, though: that music is a fascinating thing; that making a living in music demands perseverance, accommodation, ingenuity, a sense of humor, open-mindedness, and practical ways of dealing with creativity and inspiration. No one person's career can be a perfect model for others, nor is this book more than incidentally autobiographical. But perhaps some of the experiences will resonate with those of the reader. The more instructional articles are written for various levels of development; a reader can discover for himself or herself what is appropriate. A lot of printed music has been added to illustrate various matters, and many original pieces receive their first publication.

Piano Pro may be read from the piano rack as easily as in a comfortable chair, but you don't have to play this book in order to get into it. If you do, however, the additional dimension may be instructive, entertaining, or both.

The author expresses his sincere appreciation to Stuart Isacoff, who was confident that there was a book here, and to Julia Peña, whose meticulous editing brought it to completion. Thanks also to Bobbe Stultz and Anita Tumminelli for the elegant design and graphics. Finally, a deep bow to Ed Shanaphy, the publisher, a most supportive friend and colleague.

Dick Hyman

PART I

AS I RECALL...

*"By 1948,
52nd Street
had passed its
golden age..."*

STRANGE GIGS AND WEIRD SCENES

By 1948, 52nd Street had passed its golden age, as far as jazz was concerned, and in the dozen or so little clubs which remained, names such as Art Tatum, Coleman Hawkins, and George Shearing were being swiftly replaced by those of so-called exotic dancers. Since this was the time I began my professional career, the only 52nd Street gig I can claim to have played was just one night as accompanist to a dancer known as Zorita.

As I diligently read my piano part, playing as a member of a trio led by Sol Yaged, the Benny Goodman-style clarinetist, I became aware out of the corner of my eye that Zorita was wrapping a live boa constrictor around her torso in various lascivious poses. Seated at a table near the bandstand, Julia (we were newly married) sipped a Coke and admired the dancer's skill in lending an apparent semblance of life to a stage prop. Later on, when I told her that the snake was indeed live and that it contributed its own muscle volition to the act, she was horrified, and she remains so to this day.

Although I didn't make much of a mark on 52nd Street, there were many other clubs to play in, and I worked Wells Music Bar in Harlem (solo piano and in duet with organist Charlie Stewart), Cafe Society Downtown with Tony Scott, the clarinetist, and Bop City with vibraphonist Red Norvo.

The Christmas season of the following year saw the opening of Birdland, the Broadway club which featured Charlie Parker, Dizzy Gillespie, and other legendary boppers. For its first show, an ecumenical billing, never to be repeated, included trumpeter Max Kaminsky and his Dixielanders, of whom I was one. When Max's engagement came to an end, I stayed on for some months as a houseman, playing in particular with Lester Young and then with Flip Phillips, the reigning kings of the tenor sax. One night Bud Powell came in late, so I subbed for him on a set with Charlie Parker and Miles Davis.

I continue to work with Flip Phillips here and there. At the time of the present publication, we've just completed a CD which I arranged for him, using a large string orchestra. He is a master and plays better than ever.

As for Lester Young, I was with his quartet, which included Jo Jones on drums, for the opening Birdland show and for some others in addition, and I also recall playing a Black dance in Newark with him around that time. He was in the final phase of his career, his playing less incisive than the early years

with Basie, still swinging, but somehow weary and more repetitious, particularly in his selection of tunes.

One night he surprised us by calling for "Lavender Blue (Dilly Dilly)", a quasi-folk pop song of the period, no hipper than a nursery rhyme, and I couldn't believe it. More often it was "Three C's and Four F's", an accurate description of a modulating series of blues choruses.

I was asked to go to Chicago by his contractor, but the money was very low, and I had other commitments. The following did *not* happen to me, but there is a famous Lester Young story which expresses the identical situation:

The sideman says to Lester, "I'm sorry, Prez, but I can't go on the road for $45 a week! How can I live?" To which Lester replies in his funny, high-pitched voice, "You got to save your pennies if you want to work with The Prez!"

It was a glorious time artistically, but when many of us celebrated the opening of Birdland thirty years later by revisiting the site of the club, which had become a disco, I remembered the long hours, the short pay, the funkiness, the rumors of gangland presence, and the menacing quality of some of the bar patrons. (Someone was shot one night; I happened to be off.)

Immediately to the left of Birdland there was another club known as Iceland. At this location folks came to see ice shows of scantily clad girls on skates. My old friend Charlie Stewart was playing there in between the skating shows, and he arranged for me to join him and reconstitute our organ-piano duo, even though I was already engaged at Birdland on a schedule that ran from 9:30 P.M. to 3:30 A.M. I don't believe anyone else was ever foolhardy enough to attempt to double between Birdland and Iceland in one evening, but I managed several times to run over to the latter in between my sets at the former and add my keyboard to Charlie's. I did not undertake this double schedule more than one night, and whether the limited run was due to exhaustion or to the indifference of the Iceland management I cannot recall. Most likely, Charlie's engagement simply came to an abrupt end, as gigs still do.

A few years later my schedule had become completely turned around. I had joined the orchestral staff at NBC, and for a long time my chief duty was to show up daily in time to play a live radio show at 7:05 AM. Eddie Safranski, the late and great bass player, led the band, the rhythm section of which included Mundell Lowe on guitar and Don Lamond on drums. The best part of this program never reached the air waves. Most of the laughs took place as we consumed great quantities of coffee, while records or commercials were being played.

Safranski's band had also done some outside recording work, and on one occasion we used one of these records for a ghastly practical joke on the leader. After Allyn Edwards, the host, introduced one of our performances, we began to play with a deliberate sloppiness which degenerated into unthinkable mistakes along with obscene bickering and name-calling. Safranski turned pale and took some time to recover after the engineer revealed to him that a flawless recorded performance was going out on the air.

A bit later, in the early '60s, I played organ in a television combo led by Lou Stein, the pianist, on a weekly children's circus show called *Magic Midway*. The band members were occasionally seen on camera, each of us wearing a gaudy outfit topped by a beanie with an attached propeller. Elephants, jugglers, and acrobats did their acts perilously close to our bandstand.

The oddest act, undoubtedly dating from the bygone years of circus and vaudeville performing, consisted of a man and a Model T Ford. The man put the apparently driverless car through various maneuvers, standing imperiously before it in the manner of an animal trainer commanding a reluctant bear. The car would occasionally let forth with a protesting *aruga*.

By the 1970's I was composing music for various commissions, and one day received an assignment to write a piece on the occasion of the Chinese New Year. Madame Kwo, the proprietress of the Lichi Tree, a restaurant in Greenwich Village, explained to me that her chef was able to beat out a compelling rhythm on a chopping block, using a meat cleaver in each hand. What was needed, she felt, was a suitable musical composition to accompany this skill and in so doing to honor the Year of the Monkey. I had previously written plenty of music for TV commercials, from tooth-brushing to cigarette-puffing to beer-guzzling, so cleaver-chopping did not present an entirely alien challenge.

I wrote a piece for xylophonist, vibraphonist, and cleaver-player, and engaged two percussionists, Doug Allen and Warren Chiasson, both of whom assured me that they enjoyed Chinese cuisine, to work with the chef. At nightly banquets at the Lichi Tree I conducted the trio with a long chopstick as the chef repeated his one pattern interminably:

Right Cleaver
Left Cleaver

(See next page.)

Madame Kwo's expert public relations people got several radio and television news programs interested in the festivities, and within a few days, as the celebration of the Year of the Monkey continued, various powers had arranged for an appearance by Madame and her chef on the Johnny Carson Show. I quickly arranged my "Concerto For Cleavers" for Doc Severinsen's band, and, ignoring the raised eyebrows of several friends who were playing in the band, I guest-conducted a memorable performance during which the chef's beat, never very regular, diverged noticeably from that of the orchestra. Carson watched the proceedings with a bemused expression. I think he suspected that he had been had.

Time passed, Neil Armstrong walked on the moon, and I received a call from a man who said he was looking for music for his new dog act, which was about to premiere in Las Vegas. The caller had come across my first Moog record and thought that one of the tracks would be just the thing to accompany a spectacular canine presentation in which dogs clad in space suits descended in a rocket ship onto a specially constructed lunar terrain.

The catch was this: Due to tight union regulations in those days, the music had to be played live by the Las Vegas house band. I regretfully explained that the overdubbed synthesized sounds could in no way be performed by a conventional orchestra. (Interestingly, this project could be easily accomplished now, using today's more performance-friendly synthesizers.)

"However," I told him, "do I have a score for you!" I then described the Cleaver Concerto and mailed him a cassette of the Carson performance.

I never heard from him again.

Concerto For Cleavers

(in celebration of The Year of the Monkey)

DICK HYMAN

HONKY-TONK PIANO

Back in the 1950's there was a vogue for records of a sort of piano playing best known as honky-tonk. Always performed on a fairly out-of-tune upright piano, the music recalled countless movie settings of Western saloons and Tenderloin barrooms, its tinny tonality instantly evoking images of pitchers of beer, dance-hall girls with bright red garters, and cowboy shoot-outs. Whether these old-time pianists actually played in the now well-defined honky-tonk style remains in some doubt.

The first record in this craze was played by a mysterious German pianist billed as Crazy Otto. Following the cutthroat practice of record companies of the '50s, a competitive label immediately released the *Crazy Otto Medley*, played by Johnny Maddox. The success of this record led in turn to a series of albums by Joe "Fingers" Carr, and soon other record labels sought to get on the piano-wagon with their own honky-tonkers.

As a freelance studio player willing to play in pretty much any style anyone requested, I joined the fray. I never learned who Crazy Otto was, but Joe "Fingers" Carr was known to be the late California pianist/arranger Lou Busch. Most of the other fanciful pseudonyms protected the identities of a number of New York studio pianists, among them Billy Rowland, Moe Wechsler, Lou Stein, and myself. After thirty-five years, I think it is safe to acknowledge that my own honky-tonk ticklings appeared on various labels under the *nommes d'ivoire* of Knuckles O'Toole, Willie "The Rock" Knox, Rip Chord, Puddinhead Smith, Slugger Ryan, Good Time Charlie, and possibly others.

To confuse matters, I must point out that there were actually two Knuckles O'Tooles. Billy Rowland was the other one, and it is difficult by this time to be sure who did what. I can warrant, however, that I recorded the likes of "Twelfth Street Rag," "Yellow Rose Of Texas Rag," "My Gal Sal," "By The Beautiful Sea," "School Days," "I Want A Girl," "Row Row Row," "Tiger Rag," "The Sidewalks Of New York," "She's Nobody's Sweetheart Now," "New Orleans Rag," "Honky-Tonk Man," "Maple Leaf Rag," "Some Of These Days," "Darktown Strutters Ball," "Honeysuckle Rose," "Margie," "Wild Cherries Rag," "Mississippi Rag," "Black And White Rag," "Raggin' The Scale," "Ragtime Razzmatazz," "Ragtime Revelations," "Canadian Capers," "Nola," and a bunch of other red-hot items.

The repertoire itself defined the style. Songs of the Gay Nineties were favored not only for their period flavor, but because they were in the public domain and consequently required no royalties to publishers. Other old-time songs of the '20s were included, as were some instrumental rags and novelty pieces.

Not only were performances by Billy Rowland and myself intermixed on certain albums, but performances ostensibly by Knuckles O'Toole, Willie "The Rock" Knox, Rip Chord, and Puddinhead Smith were identical tracks issued on several different labels by the same producer. For example, Willie The Rock's "New Orleans Rag" (one of my own tunes) was issued on Waldorf Music Hall Records, but it was also released on a different Waldorf record by Puddinhead Smith, and on Audition Records by Rip Chord. The latter recording also included "Honky-Tonk Man" (another original), which subsequently appeared under Knuckles' name on both Grand Award and (much later) ABC Records. Enoch Light was the producer in all these instances, and his complex business arrangements were the reason for this discographical intricacy.

The appeal of honky-tonk albums was probably a combination of the aura of the mythical good-times saloon and the novelty of the recorded sound of the old upright pianos on which we played. They were deliberately kept out of tune, and often had tacks or staples inserted into the hammers. Sometimes a piano came equipped with an authentic "mandolin" attachment, which consisted of a row of metal-tipped tabs suspended from an overhanging rod. The tabs dropped down into a position where the hammers' movement jammed them against the strings, producing a jingling effect. Each recording studio at that time had its own honky-tonk piano, and playing on any of them deadened the urge to go after any artistic finesse.

Although some ragtime authorities consider honky-tonk to be an authentic representation of historical ragtime, my own feeling, though I'm grateful for their opinions, is that we knew better than to consider it genuine. The style developed quickly, or maybe it had always been around (I'm not sure which), full of tremolos, "Kitten On The Keys" figures, and occasional lifts from Jelly Roll Morton, but there was never any attempt on our part to be historically accurate. It was fun music, without a doubt, and part of the reason we had such a carefree attitude was that we were playing under pseudonyms. Since then, under my real name, I've recorded more responsible versions of some of the same pieces, but perhaps the artless fooling-around quality of the '50s records is valuable in itself.

I remember some dates that came out as Good Time Charlie. All of the honky-tonk records used drums, banjo or guitar, and fairly inaudible bass. I was rather naive about the whole scene at first, and thought that Good Time Charlie was the pseudonym of the leader of the dates, the drummer, Billy Gussak. It wasn't until later that I realized that I was Charlie. Slugger Ryan was a puppet creation of Bill Baird, whose work enlivened television for years. I assumed Slugger's name for a recording on the Judson label. Slugger's boss wanted a "Maple Leaf Rag," and since this was a different company from the one which had released the various Knuckles

O'Toole versions, I re-recorded it for him. By now, I must have recorded "Maple Leaf" and "Kitten On The Keys" a half-dozen times each, one way or another.

While some pianists recorded under their own names, the catchy pseudonym was more often the selling point, as was the invariably stylized cover depicting a piano player at an upright wearing a derby, sleeve garters, and a striped shirt. The tradition lingers on at Disneyland and Disney World, and in such places as the restaurant chain known as Rosey O'Grady's, where you can find young ivory ticklers dressed in the prescribed uniform. Washboards, banjos, trombones, and red-hot mamas singing "Some Of These Days" complete the scene.

Honky-tonk records are to be found in the so-called nostalgia sections of record stores, often alongside the more authentic recordings of Max Morath. You might discover others by JoAnn Castle under her own name, as well as by Big Tiny Little, whose last name, at any rate, is a real one. Other pseudonyms that I know about include Willie Gibson, who was Lou Stein, Crazy Fingers Moe and Cooky Carr, who were Moe Wechsler, and Honky-Tonk Herman, a 1970's addition to the fold, who

was Derek Smith. There are others I can't identify, but they might be any one of us.

If you want to get a honky-tonk sound out of your own piano without seriously damaging it, make a chain of paper clips and lay them over the strings. Then try a little "Sidewalks Of New York," as shown below. Try some Joplin rags as well, using the paper clip effect, but forget the classical approach which has been in favor recently. The result may not match the elegant way in which Joplin has come to be played, but it may have some kinship to the sound of the mechanical nickelodeons for which Joplin made piano rolls 75 years ago.

Learn the old tunes, work up a nervous tremolo in your right hand, encourage patrons to sing along, and you will be prepared for a genuine honky-tonk job. You will be expected to bring a derby or straw hat, or at least to fit into the one left behind by the previous tickler. Do not inquire what became of him. After too many nights spent rendering "Melancholy Baby," he may have departed for honky-tonk heaven.

"The Sidewalks of New York"

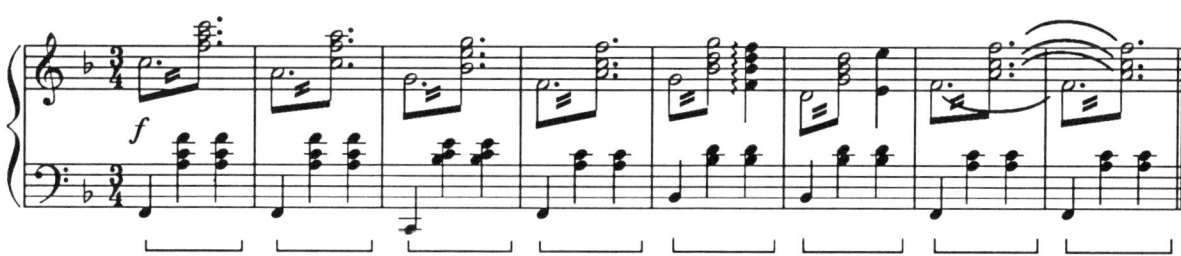

COPING WITH A GOOD CIGAR

Once I played at a particularly smokey affair. Vocalist Maxine Sullivan and a jazz quartet were engaged to entertain a group of cigar fanciers who had gathered to inspect a large collection of pre-Castro Havana cigars. These delectable items (for cigar experts the best possible product) had been deposited in Spain before the United States ban on Cuban imports took effect. They were scheduled to be auctioned off that evening. We were, in fact, the opening act for the cigars.

Our quartet was headed by Jack Lesberg, the bass player, and included cornetist Ruby Braff and guitarist Howard Alden. Tuxedo-clad, we performed on our own as well as accompanying Maxine. We played intermittently for several hours for the crowd of cigar buffs, most of whom were far more interested in the great pile of cigar boxes. The true nature of the gig was soon clear: We played, they smoked.

Early in the evening we attracted a somewhat sozzled fan who hung about near the piano exhaling great clouds of expensive smoke in my direction. He was convinced that we were there to accompany his scat-singing, and nothing we could do persuaded him otherwise. We avoided the melody; we switched keys abruptly; we moved from one song to another; his enthusiasm never faltered. Throughout the night our friend sang along with unflagging brio no matter how we attempted to elude him and despite our earnest pleas to cool it.

Our increasingly annoyed leader, Jack Lesberg, at first tried to reason with the man, who was perfectly good-natured, but as time went on, it became apparent that stronger measures were called for. Inflamed by alcohol and narcotized by nicotine, our associate was oblivious as Jack's appeals became more peremptory. Matters had progressed from "Please" to "Shut up!" when we finally admitted defeat and gave him a chorus of his own in the last set. A very cheerful drunk, our friend pointed out that he was the only one in the room who was listening to us, and I'm afraid he was right.

Carcinogen-laden clouds of smoke enveloped us in an increasingly polluted atmosphere. A reporter interviewed the band and quoted me anonymously in *The Times* the next day as having hoped that a guest would request Victor Herbert's "A Woman Is Just A Woman, But A Good Cigar Is A Smoke." (Yes, such a tune does exist; herewith is the chorus from the original edition of this 1905 novelty item. They must have had supple hands in those days to span that F^7 chord.) During the evening we played "Smoke Gets In Your Eyes," and might have gone on to "Smoke Rings" and "On Top Of Old Smokey" had there been any response whatsoever. At the end of the gig we toasted our vocalist, packed up the instruments, and departed to breathe the relatively clean air of the New York streets.

Perhaps the most important thing to be learned from such an engagement is the value of an old household remedy for removing smoke odor from garments. A recent discovery of mine, I offer it to other piano players who encounter similar hazardous duty: Hang your tuxedo in the bathroom over two saucers filled with white vinegar. After a day or so the vinegar will have absorbed the tobacco odor. What you then have, of course, is a tuxedo which smells of vinegar. Do not despair. Place the garment at an open window for a while, and the fresh air will dispel all odors. This is a professional tip of great utility. Also, learn "Melancholy Baby."

A concert soon after at The New School offered Ruby Braff and me an opportunity to play for a more attentive audience. The two of us, on piano and cornet, dueted at a twilight event improvising on old standards, as we've done at similar concerts or on records over the last few years. We have no set routines and frequently surprise each other with keys or tempos. Ruby sometimes medleys songs together unexpectedly, but we cope with each other's impulses and tie it together in one way or another. We've also performed at concerts at which I play theatre organ. A performance of this sort of duet in Pittsburgh in 1982 was taped, and released under the title, "America the Beautiful."

Our concert at The New School was a good one, we felt, and John Wilson wrote well of us in his review. We were pleased by this, because many more people read the *New York Times* than showed up to hear us. In a sense, the review made up for the coping we had to do with the cigar people.

A Woman Is Just A Woman, But A Good Cigar Is A Smoke

WORDS BY HARRY B. SMITH
MUSIC BY VICTOR HERBERT

Puff, puff, puff, puff,

Watch - ing the smoke a - ris - ing;

Puff, puff, puff, puff,

Soon you'll be re - a - liz - ing

That which the po-et has writ-ten is true. All love is a prac-ti-cal joke._____ For a wom-an is on-ly a wom-an, my boy. But a good ci- gar is a smoke. smoke._____

ON THE ROAD

I've been traveling much more in the last few years than I used to. A long time ago, before I settled into New York studio work, I went out on the road with a couple of bands, but I've been clocking more mileage recently. Many of my jazz-oriented colleagues are also traveling. What seems to have taken place is simply that the conditions under which we play for live audiences and the rewards for doing so are more attractive than they used to be.

Not many years ago, jazz concerts were a rarity. Solo jazz recitals were even more uncommon. Jazz was not often booked as entertainment, and since school jazz education did not exist, there were no college concerts or clinics. Also, of course, the players in my age group were not individually as well known back then as many of us have since become. Merely because we've hung around so long, we've publicized our names and increased the demand for our services. Now we have to get used to greybeards coming up to the bandstand to tell us that they have been following our careers since they were at their mother's knee.

In the old days the road scene for musicians mostly meant endless one-nighters, riding the band bus from one location to another and stopping at cheap hotels en route for a few hours of sleep. I did comparatively little of this (the time of the big bands was pretty much over by the time I started working), but I went through enough to want to get out of it. Although I regret missing the reputed glory of the big band era, I have always considered myself lucky to have begun studio work so early. After I'd gotten on staff at WMCA, a local radio station, and had begun to play jingles and record dates, I rarely found any good reason to leave New York until the late '70s.

The tone of traveling is very different now. Our new mobility is due to usually efficient airlines and (let's be candid) a higher pay scale. We live better on the road these days. Air travel enables us to play anywhere in the country in a few hours, and even trips to Europe, Japan, and Australia have become commonplace. Jazz concerts and festivals featuring masses of musicians take place all over the map, soloists are regularly booked in smaller halls, and an entirely new area of performances has opened up in the schools for many players.

When it comes to accompanying singers, bassist Milt Hinton assures me that conditions are a lot better than they were fifty years ago when he was on the road with Cab Calloway. For Black musicians as senior as Milt, there are contrasts both dramatic and ironic between what we take for granted today and the racially segregated practices that were applied to trains, hotels, and restaurants not all that long ago.

Most of the mainstream musicians with whom I tend to hang out make their own booking schedules. We deal directly with concert promoters or with other musicians who act as contractors, and for some events we work through non-exclusive agents. We play with and for each other in varying combinations and situations. Some of us have organized groups which overlap and interlock with one another. Other players function more often as individuals, star soloists with whomever they play.

We frequently come together as soloists in what has become known as the jazz party. At these non-profit affairs, which were begun in the 1960s by a Denver fan and entrepreneur named Dick Gibson, between fifteen and fifty players are typically engaged for a weekend and are brought together in various impromptu combinations for both afternoon and evening sessions. The personnel changes with each 45-minute set, and a lot of the fun for both the players and the audience is in this fluctuation. Invited guests pay their way for the total event, often flying in from other parts of the country. The action takes place in a hotel ballroom where the atmosphere is more structured than a jam session but less formal than a concert. A number of jazz parties now take place annually in various places, and all of us musicians look forward to meeting one another as well as many of the same guests in regions as far-flung as Colorado, Texas, Arizona, Florida, and California.

Many of us perform at the big festivals packaged by George Wein's Festival Productions, the giant in the field. These events take place all over the world, particularly in the summer months. Smaller producers reach individual players directly or through musician contractors, while leaders of groups carry their own players from concert to concert.

In the field of solo recitals, pianists have the advantage of being able to present events all by ourselves. Guitarists like Bucky Pizzarelli also perform this way, however, and for some occasions duos and trios are appropriate, particularly in smaller halls.

In addition to jazz gigs, there are other jobs which have lured me out of New York. Arrangers sometimes have to go to where a singer or a show is, and for this reason I once spent a week in East Haddam, Connecticut. A Broadway-bound musical, *Noel*, which I was orchestrating, was in its final week of rehearsal. An orchestrator gets to do his job last, after all the elements of song, dance, and underscoring have been exactly set in rehearsal. Much energy and expense went into *Noel,* and we no doubt fueled the economy of East Haddam, where the Goodspeed Opera House was located, but the show never made it to Broadway. For *Sugar Babies,* a much more successful vehicle, I put in comparable time in San Francisco, Detroit, Boston, Atlanta, and Philadelphia as the show made its way around the country prior to the New York opening, acts and songs dropping in and out.

A concert area which is unique is the world of the theatre pipe organ. In another article I've described some occasional ventures onto this circuit. In most locations a literal highpoint is achieved when the console with the presiding player ascends from somewhere below the stage. It is expected that the player will be rendering a stirring opening selection as he rides upward. At the very top the transport mechanism clicks off, the console platform shudders as it comes to a stop, and the audience cheers. I've always felt as though I were sitting on top of a flagpole, and I go about my business trying not to look down.

A very different road event took place under unusually pleasant circumstances when, some years back, my Perfect Jazz Repertory Quintet checked into the Kaui Hilton for a ten-day booking. This Hawaiian island is the archetypal tropical paradise, and a vacation there for the IBM people who had hired us was a combination of Bali-H'ai and *The Love Boat.* Still, performing for a group of corporate executives required something more in presentation than merely playing. In a word, we needed to be entertaining.

We performed our show three times for three different company groups, basing it on an Irving Berlin presentation we had worked out at Michael's Pub in New York, where the IBM representatives had first seen us. My arrangements for the Quintet establish a rehearsed framework, although many sections are left free for improvisation. The entire show was carefully structured with the help of the IBM production staff, and I went over my spoken introductions with some care.

The Quintet, which was then made up of musicians each of whom had an active career other than coming together for this occasion, included the late PeeWee Erwin, cornet; Phil Bodner, clarinet, alto sax, flute, and piccolo; Milt Hinton, bass; and Bob Rosengarden, drums. We played my arrangements of "Alexander's Ragtime Band," "Say It With Music," "Marie," and other tunes the audience was sure to know. I did a piano solo on "Russian Lullaby" and in the interest of showmanship even sang a couple of antique Berlin comedy songs. PeeWee soloed on "How Deep Is The Ocean," Phil on "The Piccolino," Milt on "Blue Skies," Bob on "Soft Lights And Sweet Music." The IBMers responded appreciatively. We've found that people who are not precisely jazz fans nevertheless enjoy virtuoso improvisations on songs they know.

Surrounded by beaches and palm trees in the glowing ambience of a perfect climate, slurping our piña coladas, we observed that life on the road is not what it used to be, thank goodness.

EUROPEAN PIANOS, 1983

I liked the idea of getting on a plane in New York in the morning and playing a gig in London that night. It might be a way, I thought, of including a European performance in my New York psychology and perhaps avoid the wrenching shift one feels moving across several time zones. I warned Peter Boizot, the proprietor of the London club called Pizza On The Park, to expect me late. We would have the official opening the following night, but would do a trial run whenever I arrived.

My tour began with a 10:00 AM flight which touched down at Heathrow Airport six hours and forty minutes later. The local time was then 9:40 PM. I was delayed a bit by British immigration officials who were unable to locate my labor permit, so it was not until twenty minutes to midnight that I arrived at The Pizza. In New York it was only 6:40 PM.

As I came down the stairs, Eddie Thompson was holding forth impressively at one of two Yamaha grands. When his set was over, I was introduced, and I played until closing time, which occurs in London at the decent hour of 12:30 A.M. The evening's brief performance was considered merely a warmup for the following night, which was the official publicized date.

My travel agent had booked a hotel for me on the strength of its being within walking distance of the club. It wasn't, quite, and the bedroom was not much larger than the meager bathroom, but I was grateful at least that my reservation had been held for late arrival. A trans-Atlantic crossing always involves an adjustment of your sleeping pattern. Predictably, I found myself wide awake about four hours after I had retired. Although I eventually fell asleep for another shorter period, it would be a week before I would be able to sleep straight through the night. Daytime naps became a necessity.

The next morning I gave up trying to coax myself into any more shut-eye and got up early, taking care not to bump into the walls of my tiny chamber. I headed toward Piccadilly Circus and surprised myself by stumbling onto my destination, Kettner's, the non-pizza restaurant where Peter Boizot had invited me for lunch. A pianist named Johnny Parker was playing, and he proved to be very knowledgeable in stride and blues styles. Soon I joined him at a second instrument, a Petrov, and in no time we were doing a creditable impression of the old boogie-woogie team of Albert Ammons and Pete Johnson.

That evening I doubled up by playing a bit for the pre-theatre diners at Kettner's and then returned to Pizza On The Park for the main event. Eddie

Thompson and I alternated sets and got together for some stimulating two-piano duets. He proved to be a formidable technician and a sensitive team player. Toward the end of the night we both accompanied the legendary singer Adelaide Hall, who happened to be in the audience.

Early the next morning, a bit less than 36 hours after arriving in London, I was airborne again in the direction of the Netherlands. At the Amsterdam airport I was met by representatives of the North Sea Festival, who drove me about an hour to The Hague, where, in a first-class hotel this time, I slept through the afternoon. That evening I was scheduled for yet another two-piano performance with my old friend Dick Wellstood. Our two sets of double stride piano were but one element in a mammoth weekend affair during which up to ten events were taking place simultaneously in an enormous art and convention center. Other acts on the bill included Oscar Peterson, vibraphonist Lionel Hampton's orchestra, the Art Ensemble of Chicago, and hundreds of other groups and individuals, both American and European.

All of this went on until 4:00 A.M. in a non-stop barrage intensified by taped music, television monitors, and the sounds of record and instrument shops. Through it all, thousands of people crowded in and out of the performance areas and snack bars. Dick Wellstood and I were surprisingly relaxed in the midst of this bedlam. We were even able to adjust our playing to two grotesquely mismatched instruments, a seven-foot Bösendorfer and a Baldwin upright, something like a Great Dane and a Pomeranian. Dick and I played as a team occasionally, and our playing style, based on Fats Waller and James P. Johnson material, might be described as mutually deferential; one of us frequently laid out so that the other could solo for a chorus or so.

This time we were so relaxed and deferential that Dick suggested that we not tell each other what we intended to play. We would take turns starting off numbers, each of us choosing pieces he expected the other to know. This system worked well as a demonstration of sublime mutual confidence, but Wellstood swore at me under his breath when I launched into "Jitterbug Waltz," which, it developed, he hates. Too late.

The next evening I was in charge of the Classic Jazz Band, a group of all-stars I'd been putting together annually for festivals. Doc Cheatham (trumpet), Kenny Davern (clarinet), Eddie Jones (bass), and Oliver Jackson (drums) were joined by a Dutch trombonist, Kees Tanger, when we learned that our regular man, Vic Dickenson, had become ill and had stayed in New York. Eddie Jones was also a sub, since Major Holley's festival schedule had him playing elsewhere when I expected him to be with us. A talk-over backstage let us know what tunes and keys everyone was comfortable with, and we put on two good shows. The Bösendorfer was very nicely responsive.

In addition, I was drafted to play for the humming-and-bowing bass team of Major Holley and Slam Stewart. Slam was, as we say, somewhat out of it on this occasion. I had never before heard him introduce titles in the pseudo-language children used to call Double-Dutch. To an audience for most of whom English was a second language Slam solemnly intoned, "We will now play for you 'Sagatin Dogoll'." Somehow, though, "Satin Doll" got mixed up with "Perdido," and we finished it as such. I was startled to hear Slam then announce that our next number would be "Sagatin Dogoll."

"We already played 'Sagatin Dogoll'," I called out, rising to the occasion. Too late again. We were off and running, bass rosin dusting the air.

The Nice Festival takes place on ten evenings from 5:00 P.M. to midnight, on three widely separated outdoor stages in an old Roman park known as Cimiez. One performance area is actually within the original arena, and the presentations there take on a dramatic character due to the ancient stone masonry. The personnel on each stage changes hourly according to an intricate schedule, and many musicians are seen in Nice for only a portion of the ten days as they move in and out to other events.

The cast of characters was huge, and many of us had already played The Hague. Woody Herman, Tito Puente, and Fats Domino were among the headliners, and there was a large pool of individual musicians, all of whom were capable of whipping through an hour of playing with no rehearsal. My duties were once again with Dick Wellstood on two pianos in the arena and with the Classic Jazz Band, but additionally all of us were formed into an assortment of small units or scheduled as soloists with various fixed groups.

All of us musicians wandered around the park digging one another. Among a lot of memorable sets, I recall seeing Dizzy Gillespie joining V.S.O.P. II, a group that included Herbie Hancock and the Marsalis brothers, and James Moody sitting in with Jimmy Smith's organ trio. About the only drawback in the midst of all the fun was that the considerable humidity affected the pianos adversely. Among the Steinway, Bösendorfer, Pleyel, and Gaveau instruments there were also a couple that even at their best ought to have been hauled down the mountainside and mercifully sunk in the blue Mediterranean.

The tour ended for me in Nice. I set the inner clock back the other way and headed for New York.

Since then I've flown to London on the Concorde in three-and-a-half hours. One could play a full evening in Pizza On The Park, at that rate.

A tragic number of colleagues mentioned in this article have passed on: Eddie Thompson, Dick Wellstood, Vic Dickenson, Major Holley, Slam Stewart, Woody Herman. I miss them all.

THREE WEEKENDS

982 began gloriously with a gig in sunny Antigua, far south of New York's winter chill, where we played dance music for vacationers from up north. Without undue emphasis, I can state that Julia and I were delighted to be there.

Although Bob Alexander's quintet, with whom I was working, had many set arrangements featuring the leader's trombone, a lot of what we played was the usual faking of standard tunes. In the time-honored fashion of such gigs, we would call titles and keys to each other and string together long medleys, generally two choruses on each song with piano modulations in between.

The job was typical in another sense in that it contained a built-in and age-old problem: If there are jazz players in such a dance band (and in this case all of us were), it is not enough simply to accommodate the dancers with recognizable melodies and danceable tempos. In addition, jazz people want to play hot.

Even back in my high school days, I remember, it was always thus. Some jobs were lost because management couldn't recognize the melody and dancers complained about tempos. Other gigs, in which we restrained ourselves, produced a low degree of morale for those of us tuned into the jazz message. Gradually we were forced to learn what jazz tempos are good for dancing, and how much non-melodic improvisation dancers can tolerate. Back then we were always hoping to find a restaurateur or club owner of whom it could be said, using the vernacular of those days, "It's cool to blow, the boss digs jazz." We really did try to be that hip.

With a little accommodation, such as being willing to play a cha-cha now and then, it is possible to have it both ways, and in the Antigua job we did our best to keep the dancers happy while satisfying ourselves, pretty much. After the dancing ended at 11:30, the hotel owner, who really did dig jazz, would gather friends near the bandstand, and we would play a while just for listening.

The personnel changed over the course of the three weeks I was there. On my final weekend, Bob Alexander himself had flown back to New York for some concerts with Frank Sinatra, and I was left in charge. In turn, Tony Monte arrived as my replacement, since I was due to leave on the following Monday. Since he came down a day early, we took advantage of the two grand pianos on the bandstand (the boss also dug piano) and rendered a few impromptu duets.

The next day, Julia and I flew north, stopped in New York, and on Friday we arrived at Decatur, Ill., home of the Central Illinois Jazz Festival. Snow was on the ground, and we thought wistfully of Antigua. I was part of a contingent of players known as the New York All-Stars. We included Warren Vache, Jr.

(cornet), Johnny Mince (clarinet), George Masso (trombone), Milt Hinton (bass), and Ron Traxler (drums).

Festival concerts were scheduled on Friday and Saturday nights as well as Saturday and Sunday afternoons and took place in an immense Holiday Inn motel. The rest of the bill consisted of organized Midwest bands, heavily traditional in style, often using tuba and banjo. Milt Hinton and I also played with a group featuring the fine Milwaukee clarinetist Chuck Hedges. In such an ambience, even swing is considered progressive, and our group kept to the conservative side. I played almost entirely in pre-bop styles. For solos I performed pieces by Fats Waller, Jelly Roll Morton, and Willie "The Lion" Smith.

On Saturday of the following weekend I was at a Manhattan television studio where the soap opera *As The World Turns* is taped. I had been called to play some organ cues, but the exact nature of what I was to do was not clear. In any case, from past experience I knew that the session would be slow-moving, because that's the way it is with dramatic productions. Many elements must be planned, assembled, and rehearsed, of which music is only one.

Soap operas, on both radio and television, formerly employed organists to underscore scenes and to bridge transitions, and there were a few players such as Eddie Layton who rushed from one TV program to another, taping two in a day. In the days of live radio, Paul Taubman was an organist who was able to schedule as many as four programs daily. (At that time radio soaps were only fifteen minutes long.) The old-fashioned Hammond organ cliches are still fondly remembered and often parodied — the lachrymose theme, the dramatic accents ("stings"), and the somber low underscoring leading to a minor chord resolution.

Those days are gone forever, but now and then an organist is still needed to provide music for realistic scenes which actually call for organ music. I have participated in several church weddings and funerals among the troubled characters of soaps, sometimes appearing on camera as the church organist. In the case of Saturday's taping, a bizarre plot, the beginnings of which were incomprehensible to me, called for a diminutive actor to play the role of the ironically named Mr. Big, a sinister fellow indeed. Mr. Big amused himself, as he plotted his fiendish plans, by noodling on an old pump organ to which the set designer had added certain menacing Gothic decorations. Of course, this characterization is in a hoary tradition of organ-playing villains. Remember Captain Nemo, for one, aboard his submarine in *Twenty Thousand Leagues Under The Sea.*

On the same weekend I attended a birthday party

for Eubie Blake, who was then 99. Eubie's incredible endurance and good spirits were as much an inspiration as his playing, which recalled the days of ragtime. Many friends and associates were there, and the pianists present included McCoy Tyner. With both men in the same room one had a sense of jazz history from its beginnings to the most contemporary style. It fell to me to play "Happy Birthday" to Eubie, and I thought it would be appropriate to rag it up a little in his honor.

ON STAGE WITH EUBIE

Eubie Blake's one-hundredth birthday occurred in 1983. I was privileged to have become friendly with him during his last decade. Our get-togethers mostly took place on stage, where I would be conducting one concert or another in which Eubie would emerge from the wings and effortlessly steal the show from all the other participants. His stage manner was always very different from his quiet demeanor backstage, where he appeared to be gathering his energy for the performance to come.

At Carnegie Hall I offered him a supporting arm, expecting to help him make his way deliberately to the piano. To my astonishment, as soon as his name was announced he leaped from my grasp like a gazelle, dashed out into the limelight, rushed to the keyboard, and played with the boundless energy which enabled him to span all the eras since ragtime was America's popular music.

Already in his tenth decade at the time of this concert, Eubie immediately won the audience with the charm of an outgoing and perfectly confident performer, not at all concerned with the stage director's notion of limiting his spot to ten minutes. Eubie played and reminisced for twice that. Nor did the fact that the concert was billed as a George Gershwin evening inhibit him from playing a full-length rendition of his own "Memories Of You." He even drifted into the slow theme from the "Rhapsody In Blue", somewhat stealing the thunder from the full reading of that work which I was to conduct later with Lorin Hollander as soloist.

Eubie must have been conscious of his increasing fragility at the RCA studios where he was reciting the text of Scott Joplin's "School Of Ragtime" as part of a set of recordings I was doing of Joplin's complete piano works. The only survivor of the ragtime era was reading Joplin's defense of his music against its detractors as I demonstrated Joplin's brief examples of syncopation. As we helped Eubie up onto the high stool in front of the microphone, he cautioned, "Careful, I've only got one fall."

It must be wonderful to attain that advanced age at which people will allow you to do just about whatever you want, and it must also have been a satisfaction to Eubie to have come out of retirement in his 80s and attain far more celebrity than he had even as a highly successful younger man. And how ironic it must have been to him that, having done his utmost to progress from the status of ragtime professor to Broadway composer, he was rediscovered in his old age as the personification of the ivory tickler. Nevertheless, wise to the ways of show business, and with the shrewdness of one who has seen it all, he seized the opportunity and played his "Charleston Rag," written in 1899, on *The Tonight Show* with an authenticity that Marvin Hamlisch and the rest of us would not dare to challenge.

At one of the Kool Jazz Festival events, Eubie, a bit more frail, was slowly helped onstage and assisted to a chair center-stage from which he listened approvingly to the finale of a concert in his honor. His energy appeared to be at a low ebb, and none of us expected him to perform, but with the stubborn determination that marked his whole career, he insisted on topping our best efforts by stopping at the piano on his careful way offstage to render once more a chorus of "Memories Of You."

He attended the Nice Festival in France in 1978. The usual travel schedule to this annual event involved leaving Kennedy Airport around 8 PM and flying to Paris. Then there ensued a wait of an hour and a half or so before the flight to Nice. One arrived in the south of France in a state of exhaustion from which it took most of us several days to recover. Although Eubie permitted himself to be trundled through the various airports in a wheel chair, he was noticeably more chipper than the rest of us, sitting up in the plane, chatting, and smoking through the night. At Nice, once the concerts were under way, he apparently required less sleep than we youngsters do. He could be found holding court in the little lobby of the Hotel Mercure until 2 AM, long after Terry Waldo, his ragtime colleague and traveling companion, had hit the sack.

Once, from the vantage point of one who had survived it all, he looked at me and remarked drily, "You know, I wasn't always this old!"

EUBIE'S FINAL BOW

In May of 1983 the Public Broadcasting Service aired a ninety-minute special entitled *Eubie Blake: A Century Of Music*. The program had been seen earlier by a smaller audience on cable television soon after it was taped as a live concert at Kennedy Center in January. It was to be Eubie's last public appearance. The camera picked him up as he sat in the Presidential box, watching the presentation of his music. He made his characteristic triumphant boxing gesture, hands clasped together, though not quite so high as when he was younger.

I was the musical director of the event. I became part of the operation when the producer, Ron Abbott, called me toward the end of the previous summer. We began discussing a production that would eventually have much of the complexity of a Broadway show, but without nearly the budget or the amount of rehearsal time which gives such productions a healthy safety margin. Professionally speaking, we would be living dangerously.

Some years back, on the occasion of another show, I was solemnly advised by a good friend that the term "musical director" was gauche. He explained that a director of music is by definition expected to be musical, and that all of those attention-getting posters with my name that had been pasted onto flat surfaces around midtown Manhattan should properly have referred to me as "music director." My friend may have been correct, much present usage notwithstanding, but I told him that such a grammatical distinction is the very least that a director, musical or otherwise, has to worry about.

What does concern the music(al) director is his or her responsibility not only for the best possible performance, but for all of the preparation that leads up to it. The director will be concerned with arrangements, orchestrations, copying of parts, casting, working with the choreographer, seeing to the physical setup of the orchestra, scheduling rehearsals, contracting the musicians, consulting with union representatives to sort out the tangle of applicable pay scales, checking with the audio engineer to make sure everyone will be heard, with the lighting engineer so everyone will be able to read the music, and in general trying to expedite the ideas of the producer, director, composer, and writers.

Becoming a music(al) director is a fate that befalls piano players fairly often, since keyboard work is very good preparation for arranging, and arranging inevitably leads to conducting. Although there are instances when another person may be designated as the conductor, this is almost always the most visible function of the director. He may also be the vocal arranger, the dance arranger, the orchestrator, or even one of the players.

When Ron Abbott and I had the first of our many

meetings, we needed to settle on the size of the orchestra. According to the budget, what turned out to be affordable was 19 players. I decided not to use what would be at best a puny string section, but instead to plan on a generous assortment of wind instruments — reeds, brass, and French horns, plus rhythm and extra percussion. It was also clear that with our modest production budget, we could not afford full orchestrations of the 25 or so selections, some of them lengthy dance pieces. Our solution was to find appropriate ways of performing certain selections with less than the full orchestra. This we did in the early ragtime-flavored part of the show by creating a small ensemble of two pianos plus rhythm. We used common parts on these tunes, Frank Owens and I improvising in old-time two-piano fashion. Another budget saver was Frank's solo accompaniment to Joe Williams singing "A Dollar For A Dime," one of the most appealing moments of the program.

Finding the songs which would make up our repertoire was a special and intriguing problem. Eubie's catalog of songs is vast, but only a comparative few of the tunes are well known. We needed to locate many others, and we wanted our selection to extend beyond those that make up the score of the Broadway musical known as *Eubie*. I knew some obscure pieces, and Blake specialists Terry Waldo and Carl Seltzer provided us with others. We also referred to the encyclopedic list of titles printed in *Sissle & Blake*, the invaluable reference book on Eubie and his partner Noble Sissle.

Carl Seltzer and I drove out to Eubie's Brooklyn brownstone one fall day to search through his song files. We found Eubie sitting at the kitchen table in his bathrobe reading a newspaper. He seemed tired, and it was difficult to converse with him because his hearing aid was not functioning. A cheerful nurse was there to look after him. A hospital bed was set up in the small living room with the television set and grand piano nearby. Eubie was no longer able to climb the stairs to the upper floors of the house. It was obvious that he would be unable to help us in our search for material. Carl and I descended to the basement, where, not far from the oil burner, office files and cabinets rested on a cement floor. In them was much of Eubie's life work. More than anything else, the enormous collection of paper demonstrated that for all his talent as a performer, Eubie was at heart a songwriter. I wondered if, judging by the sheer quantity of material in the files, Eubie might not have averaged a song a day for his entire hundred years.

We found many of the titles that had intrigued us and stumbled onto other usable songs. There were additional notebooks of unpublished and untitled melodies. I sent one melody from this treasure trove to Sammy Cahn, the lyricist, who in a matter of weeks wrote marvelously appropriate words, entitling the song "It Was Well Worth The While." I subsequently arranged this for the great 90-voice Morgan State University Choir, and their performance of Eubie's last published work provided a moving moment.

Soon Ron and I were assigning the various songs to the performers who were being booked for the presentation. I made lead-sheet vocal arrangements of each item and strained my limited vocal demo technique by recording numerous cassettes which were then sent out to Las Vegas, Los Angeles, Toronto, or wherever the performers happened to be. I reached a new plateau in audacity, if not in vocalizing, by working up the nerve to demonstrate songs to Cab Calloway, Joe Williams, Rosemary Clooney, Phyllis Hyman, and Patti LaBelle.

Around the same time, the selection of chorus people who could both sing and dance was getting under way. A general call for such talent was placed in the theatrical trade papers, and, in company with the choreographer and the producer in a funky rehearsal hall on 8th Avenue, I had my first experience on the judging side of that ancient show-biz ritual lovingly known as the cattle-call. In order to ensure that the vocal standards would be reasonably high in our dancing-singing chorus of eight persons, I sat through brief performances by nearly three hundred aspirants in one marathon day. An unflappable pianist, Don Sosin, who was to become our dance arranger, effortlessly sight-read or faked accompaniment for all of them. One learns a lot about auditions in such a day, but I'd just as soon not do that again too soon.

The next day the choreographer quit the show, for reasons I never learned, and the new man started his own talent search. The eight lucky winners who were eventually chosen proved to be good people who, with their interminable rehearsal hours, put in more hard physical labor than many athletes do. Theirs is a hard job. The dancers began working with the new choreographer, whose domain also included staging, and Don Sosin and I established a careful working procedure. As the choreography became set in terms of accents, tempo, and overall contour, he would feed the day's results to me so that I might if necessary recast sections into a characteristic Eubie Blake style. The next day Sosin might make modifications on my modifications, and so on. The vocal arrangements also underwent revisions in rehearsal. A chorus of dance might be inserted into a song, for example, or lines might be transferred from one performer to another. We had a few changes in the cast, moreover, which required that some songs be transposed to other keys. I kept on top of this, because only when everything was absolutely set could I begin the orchestration process. I did much of the orchestration myself, but the limitation of the number of hours in a day convinced me that help would be needed. Jon Charles, Sy Johnson, and Dick Lieb were the expert orchestrators I called on.

Eventually all of the music was ready, having been copied and prepared by two veterans of this game, John Mical and Pat Kondek. We flew to Washington for the first orchestral reading, having contracted excellent local musicians supplemented by our New York rhythm section of Frank Owens, Milt Hinton, and Ron Traxler. With a few of the inevitable mishaps, the stop-and-start dress rehearsal went fairly well, and the evening concert was of course much better. Following this, the music(al) director enjoyed a good night's sleep and returned to New York the following morning.

There was more than enough material on videotape, so that post-show editing could remove the least effective numbers as well as tighten up the stage waits and announcements. Back in New York I supervised the dubbing of one of Eubie's recordings under the opening titles and led some of the singers in an overdubbing session where we beefed up the vocal efforts of the chorus.

I last saw Eubie in his wheel chair, being pushed down the great corridor of Kennedy Center. He died not long after, having achieved his goal of living to be 100.

THINKING ABOUT TEDDY WILSON

Back in 1947, when I was going to college at Columbia in New York, word came my way that a local radio station was sponsoring a jazz piano competition. The contest was announced on WOV by Fred Robbins, a popular dee-jay whose name is forever inscribed in the annals of hip as the dedicatee of the tune named after his show, *Robbins' Nest*. The winner of the contest, I learned, would receive private lessons with Teddy Wilson, while the runners-up would study with Mary Lou Williams. Even at that time both names were legendary. I had various 78 rpm Decca records of Mary Lou playing in the full swinging style which she would later modify in the evolution of her musical thinking, and I had been hearing Teddy's crystalline performances with Benny Goodman since I was a little boy.

The great evening arrived, and I abandoned whatever homework I was supposed to be doing and hurried down to WOV. The competition took place in the radio studio and was broadcast live. The panel of judges included not only Teddy Wilson and Mary Lou Williams but producer John Hammond and other distinguished names from the jazz establishment. Much as I would like to recall every detail of my first broadcast (previous experience at the Columbia radio station didn't really count), I can't remember much except that I don't think I was nervous, and that I won first prize. I performed Irving Berlin's familiar "Always" as my offering, and when I got home my mother, who had tuned in the Zenith console radio for the great moment, asked me what it was I had played. When I told her the title, she expressed considerable astonishment. In those days melody was not a big thing for me.

Teddy was doing a lot of teaching at that time, both privately and at the Juilliard School of Music. I embarked on a series of twelve lessons with him, first at his apartment on St. Nicholas Avenue and later at a studio downtown. He showed me fingering for the Wilsonian runs which were to become the standard vocabulary for a generation of pianists. He suggested chord substitutions which greatly improved the classic pop songs such as "Body And Soul," "The Man I Love," and "I Surrender, Dear." He demonstrated some of the patterns used by his friend Art Tatum, and talked about him with reverence. He illustrated all of these things with the Mozartean touch which was so characteristic of his playing.

When I began lessons with Teddy, there was no question about my being able to improvise, but Teddy helped me refine and direct whatever ability I had. I believe that a successful teacher manages to get the student to teach himself, and this Teddy did. The most profound thing I learned from him was his response to my worrying that my playing was inconsistent: Sometimes it was good enough to win a piano competition, while at other moments I didn't really feel that I was making it. His answer was a truism, but none the less valuable for that: Try to become good enough so that even on those inevitable days when you slip, your level will still be high.

Young musicians often have not had the opportunity to learn that their idols and role models are human, after all, and that it is impossible for anyone to maintain the highest possible level of performance at all times. Learning from records, furthermore, tends to awe beginners, who cannot be expected to realize that a recorded performance usually displays the most error-free work of any musician. What you do not often get to hear are the previous takes, the breakdowns, the fluffs, the totally rejected selections, or, for that matter, the lifetime process of putting it all together.

As to the other WOV contestants, Bert DeCoteau, the runner-up, who became a busy New York arranger, received twelve lessons with Mary Lou Williams. In my case, even after the lessons with Teddy were finished, I continued to study his playing in an ongoing process which continues to the present time. I have assembled a bit of what I was able to learn from him in an original piece called "Pass It Along." Teddy did that with me.

Pass It Along

(dedicated to Teddy Wilson)
from Etudes For Jazz Piano

DICK HYMAN

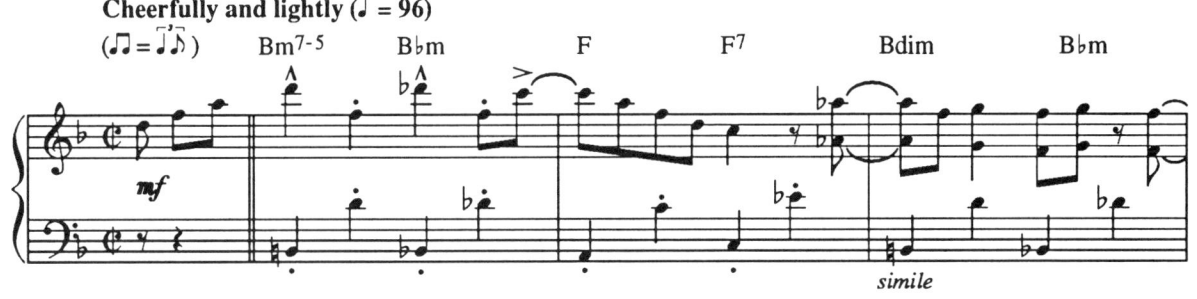

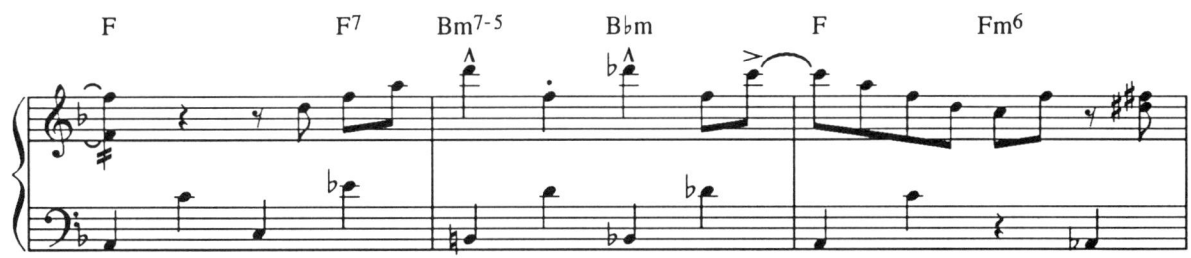

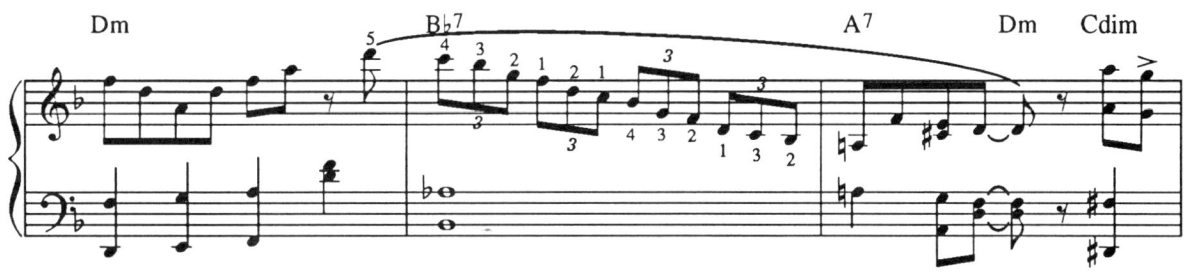

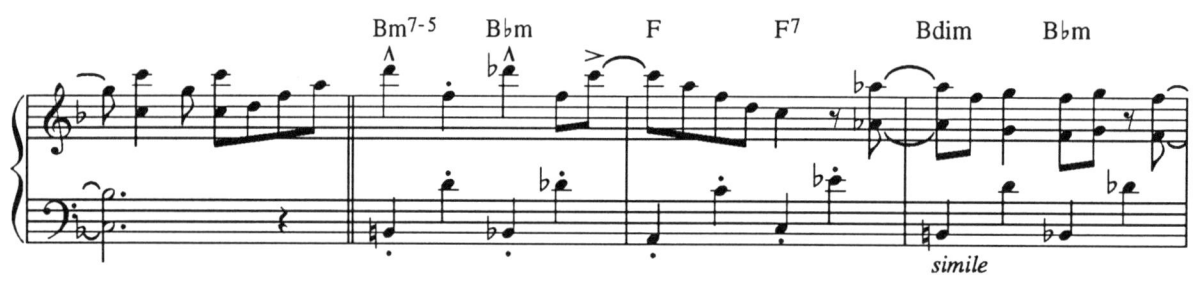

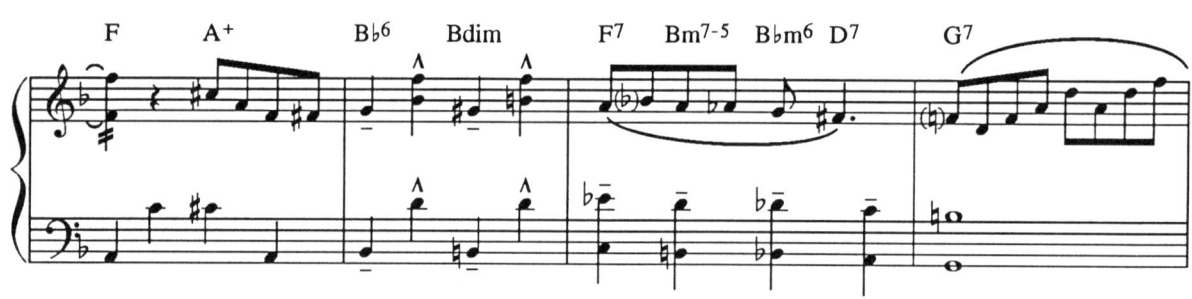

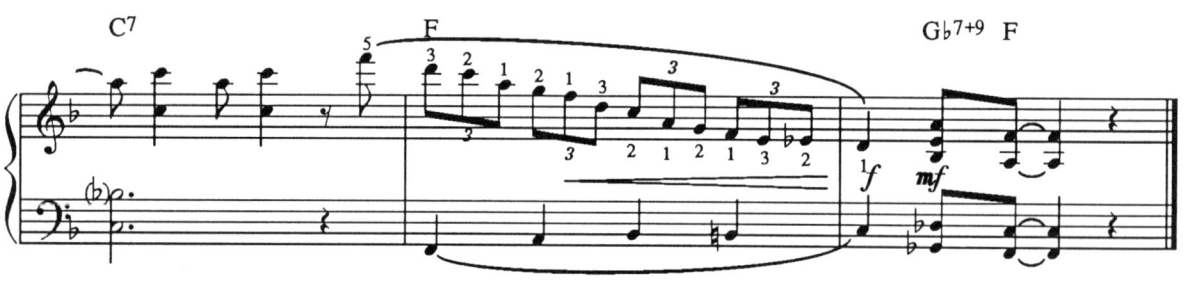

THINKING ABOUT JAMES P. JOHNSON

When I was not yet a teenager, my big brother Arthur went off to Harvard and, having been exposed there to the great world of culture, returned one vacation with an armful of 78 rpm jazz records, mostly reissues of music from the classic 1920's period. This was not the sort of learning for which Harvard was noted, but, from whatever source he had acquired the virus of what was in those days known as hot record collecting, Arthur soon passed it on to me.

A lot of what I now know I picked up from those old records. I played clarinet when I was a kid, and I would jam along with Louis, Bix, and the rest for hours, stopping only to sharpen my cactus needle. When I probably should have been doing my homework, I would look for old records, prowling in Salvation Army outlets, junk stores, 5-and-10-cent stores, and those few places where you could buy new hot records. I'm convinced that I would have become a full-time collector and dealer as an adult, had it not been for my piano playing.

As I became a professional musician, the collecting instinct diminished, and the clarinet fell by the wayside as well, although what I learned from playing it along with the old records is with me still. One Victor record of the late '20s which is still on my shelf is by a group called the Louisiana Sugar Babes. This pick-up orchestra plays "Thou Swell" on one side and "Mountain Greenery" on the other, both from Rodgers & Hart shows of the period. The performances have an old-timey charm to me even now, and I must have played the record so many times that I know every note on both sides.

My brother had given me a copy of Charles Delaunay's "Hot Discography," the first scholarly listing of jazz recordings, and by consulting it I learned that the band included both Fats Waller on organ and James P. Johnson on piano. This must have been my first awareness of Johnson's playing, although Fats was familiar to me, since his piano and vocal records were being played on the radio at that time. Fats' recorded organ style became the basis of my own later exploration of the theatre organ, but the other keyboard player on the record-

ing proved to be no less influential on me, and, long before I stumbled on his records, on a whole generation of pianists.

Johnson's greatest pupil was Waller, whom he tutored in the intricacies of stride piano while the latter was still in knee-pants. They became a team not only in recordings but in the pit orchestra of *Keep Shufflin'*. Together with Willie "The Lion" Smith, they were the champions of the legendary after-hours piano cutting contests which took place in Harlem in the '20s and '30s.

While I was going to college in New York, I learned that a direct subway route would take me from Columbia down to Greenwich Village, and there I discovered James P. playing intermission piano in a club called the Pied Piper. In a billing that gets more wondrous as time goes by, Willie "The Lion" Smith was also working there in Max Kaminsky's band. I began to hang around steadily enough to be allowed to sit in one memorable night.

Still, I had pretty much gotten away from this kind of playing until the Scott Joplin renaissance, about twenty years later, which led to a greater interest in the music of such pianists as James P. Johnson. Finding a revived demand for stride piano, I learned or re-learned Johnson pieces such as "Carolina Shout," "Jingles," "You've Got To Be Modernistic," and "Caprice Rag," and recorded them in a Columbia album entitled *Charleston* (M-33706), after Johnson's biggest song hit. My appreciation for the man grew as I discovered that in addition to the stride pieces he was a composer of many songs, shows, and symphonic works.

I've tried to combine a few of the things we've all learned from James P. in a piece of my own called "Cuttin' Loose," which I wrote in tribute to him. Included are Johnson's contrapuntal stride bass and many of his characteristic right-hand figures. Eighth-notes are to be played with a triplet feeling, not with the evenness of ragtime. The tempo may be more or less bright, but it must swing.

The album has been reissued, along with a Jelly Roll Morton set from the same period, as a CD on Sony Classics.

Cuttin' Loose

(dedicated to James P. Johnson)
from Etudes For Jazz Piano

DICK HYMAN

THINKING ABOUT ART TATUM

One of my first gigs around New York was playing with Tony Scott's Quartet at Cafe Society Downtown. The club had been established by Barney Josephson, who succeeded not only in presenting jazz and cabaret performers whose names were or would be among the most important in show business (Lena Horne, Zero Mostel), but in breaking down the color barrier which in 1949 still prevented Black people from attending most venues.

Tony Scott's group was the house band. The other musicians in the quartet while I was with him included Irv Kluger, drums; and, at different times, Irv Lang and John Levy, bass. The club was located in the basement of an apartment building on Sheridan Square in Greenwich Village. Leonard and Jane Feather lived upstairs. Cliff Jackson played intermission piano, and our quartet provided dance music from 9:00 on, performed a feature number or two in the floor show, which occurred twice during the evening, and accompanied the acts as needed. The night ended somewhere around 3:30 or 4:00 AM, and I recall the management once encouraging the departure of the last few patrons by shutting off the air conditioning.

The stars that I can remember working with included comics Jack Guilford, Jane Dulo, and Lord Richard Buckley; singers Josh White, Thelma Carpenter, Ruth Brown, and Muriel Gaines. There were after-hours guests, too, such as Tony Bennett, who was still known as Benedetto in those days, and Calvin Jackson, the pianist, whose playing and arrangements very much impressed me. The performer, though, whose memory is most vivid is Art Tatum. Nightly we would finish our opening numbers and then sit to one side while Tatum would perform his program, playing with his usual astonishing facility, simply playing; I do not remember his announcing titles or making any attempt to ingratiate himself with the audience. He had no need to. We sat there reverent and dumbfounded, and when the show was over, John Gary, whose piano-moving expertise had won him mention in the New Yorker, would roll the instrument so recently blessed back to its bandstand position, and our quartet would play more mundane dance music. It was a great lesson for me in music as well as humility.

I did not ever speak with Tatum beyond polite greetings when Tony introduced us. Nevertheless my impression of him was one of kindliness and encouragement. It wasn't until years later when a friend and fan, Siegfried Mohr, made me aware of the radio interview which Willis Conover conducted with Tatum in which, when asked who his favorite pianists were, Tatum included me, as a "new kid" (I was 22), probably to avoid having to make a selection among his peers. Even so, this accolade, discovered so long after, touched me.

I remember watching Tatum do one of his descending runs in which the thumb slid down the white keys while the four fingers articulated the black ones. I've since learned how to do a slower version of this one myself, but at Tatum's tempo, the thumb appeared to be a pure glissando. Ever since those days I've tried to grasp as much as possible of Tatum's playing, but one learns one's limitations.

I've always been amused by Tatum's propensity for making up dummy verses when he needed them and apparently didn't know the real ones, very much as George Burns used to do with his rapid patter universal verse.

Tatum's choice of keys constitutes a study in itself. Obviously certain keys lend themselves to particular technical devices. This tendency can lead to cliches, but Tatum rose above the problem. He deliberately chose out-of-the-way keys such as E, A, or Gb in order to use the devices of, say, Eb, Ab or G in unexpected chromatic digressions. The familiar runs could thus be used in strange territory. Furthermore, he combined the basic vocabulary of his runs and scales so that they were never textbook exercises.

His linear improvisation developed from this constant reconstituting of his material. In a sense I agree with the theory expressed in Arnold Laubich's notes to *Pieces of 8* that his single note lines, when slowed down, anticipate Bird and maybe even Coltrane. In my opinion, the advances in harmony of the boppers were simplistic compared to Tatum's usage.

For all of his musicality, Tatum did not appear much interested in composition. Embellishment and arranging (or rearranging) were his metier. Those few pieces which he recorded or published seem either variations on common material or merely Christmas decorations waiting to be hung on a nonexistent tree.

He shared, in my judgment, a harmonic world with George Gershwin. Both explored the outer reaches of chromaticism. It is admittedly difficult to hear the basis for this notion in Gershwin's piano-roll-styled solo recordings as compared with Tatum's elegant playing of 15 to 20 years later, but I maintain that the similarity is there throughout the score of *Porgy and Bess*.

What did Tatum not do structurally which he might have? Nothing that he needed to do, certainly. However, if one wanted to speculate academically on areas which held no attraction for him even with his prodigious and—at least in jazz—his unequaled musicality, one could point out that he rarely made complete key changes, for example modulating a half-tone or a fourth higher for the climactic final chorus. Of course, this was not at all necessary since he was constantly modulating in and out of home tonality in any case.

Piano technique is a vast territory, and as astonishing as was Tatum's, there are areas which are not explored in his playing. It appears that his preferred cushioned tone and his emphasis on velocity precluded fortissimo or percussive qualities. Nor was he concerned with rapid octaves or certain other technical problems dealt with in Czerny. (Consider, for example, DeFalla's *Ritual Fire Dance* or Chopin's etude in octaves.) Additionally, he was never required to project above symphonic accompaniment, a skill necessary for a player of piano concerti. These observations are not an attempt to reduce his status; one cannot diminish achievement as great as Tatum's. Nevertheless, it is interesting, in attempting to understand what he accomplished, to note what he did not set out to do.

I have never understood Tatum's bow to Lee Sims in one or another interview, and I've listened recently to many of the latter's recordings. I can only conclude that Tatum had not heard anyone before Sims treat a popular song with a certain solemnity which raises a performance from the level of a barroom request and demands the listener's full concentration. Also, he may have been intrigued by Sims' somewhat pretentious use of chords of the 9th and 13th. To my ear, Sims' sense of harmony was unso-

phisticated compared to the mastery of Gershwin, or of Bix Beiderbecke in the latter's pieces for piano of the late '20s. Tatum's link to Waller is much clearer, as he noted. Tatum was essentially a stride pianist who adorned that style with fantastic linear and harmonic embellishments. At the same time, in a much less decorative mode, he could demonstrate his ease with simple blues playing and his perfect familiarity with that tradition. Still, he was unwilling to sacrifice what Whitney Balliet termed his pneumatic touch in an attempt to emulate earlier players.

Most of what I've learned about Tatum's playing is from recordings rather than from the Cafe Society days. I wish I had been able to have been more analytic at the time, but I was simply too dazzled by the experience to recall whether he changed his program from show to show, how he dealt with chatters, and other practical aspects of night club performing. As Fats Waller remarked, God was truly in the house, and one didn't bother with small things.

In the following, "Onyx Mood," I've composed a brief piece using many characteristic Tatumisms. On page 119 of this volume, <u>Art Tatum in Slow Motion</u> analyzes some aspects of the Tatum technique.

Onyx Mood

(dedicated to Art Tatum)
from Etudes For Jazz Piano

DICK HYMAN

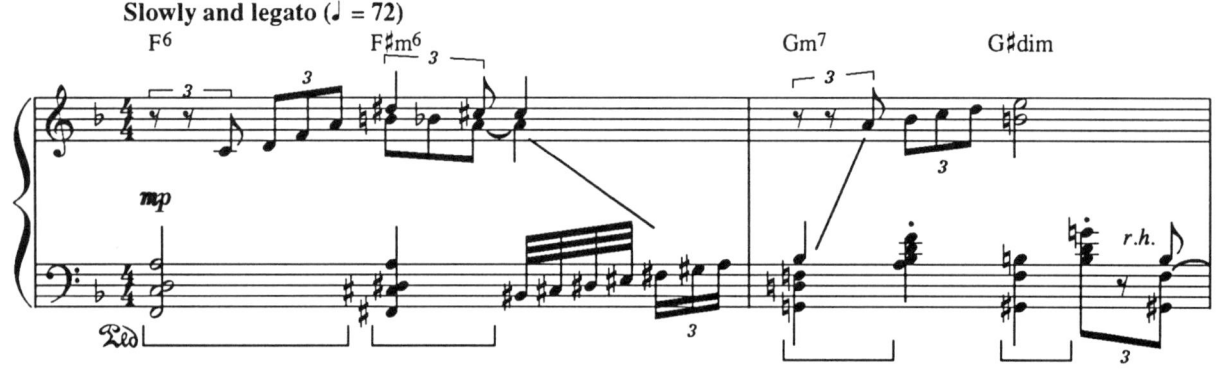

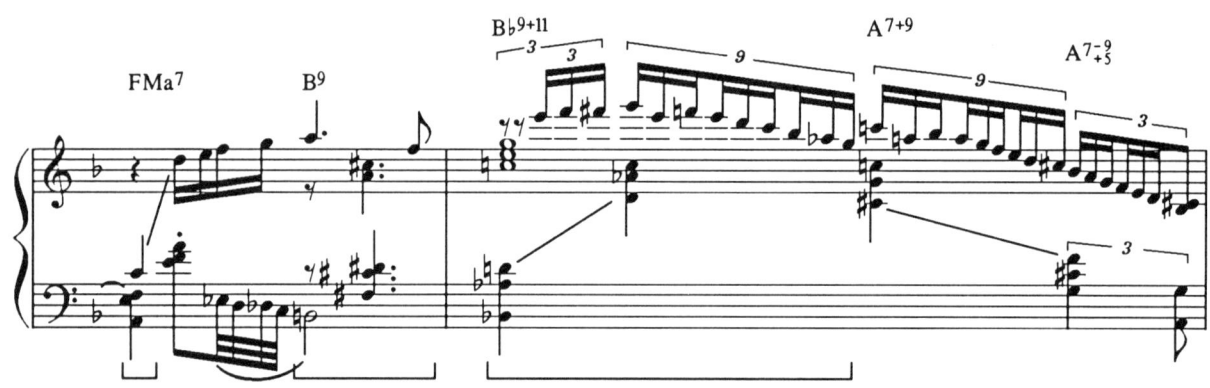

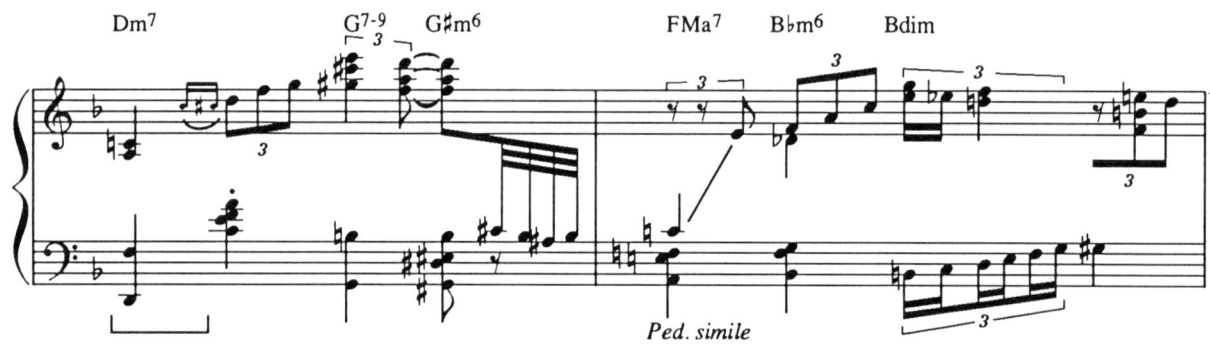

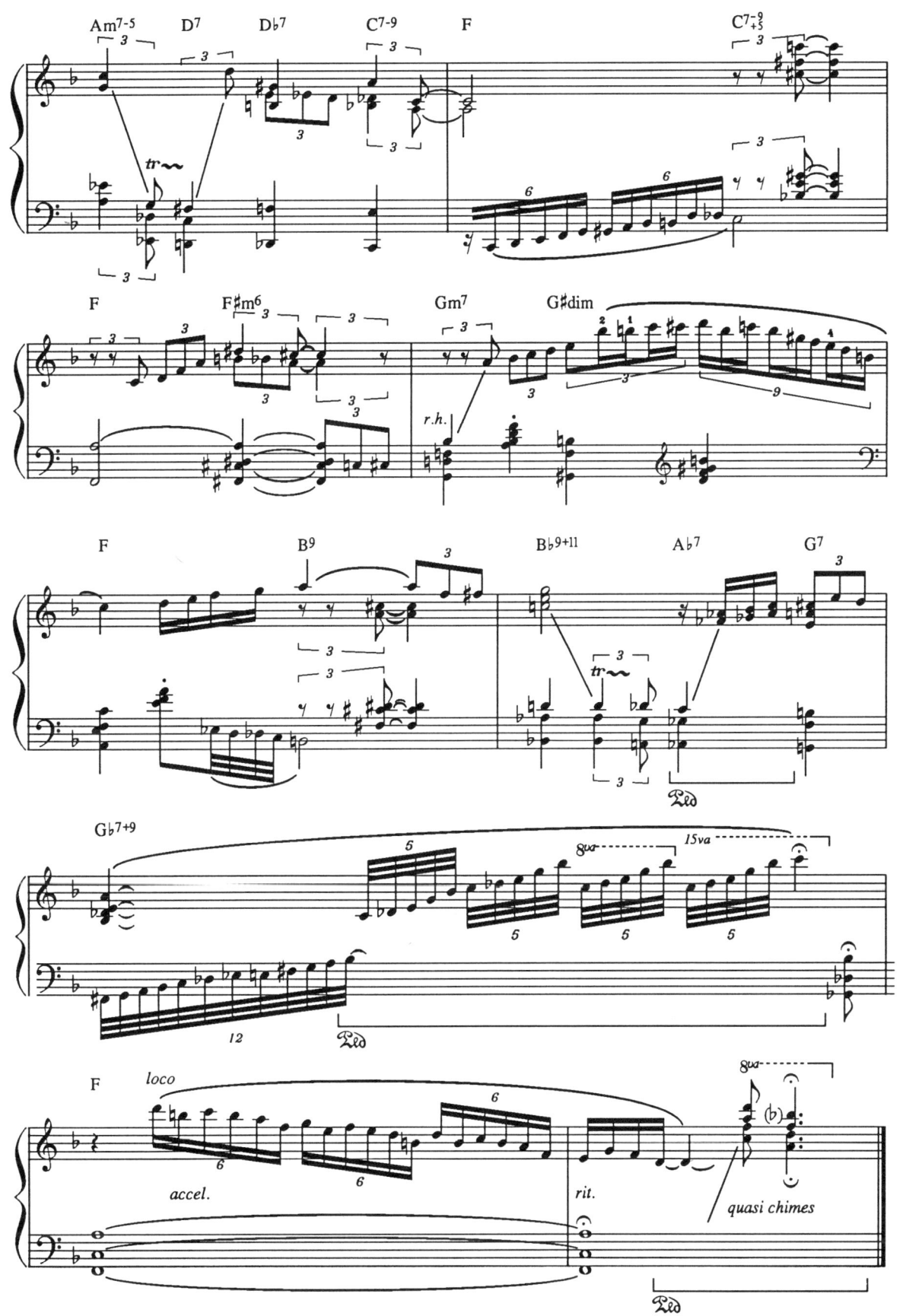

THE ART TATUM TRIBUTE AT TOWN HALL

On July 1, 1981, as one of the events during New York's Kool Jazz Festival, Billy Taylor and I co-produced a special concert at Town Hall. A tribute to the artistry of Art Tatum as well as an exploration of his playing and an expression of his musical influence, the concert was a labor of love on our part. This feeling was no less evident in the contributions of the other pianists: John Lewis, Jaki Byard, Adam Makowicz, Dick Wellstood, Barry Harris, and Ellis Larkins. All of us share a musical heritage in which Tatum is the transcendent figure.

Art Tatum's playing was no less revered by bassist Slam Stewart and guitarist Tiny Grimes, the other members of his original trio, who were on hand to help us pay tribute to their former leader. Saxophonist Eddie Daniels, less directly a part of the Tatum tradition, also joined us to demonstrate the extent of that influence on a musician of a later generation who plays an instrument other than the piano.

In planning the concert, our first decision was to use two pianos in duets from time to time, as well as to feature solo performances. We also decided to take advantage of the relatively modest size and good acoustics of Town Hall by not artificially amplifying the pianos. While there were microphones on stage, they were used only for taping the event for the National Public Radio program *Jazz Alive*.

Beginning the evening with a 1939 film clip of the Tatum Trio, immediately followed by Tatum's solo recording of "Get Happy," Billy and I set up the first half of the concert so that each pianist played one solo. In our dialog we introduced each player and attempted to suggest the specific influence of Tatum's pianistry. Ellis Larkins, for example, played "Blues In The Night," a selection from the show tune repertoire Tatum favored, showing off his great delicacy of touch as well as the kind of harmonic alterations that Tatum explored so notably. The same qualities of touch and harmony were found in John Lewis' "Sacha's March," an inventive original composition which also expressed the essential economy of John's playing, something *not* characteristic of Tatum.

Still, a degree of economy was increasingly evident in Tatum's output as he grew older. His earliest recordings are jammed with whirlwind flourishes that were trimmed considerably by the time of his mature efforts. A tendency toward economy of expression is a common process for most artists. The problem for Tatum's critics, however, was that his technical command was so great that he played, even when he cut back, with what some listeners felt was an excessive and even unrelenting facility.

As time has gone on and we have learned better what he was up to, this criticism has seemed less valid, certainly in terms of his best later work.

Barry Harris is particularly adept at playing the rapid single-note line that Tatum often used and that, as developed by Charlie Parker, evolved into the bebop piano style of Bud Powell. In a medley of "Would You Like To Take A Walk" and "Willow Weep For Me," Barry framed his characteristic style with authentic Tatum harmonies and figurations. Jaki Byard's pixyish manner suggested the sly humor of much of Tatum's playing. Jaki played his "European Episode," which includes unexpected rhythmic devices, Tatumesque harmony and rapidity, and a bit of the stride left hand that Tatum learned from Fats Waller.

More stride was displayed in Dick Wellstood's "I Would Do Most Anything For You." Dick was capable of incorporating large measures of Fats Waller in his playing, although he could also go in quite different directions. The Waller in this solo helped to illustrate Tatum's historical antecedents. Adam Makowicz is a clear example of Tatum's international influence and a first-rate practitioner of the Tatum tradition. An American citizen now but Polish born, Adam demonstrated his beautifully fluent technique on "Lover."

All of us played differently, but all had a specific heritage in common. Some played more in the Tatum manner; others had taken different paths. But all of us had been exposed to Tatum and had worked out our individual solutions to the inspiration his playing represented to us. I felt that we all shared a privileged tradition and that the audience sensed the unity of purpose among us.

At the conclusion of the first half, Billy and I attempted two re-creations of records by the Tatum Trio, with Slam and Tiny joining us. The original trio was a setting in which Tatum sometimes led his partners a merry chase, and clearly had a lot of fun doing it. During their respective solos, Tatum, Tiny, and Slam each tried to outdo the others in quotes from whatever songs or concert pieces came to mind, and their ensemble arrangements included references to an eclectic range of musical material. It has always been common practice for jazz improvisers to make use of phrases from melodies other than the one being performed, but the Tatum Trio probably carried this practice to a more joyful extreme than any comparable group.

Billy played "Flying Home" as the original trio had; I re-created "Body And Soul." Getting in touch with these recordings again during rehearsal, we worked out all the humorous quotes, and it occurred to me to compile a list of them, as best I could. The quotes in "Flying Home":

"Rhapsody In Blue"

"That's What I Like About The South"

"Martha"

"Rockin' In Rhythm"

"At Sundown"

"A Big Fat Mama"

"Old Man River"

"Shave And A Haircut"

And in "Body And Soul":

"I Got Plenty Of Nothin'"

"When The Caissons Go Rolling Along"

"I Don't Want To Set The World On Fire"

"Don't Get Around Much Any More"

"Merrily We Roll Along"

"Vesti La Giubba"

"Yes, We Have No Bananas"

"Love In Bloom"

"Stumbling"

"How Much Is That Doggie In The Window?"

"Humoresque"

The second half of the program began with another film clip, a jam session scene from *The Fabulous Dorseys* in which Tatum is surrounded by a group that includes the Dorseys (Jimmy on clarinet, Tommy on trombone) as well as Charlie Barnet (tenor sax), Ziggy Elman (trumpet), and other stars of the early '40s. Following two short excerpts from Willis Conover's Voice Of America interviews with Tatum, we merged into various two-piano teams for a series of duets: Lewis and Byard, Taylor and Harris, Wellstood and Hyman, Larkins and Makowicz.

After all this piano playing, we felt that the audience would be refreshed by some novelty. On the theory that Tatum's incredible velocity had influenced the playing of John Coltrane, specifically in the direction of what has been called Coltrane's "sheets of sound," we asked Eddie Daniels to play his tenor sax entirely unaccompanied. Daniels, who has absorbed much of Coltrane, perfectly expressed the relationship in a memorable five-minute solo on "They Say That Falling In Love Is Wonderful." (Since then, Eddie has concentrated on a more individual but still highly technical clarinet style. It's interesting to recall that he was an equally proficient saxophonist and flutist.)

In conclusion, with Slam and Tiny playing, all of the pianists did a round-robin at the two keyboards, even at one point teaming up with two or three players at each piano. Eddie Daniels added his saxophone to "Indiana" as a truly grand finale.

Art Tatum was always interested in hearing other pianists, even those who were far less accomplished than he. While concentrating on such a player on one occasion, he was asked what, considering his mastery, he could possibly be learning. "Everybody has his own story," he replied.

THE RETURN OF *SING ALONG WITH MITCH*

In the early 1960's, *Sing Along With Mitch* was a popular television program. Built around a 25-voice male chorus conducted by Mitch Miller, the record producer and oboist, the weekly NBC show ran for several profitable seasons before falling a victim in 1964 to changing tastes. Even then, the recordings of Mitch & The Sing Along Gang continued to sell impressively to an audience not at all affected by the growing appeal of rock music.

In addition to featuring the chorus as a whole, the program permitted several of the singers to reach the public as soloists. These included Bob McGrath, since known to a generation of children for his work on *Sesame Street*. Various guest performers were also featured in appropriate television settings. Campfire scenes, country fairs, and other wholesome American venues were stressed.

The basic orchestral accompaniment to the chorus began as a combination of accordion, bass, drums, harmonica, and three guitars doubling on ukulele and banjo. In Jimmy Carroll's arrangements the folksy quality of the instrumentation complemented the virile sound of the chorus. Occasionally the orchestra was enlarged with a string section and some horns, and, as time went by, various keyboards were added. I became the resident player of harpsichord, organ, piano, and celeste.

Considering the changes which have since taken place in pop music, 1964 was quite a while ago. As we say, there have been a lot of second endings since then. It was startling one day long after to receive a call from Frank Carroll, the bass player and contractor, informing me that we were being summoned to the fray once again. A new *Sing Along* special was in the works, he said, to be shown on NBC in January, 1981, with the possibility of several more during the season. Furthermore, the original band was to be reconstituted, and as many of the original singers as were available would also be on hand.

So it was that during Christmas week of 1980, feeling as though we had stepped into a time machine, we assembled for a pre-recording session at Columbia Records' 30th Street Studio, known for many years as one of the best sound locations in New York. A former church with unsurpassed resonance as well as a spacious area, 30th Street was the site of countless recording sessions, but has since been torn down to make way for one more Manhattan condominium apartment building. In the multi-track recording technology of the present, natural resonance is no longer an asset, and big orchestra sessions, where everybody plays at the same time, have become infrequent. Accordingly, the unforgiving economics of the market place have dictated what will no doubt turn out to have been one of the more short-sighted accounting decisions of

the record industry.

Still, there we were at Christmas time in 1980, sixteen years older and somewhat grayer at the temples, but easily falling into our old studio setup: Tony Mottola, Don Arnone, and Bucky Pizzarelli on guitars, Dominic Cortese on accordion, Frank Carroll on bass, and Bob Rosengarden on drums. Only the harmonica chair, formerly held by Eddie Manson, had been eliminated. I was surrounded by my various keyboards, which now included a couple of new ones, an amplified celeste and a Rhodes electric piano.

We immediately reestablished the two patterns which were characteristic of the old days: perfect musical cooperation, and good-natured but incessant baiting of one another. Between numbers we put each other on outrageously, plumbing depths of irony and insult that only old friends could get away with. But when we played, we listened carefully to each other, modifying or correcting our parts with a minimum of fuss. Most of the arrangements were from the original shows and I found my own ancient notations throughout. This time, however, with the expertise of artistic maturity and the mellowness of middle age, we took greater liberties, playing the arrangements more loosely. The new arranger and assistant conductor, Glenn (Abe) Osser, a veteran of vast and distinguished experience, was of course aware of our modifications. We were all old friends.

Osser wrote several new arrangements for the show and was the replacement for Jimmy Carroll, who had passed away in the interim, as had his brother, Lenny, the copyist. What Mitch refers to as the Carroll Dynasty remained, however, in the presence of Frank, the third brother, and his son, Frank Jr., who functioned as music librarian.

I played a Gutenberg double-manual harpsichord on several of the old tunes, embellishing them a bit when called for. Other tunes called for various keyboards; I played a solo organ accompaniment on the studio Hammond for a choral arrangement of "Finlandia." Rosemary Clooney was to be a guest, singing her 1950 hit, "Come On-a My House," which had been produced by Mitch. We made an instrumental track for her to sing along with on camera. Osser had transcribed her original recording, which featured Stan Freeman on a famous harpsichord solo. I remember the record and suspect that I must have recreated it somewhere before this, because the part seemed very familiar. We recorded it in one take.

In all there were six recording sessions during the week. At the same time, my quintet was playing our annual four-week engagement at Michael's Pub nightly. This put me on a demanding schedule for a few days, as it did Bob Rosengarden, who was working the club with me, and Bucky Pizzarelli, who was playing elsewhere at night. On one long day the calls were from 9:00 A.M. to noon, 1:00 P.M. to 4:00 P.M., and 6:00 P.M. to 7:30 P.M. Rosengarden and I followed this with two shows at the club. Not only were we playing the music of a couple of decades ago, but we also needed to summon our youthful stamina!

The pay scale for a pre-recorded television show is peculiar. The Musicians' Union still bases it on the largely obsolete rate for live shows. The basic payment is theoretically for the telecast itself, while the time spent in pre-recording the music is considered to be a rehearsal, payable at an hourly rate. Also paid as rehearsal is the time it takes to film the action while the pre-recorded tape is rolling. In the old days of *Sing Along* we always used to consider it a misfortune to be involved in a scene in which we actually had to be on camera pretending to play. Such camera sessions often stretched into many tedious hours, for which we earned no more than if the scene had not required the appearance of a live player.

So it was again in 1980: "Come On-a My House"

needed a close-up of hands on the harpsichord keyboards, and some other tunes would show the whole orchestra in a stage setting. I had qualified my accepting the job by warning that I would be unavailable on the camera days due to a prior booking. Fortunately, Dom Cortese, who had to be on camera in any case for his solo on "Sam, The Old Accordion Man," offered to lend his hands for the harpsichord scene. For the other songs I hired Paul Mariconda, an up-and-coming recent graduate of North Texas State, to impersonate me.

At the end of the final pre-recording session, the singers had a lot more work to do, but my part was completed. Setting the time machine for fast-forward, we stepped out into the beginning of 1981. And <u>that</u> was a long time ago!

To my knowledge, the above was the last gathering of Sing Along With Mitch. Occasionally I've seen some of the shows re-run on nostalgia television. What did I think when I watched it? To paraphrase a particularly nasty slogan I've seen on T-shirts recently, "It's an old-folks thing, you wouldn't understand."

RECREATING W.C. HANDY'S 1928 CONCERT

In 1981, I conducted an unusual concert at Carnegie Hall, which was then celebrating its ninetieth season. There was a thirty-piece orchestra, a hundred-voice choir, pianist Don Shirley, and singers Bobby Short, McHenry Boatwright, Geanie Faulkner, Carrie Smith, Katherine Handy Lewis, and her brother, Wyer Handy. The latter two people were of particular importance to us, because this was an event replicating a 1928 concert, also in Carnegie Hall, presented at that time by their father, W.C. Handy. Katherine Handy Lewis as a young girl had actually participated in the original concert and was our historical link with that presentation.

W.C. Handy, who came to be known as the Father of the Blues, was a composer whose works profoundly influenced American popular music. Handy's great success lay in his ability to create such compositions as "St. Louis Blues," "Beale Street Blues," and "Memphis Blues" out of his own folk background, and, with the skills he acquired as an arranger and conductor, to notate and disseminate this idiom in the greater world of popular music. He was also a choral arranger, and his versions of many Negro spirituals are definitive.

Born in Florence, Alabama, in 1873, by the time of his concert Handy had achieved great success. His songs were being performed around the world. "St. Louis Blues" in particular was on its way to being one of the two most recorded songs of all times. (The other, according to the *Guinness Book Of World Records,* is "Star Dust.") Wyer Handy, of Handy Brothers Publishing Company, the firm which still controls all of W.C. Handy's output, estimated that there have been several thousand recorded versions of "St. Louis Blues."

W.C. Handy's own prominence as a composer was only one element in his determination to present a Carnegie Hall concert. His goal was to make the general public aware that Black American music was not limited to the blues and jazz, and that Black performers and composers had been functioning effectively in such other areas as choral music, art songs, orchestral concert works, piano compositions, and theater songs. Consequently, when he produced his 1928 concert, he included in it a variety of music, much of it composed not by him but by other Black composers. From our present point of view, what he selected constitutes a significant document of his era.

We had done this concert once before, in 1976, at the Kennedy Center in Washington, D.C. The more recent concert, five years later at Carnegie Hall, was actually a repeat performance using most of the same artists. For the more recent event John Motley assembled a New York choir; the Washington concert featured Nathan Carter's Morgan State University Choir from Baltimore. Don Shirley was the piano soloist in 1981; Alan Booth in 1976.

The research and arranging necessary to put the concert together took place in 1976 after George Wein, the producer, handed me a program of the 1928 event and left me pretty much to my own devices. The program was divided into groups of pieces: plantation songs, spirituals, work songs, blues, jazz, comic songs, art songs, piano solos, etc., much of it unfamiliar to me. The basic question was how to begin to assemble the material.

I started by visiting Handy Brothers and consulting with Wyer Handy. We found most of the choral arrangements which W.C. Handy had made of the program's spirituals and work songs. These titles were in print, but they were published with piano accompaniment only. I had optimistically hoped that we would stumble over an old box labeled "Carnegie Hall 1928." Unfortunately, looking in the most obscure corners of the back room of Handy Brothers, we had no such luck. Nor were any of the various stock arrangements of "St. Louis Blues" and the other Handy songs completely suitable. It began to be clear that I would be doing considerable orchestration on this project.

All we had to begin with, it seemed, were the choral arrangements and Handy's account of the concert in his memoirs. This source was helpful. We learned from it, that the orchestra numbered 30 musicians. Working with Dick Sudhalter on the musicological research, we discovered that there was important material in the Library of Congress. "Yamekraw," a concert work by James P. Johnson for piano and orchestra, was available from the Library, although only in the smallest of the three instrumentations which had been published. The score, which had been by William Grant Still, was missing, but the various instrumentations were clearly described on the cover of the piano-conductor part. Using a little deductive reasoning, I was able to orchestrate the additional parts which made up the fullest instrumentation.

"Yamekraw" was performed in the original concert by Fats Waller. I undertook the solo part in 1976 and again in 1981. "Yamekraw" is obviously patterned along the lines of Gershwin's "Rhapsody in Blue," which preceded it by five years. It is a quaint work filled with James P. Johnson's stride piano style. In my opinion, however, its themes are less interesting than many of Johnson's other pieces, and it may be that they were not composed by Johnson at all. His publisher, Perry Bradford, claimed authorship, later writing that he had assigned various melodies to Johnson to develop into a longer work. While "Yamekraw" lacks the originality and integration of "Rhapsody In Blue," it stands as an interesting commentary on the earlier work.

Using the instrumentation necessary for "Yamekraw," I arranged other selections from the 1928 program after meeting with the various singers, assigning material and determining keys and routines. Some additional choral writing was needed for spirituals Handy had not published, and it turned out finally that all of the orchestral pieces had to be newly arranged, with the exception of "Yamekraw."

Several of the 1928 newspaper reviews which we were able to obtain noted that the concert was excessively long, so it seemed wise to join various songs into medleys and eliminate three of the less important ones. Apart from these, we matched the original program closely and made it a point to print the 1928 program and the newer one on facing pages of our booklet. I suspect we used the orchestra more than Mr. Handy did, since I orchestrated songs which had probably been accompanied by piano only. We did retain the piano accompaniment on the two spirituals sung solo by McHenry Boatwright. On these Mr. Boatwright accompanied himself.

The old 1928 program shows Fats Waller not only performing on piano on "Yamekraw" but playing "St. Louis Blues" as an organ solo. Accordingly, I began our 1981 finale with a Waller-style organ solo using the Carnegie Hall 5-manual Allen electronic instrument. For good measure, I also accompanied Carrie Smith in the Waller manner on "I Ain't Got Nobody."

The piano solos, "Juba Dance" by Nathaniel Dett and "Bamboula" by Samuel Coleridge-Taylor, both light and elegant pieces, are still in print, and they deserve to be played. Many of the other titles need-ed to be tracked down. We got some song sheets from the Library of Congress, others from the Lincoln Center Library in New York, others from Handy Brothers. Two items of pianistic interest were the very "classical" art songs, "Spring Had Come" by Coleridge-Taylor and "Hear The Lambs A-Cryin'" by H.T. Burleigh, which were sung by Geanie Faulkner, accompanied by Kelly Wyatt.

Bobby Short's two comic songs, "Wouldn't That Be a Dream" and "The Unbeliever," are characteristically broad in their humorous use of racially stereotyped lyrics. This type of song, with lines such as "painting the White House black" and "make me whiter than snow" was an important part of pop culture in the early part of the century. Much of this material was written, in fact, by Black writers such as Bert Williams, who was also its most outstanding performer. By the 1950's, the consensus of taste had made these songs an uneasy anachronism. Now, however, particularly when performed with the suavity of Mr. Short, this material can be accepted as an historical curiosity. His great ease with the audience permitted him to get an appreciative response from listeners who might otherwise have found some of the lyrics offensive.

In the finale Katherine Handy Lewis sang a special lyric to "St. Louis Blues":

"If my papa were here tonight how happy he would be,

If my papa were here tonight how happy he would be,

To hear his music in Carnegie Hall making history."

The original history, of course, had been made in 1928.

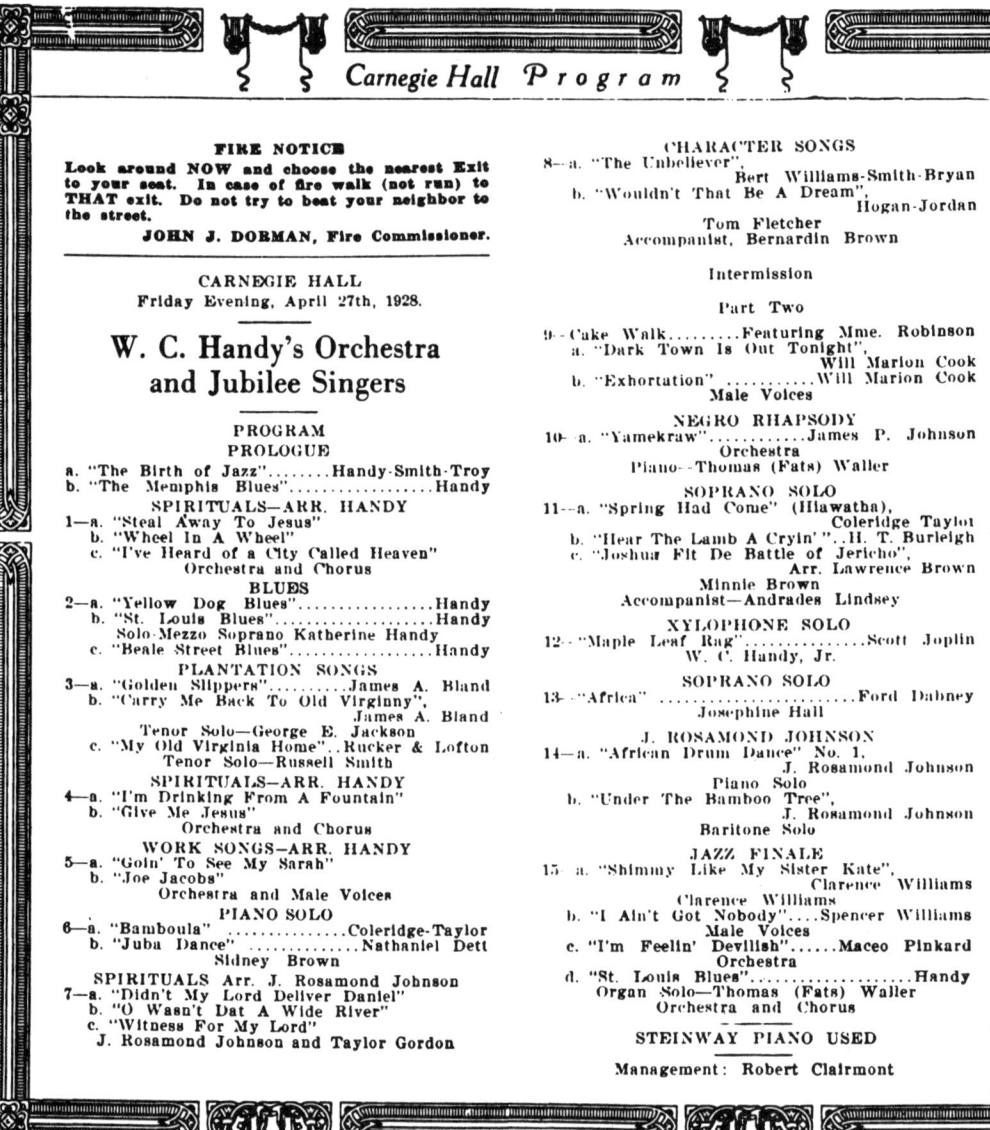

FIRE NOTICE

Look around NOW and choose the nearest Exit to your seat. In case of fire walk (not run) to THAT exit. Do not try to beat your neighbor to the street.

JOHN J. DORMAN, Fire Commissioner.

CARNEGIE HALL
Friday Evening, April 27th, 1928.

W. C. Handy's Orchestra and Jubilee Singers

PROGRAM
PROLOGUE
a. "The Birth of Jazz".......Handy-Smith-Troy
b. "The Memphis Blues"..................Handy
SPIRITUALS—ARR. HANDY
1—a. "Steal Away To Jesus"
b. "Wheel In A Wheel"
c. "I've Heard of a City Called Heaven"
Orchestra and Chorus
BLUES
2—a. "Yellow Dog Blues"................Handy
b. "St. Louis Blues"...................Handy
Solo-Mezzo Soprano Katherine Handy
c. "Beale Street Blues".................Handy
PLANTATION SONGS
3—a. "Golden Slippers".........James A. Bland
b. "Carry Me Back To Old Virginny",
James A. Bland
Tenor Solo—George E. Jackson
c. "My Old Virginia Home"..Rucker & Lofton
Tenor Solo—Russell Smith
SPIRITUALS—ARR. HANDY
4—a. "I'm Drinking From A Fountain"
b. "Give Me Jesus"
Orchestra and Chorus
WORK SONGS—ARR. HANDY
5—a. "Goin' To See My Sarah"
b. "Joe Jacobs"
Orchestra and Male Voices
PIANO SOLO
6—a. "Bamboula" ....Coleridge-Taylor
b. "Juba Dance" ....Nathaniel Dett
Sidney Brown
SPIRITUALS Arr. J. Rosamond Johnson
7—a. "Didn't My Lord Deliver Daniel"
b. "O Wasn't Dat A Wide River"
c. "Witness For My Lord"
J. Rosamond Johnson and Taylor Gordon

CHARACTER SONGS
8—a. "The Unbeliever",
Bert Williams-Smith-Bryan
b. "Wouldn't That Be A Dream",
Hogan-Jordan
Tom Fletcher
Accompanist, Bernardin Brown

Intermission

Part Two
9—Cake Walk........Featuring Mme. Robinson
a. "Dark Town Is Out Tonight",
Will Marion Cook
b. "Exhortation" ....Will Marion Cook
Male Voices
NEGRO RHAPSODY
10—a. "Yamekraw"...........James P. Johnson
Orchestra
Piano—Thomas (Fats) Waller
SOPRANO SOLO
11—a. "Spring Had Come" (Hiawatha),
Coleridge Taylor
b. "Hear The Lamb A Cryin' "..H. T. Burleigh
c. "Joshua Fit De Battle of Jericho",
Arr. Lawrence Brown
Minnie Brown
Accompanist—Andrades Lindsey
XYLOPHONE SOLO
12—"Maple Leaf Rag"..............Scott Joplin
W. C. Handy, Jr.
SOPRANO SOLO
13—"Africa" ....Ford Dabney
Josephine Hall
J. ROSAMOND JOHNSON
14—a. "African Drum Dance" No. 1,
J. Rosamond Johnson
Piano Solo
b. "Under The Bamboo Tree",
J. Rosamond Johnson
Baritone Solo
JAZZ FINALE
15—a. "Shimmy Like My Sister Kate",
Clarence Williams
Clarence Williams
b. "I Ain't Got Nobody"....Spencer Williams
Male Voices
c. "I'm Feelin' Devilish"......Maceo Pinkard
Orchestra
d. "St. Louis Blues"..................Handy
Organ Solo—Thomas (Fats) Waller
Orchestra and Chorus

STEINWAY PIANO USED

Management: Robert Clairmont

Original Concert Program

Kennedy Center Program

KENNEDY CENTER
Saturday Evening, May 29, 1976

A Joyous Bicentennial Salute to

W. C. HANDY
Father of the Blues

Performed by

THE NEW YORK
JAZZ REPERTORY COMPANY

PROGRAM
PROLOGUE
a. "The Birth of Jazz" . . . . Handy-Smith-Troy
b. "The Memphis Blues" . . . . Handy

SPIRITUALS — ARR. HANDY
1 — a. "Steal Away to Jesus"
   b. "Wheel in a Wheel"
   c. "I've Heard of a City Called Heaven"
       Orchestra and Chorus

BLUES
2 — a. "Yellow Dog Blues" . . . . Handy
   b. "St. Louis Blues". . . . . Handy
   Mezzo Soprano Solo — Katharine Handy Lewis

PLANTATION SONGS
3 — a. "Golden Slippers". . . . . . . James A. Bland
   b. "Carry Me Back to Old Virginny"
               James A. Bland
   c. "My Old Virginia Home" Rucker & Lofton
       Tenor Solo — Bobby Short

SPIRITUALS — ARR. HANDY
4 — a. "I'm Drinking From a Fountain"
   b. "Give Me Jesus"
       Orchestra and Chorus

WORK SONGS — ARR. HANDY
5 — a. "Goin' to See My Sarah"
   b. "Joe Jacobs"
       Orchestra and Male Voices

PIANO SOLO
6 — a. "Bamboula" . . . . Coleridge-Taylor
   b. "Juba Dance" . . . . Nathaniel Dett

       Alan Booth

BLUES
7. "Beale Street Blues". . . . . Handy
       Contralto Solo — Carrie Smith

SPIRITUALS Arr. J. Rosamond Johnson
8 — a. "Didn't My Lord Deliver Daniel"
   b. "O Wasn't Dat a Wide River"
       Baritone solo — McHenry Boatwright
   c. "Witness For My Lord"
     Duet — McHenry Boatwright and Bobby Short

CHARACTER SONGS
9 — a. "Wouldn't That Be a Dream"
                 Hogan-Jordan
   b. "The Unbeliever"
          Bert Williams-Smith-Bryan
     Tenor Solo — Bobby Short

Intermission

Part Two

CAKE WALK
10- a. "Dark Town Is Out Tonight"
              Will Marion Cook
     Orchestra and Chorus
   b. "Exhortation" . . . . Will Marion Cook
     Baritone Solo — McHenry Boatwright

NEGRO RHAPSODY
11. "Yamekraw" . . . . James P. Johnson
       Orchestra
     Piano — Dick Hyman

SOPRANO SOLO
12- a. "Spring Had Come" (Hiawatha)
              Coleridge-Taylor
   b. "Hear the Lamb A-Cryin'" . . H. T. Burleigh
   c. "Joshua Fit De Battle of Jericho"
           Arr. Lawrence Brown
       Geanie Faulkner
     Accompanist — Alan Booth

JAZZ FINALE
13-a. "Under the Bamboo Tree"
              J. Rosamond Johnson
   b. "Shimmy Like My Sister Kate"
            Clarence Williams
       Bobby Short
   c. "I Ain't Got Nobody" . . . . Spencer Williams
       Carrie Smith
     Organ accompanist — Dick Hyman
   d. "I'm Feelin' Devilish" . . . . . Maceo Pinkard
       Carrie Smith
   e. "St. Louis Blues". . . . . Handy
       Katherine Handy Lewis
       Carrie Smith
       Orchestra and Chorus
     Organ solo — Dick Hyman

BALDWIN PIANO AND ORGAN USED

Production: George Wein
Richard M. Sudhalter & Gus Fleming

This program is made possible by a grant from Exxon Corporation.

Recreation Concert Program

RECREATING PAUL WHITEMAN'S 1924 CONCERT

When the sixtieth anniversary of Paul Whiteman's legendary Aeolian Hall concert arrived last February, the eminent symphonic conductor Maurice Peress turned producer and organized a scrupulous recreation of the original event. Whiteman, whose orchestra was the most celebrated of the big dance bands of the 1920's, entitled his concert "An Experiment In Modern Music." He presented "melodious" popular music innovatively arranged for a large ensemble.

The original 1924 program notes regret that the music Whiteman was to perform was still known as "jazz," and take pains to distance the achievements of his arranging staff, headed by Ferde Grofé, from the earlier "discordant jazz, which sprang into existence about ten years ago from nowhere in particular." The program opens with a pejorative rendition of the Original Dixieland Jazz Band's "Livery Stable Blues," described as an example of "true, naked" jazz at its most raucous.

Whiteman was in fact presenting a pops concert, using a few elements of what we now understand to have been jazz, at a time when its definition had even less consensus than it does today. The Aeolian Hall concert is remembered, more significantly, as the occasion when George Gershwin's "Rhapsody In Blue" was first performed.

Mr. Peress followed the Whiteman program closely, obtaining the "Rhapsody" in its original Grofé orchestration ("for piano and jazz band"). He also found the score to "A Suite Of Serenades," by Victor Herbert, who was commissioned, as was Gershwin, to compose a work for the occasion. In addition, Peress located or transcribed from recordings the Grofé arrangements of such popular tunes as "Whispering" and "Yes, We Have No Bananas" and adaptations of MacDowell's "To A Wild Rose" and Rimsky-Korsakov's "Song Of India."

There was also in 1924 a solo section featuring pianist/composer Zez Confrey, who was at the time a considerably better known performer than Gershwin. Confrey played "Kitten On The Keys" and several of his other piano novelties. I was asked to assume this role. As Confrey, my contributions included "Kitten on The Keys," "Three Little Oddities," and "Nickel In The Slot," as well as a medley of Irving Berlin favorites.

By far the most important piece on the program, then and now, was "Rhapsody In Blue." The best justification for our 1984 concert was that we were able to demonstrate for modern ears the forgotten musical world from which the "Rhapsody" emerged and which, even at its first performance, it transcended. Peress engaged as soloist Ivan Davis, in whose expert hands the "Rhapsody" sounded once more as

dramatic as it had at its premiere.

With a band of top-flight New York musicians to match Paul Whiteman's original virtuoso group, we played our concert on February 12, 1984, in Town Hall, 60 years later and one city block north of the site of the old Aeolian Hall, now long since demolished. The antique arrangements sounded outrageously old-fashioned, yet elegant and perfectly balanced in the resonant acoustics of Town Hall.

There had been talk of our repeating the concert in Rome the following weekend, but, as of our Sunday performance, financial loose ends had not been tied up, and there was some doubt that the tour would take place. Consequently, Julia and I left the following day for a Caribbean vacation, gambling that our stay in the tropics would be uninterrupted. Sure enough, on Tuesday I received a call from New York informing me that Rome was off, and that I could continue to relax under my palm tree. Relieved that I wouldn't have to stir, I let myself sink into tropical torpor. On Wednesday night at dinnertime, however, I was shocked to hear from Maurice that bank credit had been received at last. We were scheduled for two performances in Rome the following weekend. So on Friday I set out, traveling on three different planes back to New York in order to board a fourth, an Alitalia flight, for eight more hours in the air.

We arrived at 9:30 Saturday morning, Rome time, close to 20 hours after I had embarked. Sleep during this time had been intermittent, with no more than interrupted dozes here and there. My most memorable awakening took place as we were passing over the snow-covered Alps at dawn.

Checking into the Imperiale on Via Veneto, I slept soundly for two hours, then walked over to the theater to do my minimum keyboard exercises. These consist of approximately an hour of muscle-strengthening finger work. The effect on a listener unfortunate enough to be in the vicinity is likely to be maddening — somewhat like being forced to attend an interminable concert of minimalist music. The reputation of the Italians as lovers of melody was reinforced when I became aware that enraged stagehands were trying to drown me out with banging and stamping, crying "Basta, basta!" ("Enough, already!"). I reasoned with them and stubbornly persisted. While Confrey is hardly as taxing technically as some other works in the repertoire, walking out on stage and ripping into "Kitten On The Keys" nevertheless requires a certain level of chops, especially if you just arrived from the tropics and have had two hours of sleep.

During that weekend, practicing, performing, sleeping, and eating were all I challenged myself to accomplish, the sights of Rome notwithstanding. I caught up on sleep whenever possible, nursed a slightly queasy stomach, and refrained from joining the gang for some notable Italian meals.

When it was all over, Maurice, Ivan, and I joined the rest of the band at a celebratory dinner. Wonders had been worked, by Maurice, who had had to cope with replacing many of the Town Hall musicians. Because of the on-and-off nature of the Roman venture, saxophonist/clarinetist Walt Levinsky had to return from California, Ivan Davis flew from Miami to New York twice, and British trombonist Chris Smith flew from London to Rome on an hour's notice. In addition, Italian musicians supple-mented our basic contingent.

On Monday we headed back to New York. On Tuesday I returned to the Caribbean for the second week of my vacation, during which I looked forward to recovering from the first. Julia was waiting on the beach.

These were the first concerts of what turned out to be five years of touring the Paul Whiteman "Experiment In Modern Music." By 1989 the charms of "Kitten On The Keys" were wearing thin for me, and, with Maurice Peress' sympathy, I called it a day.

THE PIANISM OF ZEZ CONFREY

Edward Elzear "Zez" Confrey (1895-1971) is best remembered, in a long career devoted to the milieu of popular music known as novelty piano, as the composer of "Kitten On The Keys" and "Dizzy Fingers." His was a prolific talent which both defined and enlarged the boundaries of novelty piano, an imprecise category which has come to be an umbrella term covering many styles of popular piano playing.

In its broadest sense, the term "novelty piano" designates a large repertoire of piano compositions meant to be accessible on first hearing, brief musical entertainments which were novel in the sense of being new and intriguing to the popular ear, often but not invariably influenced by the concurrent idioms of ragtime and jazz, and which were technically within the grasp of the piano-playing public which bought vast quantities of the published sheet music. Novelty piano flourished most profusely in the decades of the '20s, '30s, and '40s, when the piano was the preeminent instrument in American popular music. Its first practitioners built on many of the devices of classic ragtime, but the category had non-rag antecedents as well. Consider, for example, such late-1800's pieces as "Glow Worm," originally a piano composition rather than a song, and the innumerable waltzes and other dance pieces of the period. We might even go back as far as the venerable "Chopsticks" for early evidence of the genre. As tastes in popular piano evolved, there came inevitably to be borrowings from whatever piano styles had come to the fore: stride, swing, and various light classical approaches. In our day "Nadia's Theme" would fall within the venue, as would "Alley Cat," which appeared in the '60s and has been a staple of club date bands ever since.

What intrigued and challenged pianists in Zez Confrey's compositions, particularly those he wrote early in his career, is still apparent as one turns the pages of a collection of his works published by Belwin-Mills. Most impressive is the sense of the pianist/composer discovering and delighting in novel uses of fingering as applied to the fresh possibilities of syncopated rhythm. It is this innovative pianistic approach that distinguishes Confrey from his contemporaries. Consider the liberating effect of the unorthodox finger slides necessary to play "Kitten On The Keys" with the proper emphasis. *(See Example A.)*

It was the fingering as much as the tune itself that appealed to pianists of the '20s, and which continues to interest us today. Try to find a more comfortable fingering that works as well as the suggested slides.

Confrey was also fond of two-handed devices such as that seen in the introduction to "My Pet," a piece written in the same year, 1921, as "Kitten." *(See Example B.)*

Of course, this device was in the air at the time. It

occurs throughout Gershwin's "Rhapsody in Blue," as do other Confreyisms.

Some tricky syncopation in two hands is found in the marvelously titled "You Tell 'Em, Ivories," also dating from 1921. *(See Example C.)*

A year later Confrey was experimenting with two syncopated melodies simultaneously played by the right hand while a normal stride pattern occupies the left. This excerpt is from "Coaxing The Piano." *(See Example D.)*

In a departure from the novelty ragtime style, Confrey applied syncopation to a waltz. In "Anticipation," the melody is in the lower tones of the right hand. *(See Example E.)*

Although he was also an occasional songwriter, Confrey was at his best as a composer for the keyboard. His most lasting ideas were generated from the interaction of the fingers with the piano keys, and it is this sense of discovery which comes through even today.

I recorded "Kitten On The Keys, The Piano Music of Zez Confrey" for RCA Records around the time of this article. RCA is now BMG. To my present knowledge, this LP has not been reissued on CD, but I'm hoping.

MAKING FRIENDS WITH PIPE ORGANS

When I was scheduled to play on an unfamiliar theatre pipe organ in Ocean Grove, New Jersey, I drove down the day before to familiarize myself with it, having learned that such instruments differ greatly from one another. You can't expect, as you might with a piano, simply to slide onto the bench and start making music. Since I've become interested in these marvelous constructions of a bygone era, I've been consulting my old friend Lee Erwin, one of the few theatre organists who still accompanies silent films. Lee presided at that time at the console of an instrument at the Carnegie Cinema, which specializes in revivals of old films, and he allowed me to ask him lots of questions as I worked out on his two-manual Wurlitzer.

I was delighted when Lee expressed an interest in seeing the Ocean Grove organ, which he told me was one of the few surviving instruments built by Robert Hope-Jones, whose name is revered in theatre organ circles. Along with Don Schwing, Lee's organ technician, we left Manhattan for the Jersey shore on a hot summer morning and arrived an hour and a half later at the quaint village of Ocean Grove, a slice of nineteenth-century America which, like its organ, has somehow been preserved from the waves of modernity threatening it from nearby Asbury Park. The town has been the site of Methodist religious gatherings since the 1800's and has retained the special character of the people who founded it. Many of the scenes in Woody Allen's *Stardust Memories* were shot in Ocean Grove, and, with its carefully tended hedges, its well-kept old frame houses, and several unique streets of connected and furnished summer tents, the town seems to be a permanent stage set. At the center of the community is a large wooden auditorium, a prominent fixture of which is a truly mighty console of four manuals and innumerable stop tablets.

The temperature inside the auditorium was in the 90's as we went over the 1908 instrument, a preliminary introduction to which was provided by the resident organist, Gordon Turk. Because our time was limited, and keeping in mind that my three solos the following evening would occur in the middle of a concert of other music, we fell back on the organist's great friend, the preset pistons. Organists use these controls to prepare in advance any combination of tonal registrations and make them available instantly at the touch of a button. This eliminates the problem of hunting for each of the correct stops during a performance on a still fairly unfamiliar console.

One stop tablet intrigued me. Among the hundred or so on which were inscribed the names of such succulent organ delights as *diaphone, quintadena,*

and *tuba bombarde* was one that was simply labelled *flag.* Curious, I depressed it. Immediately, I was amazed to see overhead a galaxy of light bulbs blinking on and off, set in an enormous American flag with a cross above it. It was a spectacular sight, a light show out of the past. In the performance, I saved it, with suitable clarion fanfares, for the finale of "Ain't Misbehavin'." Fats would have been proud.

Pipe organs differ profoundly in their psychology from electronic ones. They seem to want to play a different sort of music from what I have come to expect from the studio Hammonds, Lowreys, Baldwins, and Yamahas I've played in television, radio, and recording situations. When I prepare for the occasional concerts I now play on the pipes, I have the distinct impression that the organ is teaching me what it wants to do. Since I have much to learn, I listen carefully. Naturally, I have some ideas in mind as well, so the music that results is an accommodation that the organ and I make to each other.

The tonal colors of a pipe organ are its great glory. I love the rustling string sounds and the spatial character of the various solo elements, which are separate and not electronically compressed into the confines of an audio speaker. Above all, I'm stimulated by being able to orchestrate on the spot.

There are some important physical differences between electronic and pipe organs. The former speak instantly; the latter are comparatively sluggish. Furthermore, certain elements of the collection of instruments comprised in a pipe organ may speak at different rates. The long pipes take a greater length of time to fill with air than the short ones, so that the low tones of the foot pedals will not speak immediately. And the percussion devices — real instruments such as xylophone, bells, and snare drum — may be activated at a still different millisecond. This conglomeration of time responses makes the organ an instrument which really yearns to play out of tempo altogether, which much prefers to soar *espressivamente* and *tremulando* and has to be coaxed and cajoled into the rhythmic steadiness one requires for jazz. Once you launch into a bright, swinging tempo, however, with everything somehow coordinated and the instrument sounding perhaps a beat behind your fingers, the sensation is like leading a herd of galloping elephants. You don't dare look back.

The three-manual Wurlitzer now housed in the Emery Auditorium in Cincinnati taught me a certain amount of what it wanted to do when I recorded a Fats Waller album on it. This instrument, like most theatre organs, was built for the palatial movie houses of the 1920's in order to accompany silent films. When sound films arrived, instruments such as this one lost their primary reason for being, and theatre owners in many cases abandoned them, boarded them up, or sold them for parts. Through the efforts of the American Theatre Organ Society and a band of devoted organ buffs, many of the surviving instruments have been moved and are maintained in auditoriums or private homes. The Emery organ was transported from a local movie theater to its present location, where, in cooperation with the University of Cincinnati, it is frequently presented in concert or used for silent film accompaniment once more.

I practiced on it for a couple of days and then spent another couple recording the album. I was able to make use of a curiosity of theatre organ keyboards known as *second touch*. This registration permits you to summon a different tone color by depressing a key completely (taking care to play lightly the rest of the time). The technique is useful for accents, for example, allowing you to punctuate with a chime note, a snare drum stroke, or some louder tone color. I also had some fun with the Emery organ's upright piano, which is integrated with the rest of the bag of tricks but is placed about twenty feet away from the organ console. To play the organ keys and simultaneously watch the corresponding piano keys go down a fraction of a second later is an eerie sensation. On several selections I combined the piano to good effect with xylophone and bells.

It was interesting to play the same Fats Waller pieces some time later on a completely different organ, an 1845 Henry Erben two-manual instrument located in the Old Whalers' Presbyterian Church in Sag Harbor, Long Island, not far from where I live. A church organ's role is quite different from that of a theatre organ, and many of the registrations I had used in Cincinnati were not possible here. There was a limited tremolo, no percussion except an octave of chimes (added in recent times), and, since there was no swell pedal, very little control of dynamics other than through registration.

This organ was old enough to have been built with tracker action, a type mostly supplanted by the more modern electro-pneumatic action. In both, the pipes are filled with air released under pressure from a primary source. In electro-pneumatic action, an electrical contact activated by the depression of each key signals the mechanism to release the air into the pipe. In the tracker organ, the key itself is mechanically connected by a system of levers with the valve that opens the pipe. Tracker action is harder and is liable to be irregular, but some organists claim it gives them greater control over the tone production.

Although this organ was modest in its registration and somewhat crude in its mechanism, we got to be friends after I had practiced on it five or six times. It showed me what it liked to do, and after I got the hang of the old-fashioned draw-knob stops (no presets here) it obliged me with Fats Waller sounds the like of which had never before been heard in the Whalers' Church. The console was overhead at the rear, as is customary in churches. The audience sat mostly in the balconies along the length of the building, where the organ could be seen and heard at its best.

Waller At The Whaler's... a good album title, especially when the August weather made it truly hot music.

RECORDING THE MUSIC FOR WOODY ALLEN'S *ZELIG*

The *Zelig* experience began for me with a recording session on November 3, 1981. I had been called by Woody Allen's office to arrange a song for a scene which would be shot later as part of an untitled film. Singer Marilyn Michaels, an expert Mae West impressionist, would mime during the filming to our previously recorded performance. The song, "The Wizard," by Sara Weeks and Michael Abbott, was cleverly crafted to resemble material that Mae West, the original Hollywood sex symbol, performed in her early films. However, the otherwise characteristic lyrics contained a reference to a mysterious Leonard Zelig, as well as a curious rhyming of "wizard" and "lizard." These puzzling clues constituted my introduction to the ingenious plot of *Zelig*, a film concerning a human chameleon who takes on not only the manner but the physical form of others.

Unfortunately, "The Wizard" was one of a number of examples of perfectly good music which, for non-musical reasons, ended up on the proverbial cutting-room floor. Although the singer and the orchestra both sounded fine, the filming of the scene proved unsuccessful, and film-goers will never have the opportunity to see Mae West moaning her passion for the peculiar charms of Leonard Zelig.

Two weeks later I was asked to conduct a 1920's orchestra on camera in a dance hall scene. The film was then known simply as "Woody's Fall Project." I was told that the plot called for a depiction of crazed youth hoofing to the new dance sensation, "The Chameleon", an indicator of the public hysteria attending the burgeoning and bizarre career of Leonard Zelig. Accordingly, orchestra and cast assembled one day at the Ritz, an old ballroom in lower Manhattan, which I remembered from the days when it had been used as a recording studio by RCA Victor.

The band was provided with 1920's tuxedos, and those of us who would be directly on camera were given a fast haircut and sideburn trim so that we would have the proper period look. Chuck Spies, our drummer, brought his old-time traps, complete with big bass drum and tiny cymbals, while Vince Giordano's giant tuba lent further authenticity. I was requested to wear old-fashioned metal-rimmed eyeglasses, and as an afterthought I was handed a large plastic iguana, which I impaled on my baton.

I had written an instrumental piece to inspire the dancers, who were costumed as Charleston-era flappers and their beaux. Choreographer Twyla Tharp worked with them, instructing them in weird lizard-like movements. We played my piece throughout the rather tedious day, while the dancers flicked their tongues and jerked their heads in a reptilian manner.

A month passed during which the shooting on the film continued, and on the day before Christmas we recorded again. By this time the requirements for music were more specific, and the session was a grab bag of oddities. Norman Brooks, a singer who has made a career of recreating the style of Al Jolson, was called in to perform the old tune "I'm Sitting On Top Of The World," with the lyrics slightly altered to refer to Leonard Zelig. I had by this time added my own lyrics to the instrumental piece we had introduced at the Ritz, and we recorded it as "Doin' The Chameleon" with a male trio in the manner of the Rhythm Boys, a vocal group of the '20s which included Bing Crosby and was featured with the Paul Whiteman orchestra. We also taped three other tunes of mine for which Woody had suggested provocative titles: "You May Be Six People, But I Love You," "You Have Such Reptile Eyes," and "Leonard The Lizard." In the film the three pieces underscore a montage of sheet music covers and suggest the growing *Zelig*mania. Later on, I was able to use the melody of "Leonard The Lizard" as a motif in the underscoring of other scenes.

For the recording sessions we went to considerable lengths to get a period sound. We set up three carbon microphones for the band, and when the resulting sound was better than we expected, our engineer, Roy Yokelson, mixed it with even less bass and treble. Finally, we added a hiss track to suggest scratchy 78 rpm records.

We began to plan the music which would underscore the pseudo-newsreels and the mock documentary scenes that make up so much of the film. In various meetings we agreed on the general approach, and occasionally I demonstrated thematic ideas on a spinet piano which had been moved into the editing room. Finally, when all of the prerecorded items had been positioned and the film had been edited into a basic form, I received a video cassette of it and spent a good part of the summer of 1982 scoring.

Time was passing. What would eventually be titled *Zelig* was now known as "Summer II," in order to distinguish it from another Woody Allen film in progress. There were more recording sessions before the final one came on September 21, ten sessions in all in which music was done and occasionally redone for various reasons. We used different-sized orchestras, from a small jazz band to a group of 41 players.

An authentic 1930s scene of Fanny Brice performing "I've Got A Feeling I'm Falling" occurs midway through the film. Brice appears to be singing, but the lyrics contain the obligatory reference to Leonard Zelig. In order to accomplish this, I played piano along with the original Brice performance, listening to the old soundtrack on headphones. At that point, singer Roz Harris, who is able to mimic the Brice style perfectly, sang the adjusted lyrics to my recorded accompaniment. Simultaneously she watched the original film, from which the old sound had been removed, synchronizing her performance to Brice's.

The post-filming recording sessions were played almost entirely to click tracks in order to have them synchronize exactly with the film. One very brief scene of a hand rapping on the door of a speakeasy is typical of some of the technical problems. We wanted the rapping to be included in a drum solo which would serve as an introduction to the tune "Chicago," which we would then see the speakeasy band performing. Sandy Morse, the film editor, gave me the exact number of frames in between the visible hand motions, and I used this to calibrate the tempo of the subsequent piece. The door-rapping scene was over in a couple of seconds, and the fact that no one has yet commented on it fulfills the old saying about film scoring to the effect that if you don't notice it, film music is doing its job well. There is a grain of truth to this: Music is composed in the service of the film, and it should not unduly call attention to itself, no matter how ingenious it may be.

My own favorite cue occurs toward the end of *Zelig*. We witness the hero (Woody Allen) and Eudora Fletcher (Mia Farrow) escaping from Nazi Germany in a tiny biplane, all of the Luftwaffe in hot pursuit. I called on buried memories of the music for a Flash Gordon serial I saw as a kid, brass blaring portentously under the action, and captured the comic-strip hokiness of the scene.

Although a film composer almost always accepts the length of a specific scene as a given, I asked Sandy Morse to extend the escape-from-Germany footage with more of the stock shots of Leonard and Eudora's plane flying triumphantly, although upside down, across the Atlantic. A few seconds more were needed to complete a grand phrase of "America The Beautiful," orchestrated in as stirring a manner as possible.

Woody Allen often works with specific phonograph records in mind during the editing process. Before I began to score *Zelig*, he had discovered several items in a long-out-of-print album dating back to the 1950s. These performances, by a group known as the Charleston City All-Stars, expressed to him the right relationship of music and image in certain scenes, and are now embodied in the *Zelig* score. By a strange coincidence, and with the inscrutable working of destiny and my personal *karma*, I was the All-Stars' piano-player.

The following original songs were heard in whole or in part in *Zelig*: "Doin' The Chameleon," "Chameleon Days," "Leonard The Lizard," "You Have Such Reptile Eyes," "You May Be Six People, But I Love You".

Doin' The Chameleon

from Zelig

WORDS AND MUSIC
DICK HYMAN

* breath exhalation like a cymbal

My, oh, my! Throw your best gal down right on the floor,

she'll be beg - ging you for more, and you're Doin' The Cham - el - e -

on! If you hold your breath till
Wig - gle like a

you turn blue, you'll be chang - ing col - ors like they do, and you're Doin'
sal - a - man - der, go this way, that way, all me - an - der, you're Doin'

The Cham - el - e - on! (pah!) Vo - do - do - de - o.

Chameleon Days

from *Zelig*

WORDS AND MUSIC
DICK HYMAN

49

Leonard The Lizard

from Zelig

WORDS AND MUSIC
DICK HYMAN

flash, he's go-ing to crash in-to the ground._____

On the ceil-ing, on the wall, First he's

short, and then he's tall. L. E. O. N.

A. R. D. Don't you wish that

you could be— Leon - ard The Liz - ard!

See him climb-ing right up the pole,

See him scut-tl-ing down a hole, See him put-ting on an - y old role,

Leon - ard The Liz - ard!

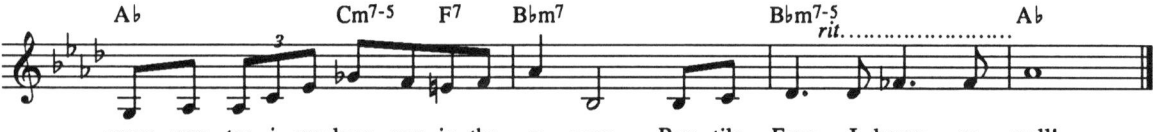

You Have Such Reptile Eyes

from Zelig

Words and Music
Dick Hyman

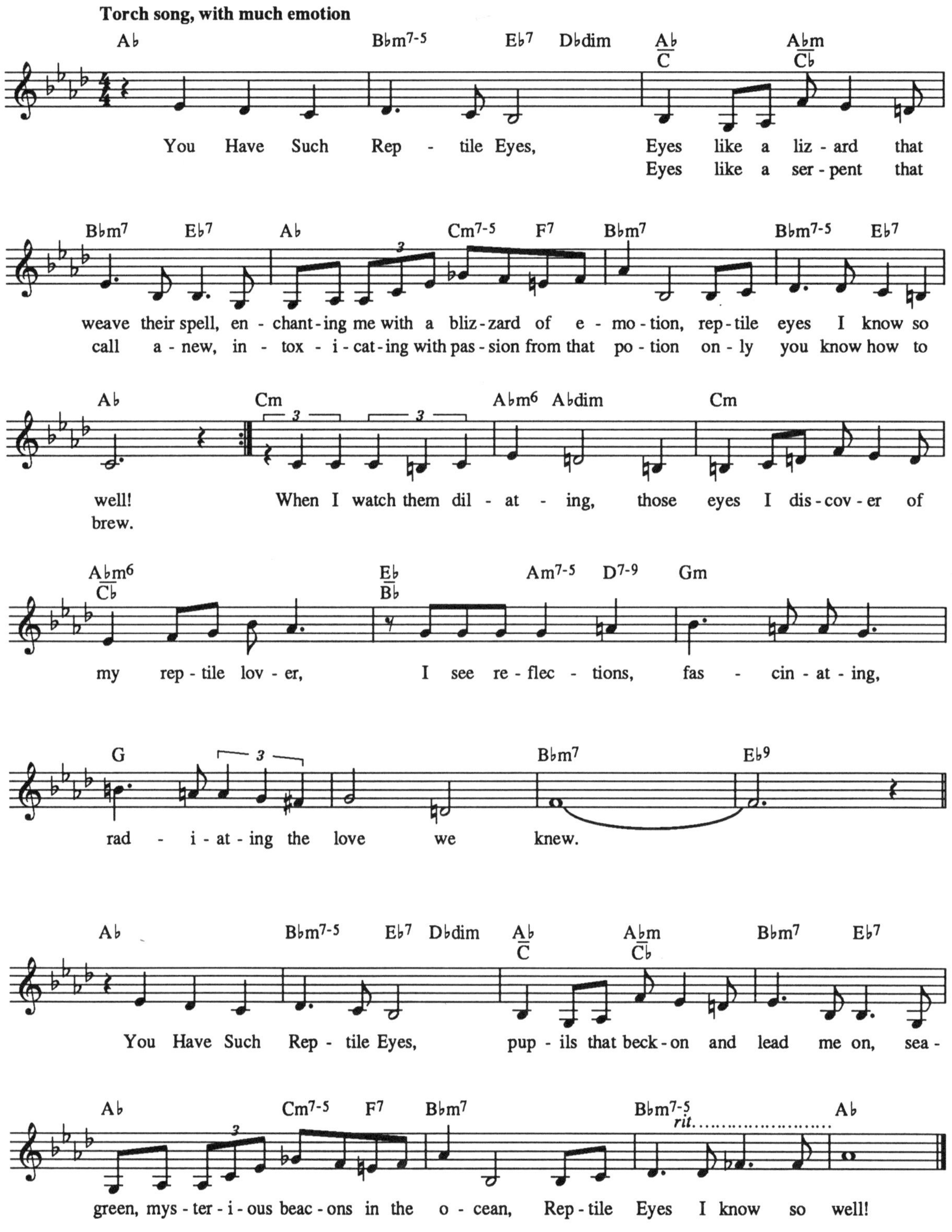
Torch song, with much emotion
Ab Bbm7-5 Eb7 Dbdim Ab/C Abm/Cb
You Have Such Rep - tile Eyes, Eyes like a liz - ard that
Eyes like a ser - pent that
Bbm7 Eb7 Ab Cm7-5 F7 Bbm7 Bbm7-5 Eb7
weave their spell, en - chant - ing me with a bliz - zard of e - mo - tion, rep - tile eyes I know so
call a - new, in - tox - i - cat - ing with pas - sion from that po - tion on - ly you know how to
Ab Cm Abm6 Abdim Cm
well! When I watch them dil - at - ing, those eyes I dis - cov - er of
brew.
Abm6/Cb Eb/Bb Am7-5 D7-9 Gm
my rep - tile lov - er, I see re - flec - tions, fas - cin - at - ing,
G Bbm7 Eb9
rad - i - at - ing the love we knew.
Ab Bbm7-5 Eb7 Dbdim Ab/C Abm/Cb Bbm7 Eb7
You Have Such Rep - tile Eyes, pup - ils that beck - on and lead me on, sea -
Ab Cm7-5 F7 Bbm7 Bbm7-5 Ab
rit.
green, mys - ter - i - ous beac - ons in the o - cean, Rep - tile Eyes I know so well!

You May Be Six People (But I Love You)

from Zelig

WORDS AND MUSIC
DICK HYMAN

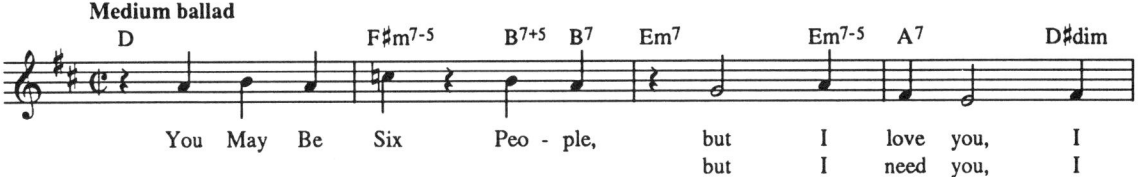

You May Be Six Peo - ple, but I love you, I
but I need you, I

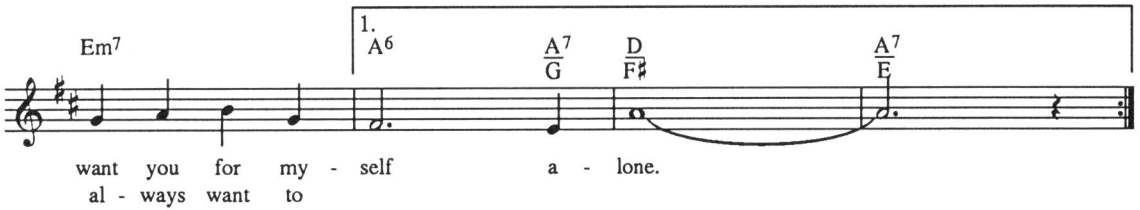

want you for my - self a - lone.
al - ways want to

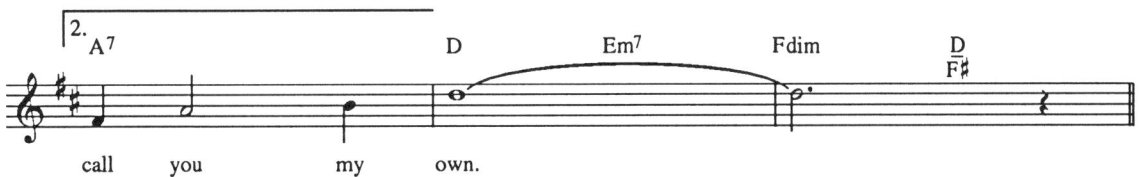

call you my own.

Each new per - son - al - it - y is a gift from up a - bove,

'Cause each new per - son gives me all the more to love.

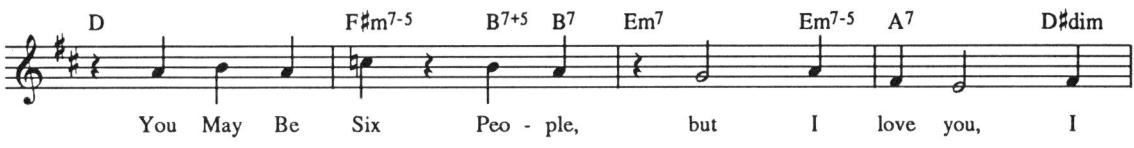

You May Be Six Peo - ple, but I love you, I

al - ways want to call you my own!

IN THE GOOD OLD 1984 SUMMERTIME

One of the pleasures of traveling from keyboard to keyboard during the summer months is being able to see the country at its most appealing. Not that musicians travel only in nice weather. I remember playing a gig in Iceland in December. But that's a different story.

June 23, 1984, was a beautiful day in Waterloo Village, a reconstructed colonial setting in Stanhope, New Jersey, where the New Jersey Jazz Society presented its annual Piano Day concert. The playing took place in a large tent, not unlike those in which some traveling circuses still perform. The audience had gathered earlier in the day to picnic on the surrounding lawn, and the grass was covered in all directions with contented munchers and guzzlers.

At 6:00 PM the piano music began. We had three grands onstage and nine pianists scheduled to perform, occasionally in two- and three-piano groupings. The players were Ray Bryant, Judy Carmichael, Roger Kellaway, Mike Lipskin, Bob Seeley, Derek Smith, Dick Wellstood, Bob Winter, and myself. I also acted as scheduler, emcee, and general traffic cop. Most of us are based in New York, but Lipskin, the stride specialist, came from San Francisco; Seeley, whose forte is boogie-woogie, flew in from Detroit; and Winter, a more contemporary stylist, joined us from Boston. We mixed it up in all sorts of combinations. Also on hand to provide a respite from the keyboards were trumpeter Glenn Zottola and trombonist Phil Wilson.

Toward the end of July, The East End All-Stars, who used to be sighted only during warm weather in the far reaches of Long Island, gathered for our annual concert on the waterfront at Sag Harbor. Most of us were summer residents of the area, and the personnel was fairly stable, with Phil Bodner on clarinet, Hal McKusick on saxophones, Toots Thielemans on harmonica and guitar, Bob Haggart on bass, and Ron Traxler on drums. We played a program of standards, featuring "What's New?" Haggart's great song from the '30s, which at that time was undergoing an important revival by Linda Ronstadt. Under the moon, the audience sat on blankets or reclined in beach chairs.

Over the summer of '84, I played solo piano every Sunday night at a restaurant in eastern Long Island called The Birches, a pleasant and informal place with an unexpectedly good grand and a sympathetic proprietor. During this period I was busy arranging and composing, and Julia and I were able to spend most of the time in the area where we have a summer house. We are about 125 miles from New York City. Whenever I looked up from the score pad, I'd

see Little Peconic Bay and the North Fork, a couple of miles across the water.

Following one of the Sunday night jobs, I drove back to New York at midnight in order to fly to Los Angeles the next day. I had been asked to record on the Pianocorder, a latter-day player piano system, and had arranged to play at a club in Hollywood that evening. Whenever possible I try to schedule recording sessions the day following some heavy playing, so I can be sure of being in good shape.

The Vine Street Bar in Hollywood had a Yamaha studio upright, and, although I'd rather play a grand, it seemed to me that with amplification the little piano was perfectly suitable for the small room. I've learned in the past that you do not play small pianos as you might big ones. Your object is to play within the piano's dynamic range. Given that understanding, the lightness of the action can be an asset, and fingers may seem unusually fleet. The trouble begins when you bear down; then the tone shatters, and the action becomes unresponsive. However, amplification can compensate surprisingly well for the small tone. The vertical (as they are known in the trade) and I got on a friendly basis, and we played two shows that evening.

On Tuesday, Jim Turner, the producer of the Pianocorder sessions, drove me out to the recording studio. Turner is an accomplished pianist himself, one of whose specialties is the stride style of James P. Johnson. The Los Angeles Olympics had just concluded, and the Angeleno weather continued to be free of smog.

We arrived at the living-room-sized studio, where I sat down at the master recording piano, a seven-foot Kawai grand equipped, I was told, with $100,000 worth of special equipment which senses every nuance of touch and pedaling. Information on the performances is stored digitally on tape and is then transferred to a data cassette. Unlike earlier reproducing pianos, which were activated by pneumatic pressure released through perforations in an unwinding paper roll, the Pianocorder's playback system responds to signals from the cassette, activating solenoids built into the piano's action at every moving part. The solenoids, in a sense, do the actual "playing."

I practiced on the recording instrument for an hour or so (my standard warmup), finding the action considerably more resistant than the lightweight keyboard of the friendly upright at the Vine Street Bar. Then we began recording. Turner wanted an hour of music, of which we would select the best 45 minutes. Considerable time was saved over a regular recording session in not having to be concerned with microphone placement or other audio requirements. It was performance in the abstract, since the playbacks would ultimately take place on thousands of individual pianos, each with its own characteristics of tone, room ambience, action, and degree of being in tune. I drew on what I'd played the night before, and the night before that, on Long Island, and we finished in about two hours.

The last week in August found a bunch of us jazz festival types in the northwest corner of Pennsylvania, playing in an old-fashioned amusement park on Conneaut Lake. Not far from the roller coaster and other crazy rides, my quintet ripped through our hottest arrangements in an ancient dance pavilion at the edge of the water. Phil Bodner was there, as were Joe Wilder on trumpet, Milt Hinton on bass, and Don Lamond on drums.

Between sets Julia and I wandered through the arcades, trying our skill at the various games. Cotton candy, candy apples, girls shrieking on the roller coaster, women intently playing bingo — all the sights and sounds of a traditional "good old summertime" surrounded us.

One attraction was a full-scale replica of a Western bar inhabited by life-size mannequins. These figures remained motionless until a direct hit was scored by a contestant using a light-beam rifle. When one's aim was accurate, a sombrero would fly into the air, a bandit would topple, a parrot would squawk, a cuspidor would overturn. And if you fixed the sleepy piano player accurately in your sight, he would leap up from his somnolent position and the old upright would blare out a few bars of ragtime. Automation, we should remember, was around even before the Pianocorder.

PLAYER PIANOS & PIANO PLAYERS

When I was very young, my big brother and I would spend hours pumping on an old player piano in our living room. There were still a lot of player pianos in homes in those days. Before that time, back in the 1920's, player pianos and the piano roll industry occupied a giant position in both home and public entertainment. In its heyday, the reproducing piano, as it was also known, functioned in several areas which have since been distributed among the phonograph, the jukebox, the easy-play electric organ, and the table-top keyboard.

To a large extent, home entertainment in America used to be centered around the piano in the parlor. Judging from the sale of tricky novelty piano pieces such as "Kitten On The Keys" and "Nola," there must have been some pretty good amateur pianists back then. Nevertheless, there were doubtless a greater number of folks who settled for pumping the bellows of their automatic pianos, while the notes cascaded forth. My brother and I would keep it up until some other member of the family couldn't stand it any longer.

Pumping was a minor skill in itself, the mastery of which yielded a certain amount of artistic control over the tempo. An artful hesitation and diminuendo could be attained by a practised pumper, but the main idea was to keep the bellows filled by means of a steady left-foot right-foot action. The air pressure thus built up caused a roll of perforated paper to pass from one revolving cylinder to another in the manner of a scroll. Each perforation in the roll selected an individual tone as it passed over a device resembling an enormous harmonica containing 88 holes (66 in the earlier models). Rubber tubing connected each of these openings to a corresponding key mechanism which was triggered into action by pneumatic pressure, somewhat in the manner of a pipe organ.

Our upright piano was the commonest type. The action of the unwinding roll was conveniently at eye level, so that the operator could watch the patterns of the perforations, which were virtually a form of musical notation. What the ear heard, the eye could see graphically in the contours of melody and the clusters of chords. Simultaneously, as one's feet settled into a steady rhythm on the bellows, the keys sank down and sprang back as though played by invisible hands.

I have a theory that the teaching potential of the player piano was never fully realized. Certainly we found it instructive to observe how the movement of the keys corresponded to the sound of the music. Furthermore, the tempo could be slowed down to a crawl, and as with audio tape, a section could be backed up and replayed for closer study. Unlike tape, piano roll pitch was unaffected by speed.

We learned quite a bit of repertoire from our collection of piano rolls. Two pieces that made a great impression on me were Liszt's "Hungarian Dance" and "It Ain't No Sin To Take Off Your Skin And Dance Around In Your Bones." The Liszt contained an octave section in which the hands spread apart in opposite directions. This was beautifully mirrored by the perforations in the roll. As to "It Ain't No Sin To Take Off Your Skin And Dance Around In Your Bones," this song did not survive as a standard, for obvious reasons, but I can still approximate the piano roll arrangement.

Various controls added to the fun. A tempo pointer enabled you to set whatever rate was printed at the beginning of each roll. Some of the classical rolls included a continuous wandering line printed along the length of the selection. If you followed its meanderings with the pointer of the tempo control (to the right — faster, to the left — slower), you achieved a sentimental rubato which we didn't much care for. My brother and I preferred to set the pointer at the cheerful bright tempo which was characteristic of piano roll style. There were loud and soft buttons as well, which changed the degree of air pressure, and some pianos came equipped with a "mandolin" effect.

I learned later that there were far better reproducing pianos than ours, grands containing electrified Ampico mechanisms capable of great subtlety of expression, and classical rolls with special perforations which controlled pedal action. Some of these rolls, when played on suitable instruments, produced remarkable performances. There were even concert hall demonstrations in the 1920's, in which the audience was asked to guess whether the performance of a concealed piano was live or mechanical.

A different principle entirely was that perfected by Edwin Welte, a German inventor who at the turn of the century built a piano player rather than a player piano. The Welte Vorsetzer ("sitter-in-front") did in fact sit at the piano, and with 88 felt-covered fingers it actually played the keyboard. The reproduction process was totally electric rather than pneumatic. On the underside of each key in the recording process a carbon prong made contact with a trough of mercury which extended the length of the keyboard. When the key was struck, the prong dipped into the mercury, completing a circuit and signaling the exact force and duration of the finger strokes by its depth. The pedals were similarly wired. Rolls were not perforated but were scored with the resultant markings, which were capable of conducting various voltages. The sensitivity of this process produced startlingly life-like reproductions of the original performances.

The above information is derived from John Conley's notes to a set of phonograph recordings made in 1963 for the Classics Record Library known as *Legendary Masters Of The Keyboard*. (Book Of The Month Club, out of print). In this collection the Welte Vorsetzer "plays" a Steinway concert grand, and we can hear with uncanny fidelity the performances of such pianists and pianist-composers of the period as Busoni, Debussy, Hofmann, Lhevinne, Mahler, Paderewski, and Scriabin. After listening to these recordings, it seemed doubtful that any subsequent development in piano roll technology could equal the Vorsetzer.

The usual piano rolls made for the pop music market were not nearly so ambitious. They were meant to be played on cruder instruments not necessarily in perfect condition. Arrangements were often doctored after the fact with extra holes which produced technically unlikely but dramatically strengthened melody lines in octaves as well as embellishments in thirds and sixths.

Pop piano rolls could not reproduce rhythms in fine detail, so a typical pop arrangement was reduced either to the relentlessly even eighth-notes we associate, probably inaccurately, with early ragtime, or to a rollicking but unswinging triple meter. In comparing the phonograph recordings of pianists such as Fats Waller with their piano rolls, we can hear a significantly greater variety of rhythmic and dynamic shadings in the former. On the other hand, the limitations of the typical pop piano roll produced in time an attractive and valid style in itself, full and busy though not very subtle, and some pianists of the '20s copied this manner in their live playing. I suspect that Zez Confrey, the composer of "Kitten On The Keys," and even George Gershwin, who cut a fair number of rolls, conformed to the recognized piano roll style as much as they contributed to it.

In restaurants, saloons, and public places the coin-operated player piano grabbed nickels and dispensed pop music as the jukebox was to do at a later time. Such pianos were often enhanced with a set of organ pipes, a xylophone, and various percussion effects. A survey of mechanical musical instruments would include these contraptions as well as the orchestrions which used to accompany merry-go-rounds, music boxes large and small, self-playing organs, violins, and accordions, and an endless gaggle of grotesque combination devices, mechanical marvels of great ingenuity left behind now in the homes of collectors and in such museums as the gigantic exhibition at Bellm's Cars And Music Of Yesterday Museum in Sarasota, Florida.

The QRS Company of Buffalo is, to my knowledge, the only survivor of the many companies which used to manufacture piano rolls. QRS still has new tunes cut on a regular basis to add to their immense catalog.

In 1969, when a Moog recording of mine called "The Minotaur" was having some popularity, the QRS people approached me to cut a long-playing roll of four of the pieces in my Command Records album. I believe that they hoped that the titles would impart to QRS some of the synthesizer mystique which was building at that time, largely on the strength of Walter Carlos' *Switched-On Bach*. By that time it was no longer necessary actually to play the original performance. Feeling that I was realizing a childhood dream, I simply arranged my tunes for three or four hands and mailed out the chart.

Soon I received a test roll which I proofed for errors on the piano of my friend, Bill Simon, a great collector of rolls and old sheet music. I caught a few wrong notes, red-penciled the offending perforations, and returned the roll to the editor. Under the title, *The Electric Eclectics Of Dick Hyman*, the title of my record album as well, the item appeared for some years in the QRS catalogue. Whether the company benefited from its association with my synthesizer record is doubtful. Shorn of the electronic sounds, "The Minotaur" and its quasi-avant-garde companion pieces were inevitably transformed into that old piano roll style, and they now seem as quaint as any other item in the QRS catalog.

I have since recorded on the ultimate reproducing piano system, that of Wayne Stahnke, whose marvelous equipment is installed in a Bösendorfer piano. I've made two programs which are available as discs to drive that piano and are compatible with the Yamaha Disclavier as well. Oddly, the reproducing piano was used as a means to an end: Reference Recordings wanted to make the first direct-to-CD recording, and only after I had played the program of Fats Waller music for the reproducing piano, did the actual recording take place. The piano played itself endlessly over an entire weekend of trial and error, until all of the recording components worked perfectly at the same time. A tuner stood by; a technician to deal with the mechanics of the reproducing piano remained on call; audio engineers dealt with microphones, balance, and ambience; others arranged for a radio transmission of the signal to be sent to the mastering studio twenty miles away, relayed through a station at Mt. Palomar Observatory en route; finally the people in the mastering studio needed a bit of digital luck to record the information flowing in directly onto virgin discs. There was no master, no tape transfer, but a processing direct to the CD.

When all of this finally came together, after numerous breakdowns, misalignments, and problems of which I have no comprehension, it was considered such a scientific triumph, that in the glowing review the recording received in one high-end audio magazine, about eight pages were needed to present the technical information, but I was disposed of after a brief mention as "the programmer" around paragraph 3. However, others noted that the playing was pretty good, too, and I've since done another such program/recording, this time of Duke Ellington material.

Two other programs of mine are in the Yamaha software catalogue of material for the Disclavier. These were made specifically for that piano. Yamaha acquired Pianocorder some years ago, and has been responsible more than any other manufacturer for returning the player piano to public popularity.

While dining one evening in an elegant Sarasota restaurant, I heard my own ghostly playing take place on an unmanned Yamaha. I was able to talk through my performance just like everybody else at the dinner table.

*"There is magic
in the sudden
surfacing in
performance of
a successful
improvisatory idea..."*

FILM FANTASIES

In a career which has been filled with the variety and craziness typical of the schedule of a free-lance musician, I've missed out on a few playing situations, I regret to say, which occurred before my time. I'm sorry that I was never able to play in a New Orleans bordello, as did Jelly Roll Morton, Scott Joplin, and the rest of our spiritual forefathers. I wish I knew how it felt to stomp it out for maybe one night in a Western frontier saloon. And, although I have accompanied some silent movies in recent years, I would like to have done so back in the Roaring Twenties, when people had no idea that sound films were about to change everything.

On the other hand, I actually played for President and Mrs. Carter on the White House lawn, and later on for President and Mrs. Bush in a series of television shows. In 1975 I conducted an orchestra in Siberia playing Louis Armstrong's music. And, while working at the President Hotel in New York in 1948, I got my hands out of the way barely in time before a drunk slammed the lid down on my keyboard. Probably I hadn't responded to his request for "Melancholy Baby." I've always felt that this was carrying music criticism to an extreme.

Since we all must live in the present, however, I take vicarious satisfaction in achieving my fantasies of the distant past by ghosting such scenes for films or television programs. Also, I enjoy solving the technical problems involved in synchronizing music with film action, as well as the specific piano-playing problems that arise.

Only rarely on films is the piano on the screen actually being played by the actor or actress as the scene is being shot, even if he or she is a capable pianist. Sound engineers prefer to record the speech, the music, and the sound effects separately in order to be able to mix them later in the proper proportions.

A characteristic piano-playing scene might take place in a restaurant. Let's suppose that a man and a woman are speaking, seated at a table; in the background there is a murmur of crowd conversation interspersed with the tinkling of glasses and silverware; at a low level we hear cocktail piano, but we do not see the pianist. All of these elements, in a typical situation, would have been recorded separately. The actors probably spoke their lines as they were being filmed, although even speech might have been dubbed in later. The crowd noise came from a sound effects recording that was added to the sound track at the sound mixing session. The piano music was very likely pre-recorded by a studio pianist in a length longer than the scene; the music editor then transferred a portion of his playing to the sound track according to the dramatic requirements.

There are several options that a music editor has in the scene we are considering. For example, if the director wants the effect of a tune beginning as the scene begins, the editor will obviously start the piano tape from the beginning. If, on the other hand, the director wants to suggest that the conversation has been going on for some time prior to our first viewing it, the editor will start the music a few bars into the tape. If it is desired to give an effect of completion to the scene, the editor will time the tape so that the music comes to an end at the appropriate point. But most often this kind of music will simply fade in and out inconspicuously.

We might even get a brief look at the pianist in our hypothetical scene. If the camera does not linger on his hands, there will be no synchronizing problem. However, the sound mixer might raise the level of the music at the moment we see the pianist, particularly if there is a lull in the conversation just then. In any case, none of these uses concerns the studio pianist, who has most likely recorded his couple of minutes of solo playing after the rest of the orchestra has finished its cues, has earned a little overtime, and has probably gotten caught in traffic on the way home.

A second grade of difficulty would involve a scene such as the above in which it was desired that the piano music both begin and end exactly with the action. This is the same basic problem, of course, as fitting any kind of music to scenes of different lengths. The composer/arranger, who might or might not be the pianist, would have timed the scene and selected one of three methods used in synchronizing music with film: (a) following the scene visually as it is projected on a screen or television monitor and adjusting the pace of the music to visual and audible cues; (b) without projection, following the second hand on a timing clock; or (c) selecting a metronomic beat which is audible to the player and/or conductor through a headset, and playing a passage with the required number of beats. This last technique is known as using a click-track, and it is the most exact method.

The most complex problem in synchronizing piano music occurs when the screen pianist's hands or arms are clearly visible. The simplest solution may be for the studio pianist to play along with the film, having familiarized himself with the music so that he doesn't have to read the part too closely, and try to do exactly what he sees the screen pianist doing. I realized one of my fantasies one time, for example, by supplying the playing for a television scene showing a Western saloon pianist at a period upright. As the actor was playing, he picked up a drink with his left hand, guzzled it down, and replaced the glass on top of the piano, all the while continuing to play with his right hand. I believe the tune was "There'll Be A Hot Time In The Old Town Tonight," a standard for Western saloon scenes. In the studio I imitated the actor, letting my left hand drop out as I watched him imbibe on the screen, but continuing the honky-tonk tickling with my right.

In the recording session for the television drama *The Dain Curse*, which was set in the 1930's, as I watched the monitor I was surprised to see Roland Hanna acting the part of a pianist in a bar. It was easy enough for me to find his tempo from the movement of his left arm. It was fortunate, though, that there were no hand close-ups, because Roland had probably been improvising, and what he had played was neither recorded nor written down. Nothing more exacting than watching his arm was demanded, except for me to apologize to Roland later on. But then, neither of us received a credit on the show.

Sometimes considerable effort must be taken to make a casual piano-playing scene look right. When the piano music is particularly important to a scene, it will probably be pre-recorded so that the actor or actress can hear it as he or she is performing the scene. Coaching by a professional pianist before the scene is shot may be helpful to the actor, but unfortunately this doesn't always take place. It may happen, because of the inaccuracies that creep into an actor's performance at the keyboard, that the studio pianist will need to re-record the piece in order to fit what the actor *appeared* to be playing.

This was the case in *Scott Joplin, King Of Ragtime*. When I saw the finished footage of Billy Dee Williams, the actor who played the role of Joplin, it was clear to me that he had not had much experience at a keyboard, and although I had pre-recorded the various pieces for him to mime, he moved his fingers in ways that had almost nothing to do with the music. In one instance, a scene which takes place in a bordello, Williams as Joplin sits at a piano meditatively composing "Solace," but using completely inappropriate fingering. The music editor and I decided to slow the film down and count each individual finger movement in terms of film frames, that is, fractions of a second, so that I could plot out a version of the required piece that would both look and sound right. I then re-recorded the piece to a click track, matching the film minutely, having worked the music out in bars of irregular length. When one is watching a finished film, situations like this go by very quickly, but sometimes enormous amounts of labor go into the apparent smoothness.

Another scene in *Scott Joplin* showed the pianist's hands trembling on the keyboard at a dra-

matic point in the narrative when Joplin's health is declining; he ends by breaking down in mid-performance. This shot was only six seconds long, so it was convenient to construct a film loop. Using the loop, we could project the same action over and over in the recording studio without having to rewind the film. I watched the film many times and shook my hands on the keyboard, making some quite Cecil Tayloresque effects. Eventually, after a number of takes, I was able to synchronize my playing with the film to the satisfaction of the director. Ever since, I've been able to give a good six-second impression of Cecil Taylor.

Still another example from *Scott Joplin* was a scene in which four pianists engage in a ragtime cutting contest, taking turns on two pianos. An added consideration was that one of the pianists, who was known in those days as "The Left Hand Of God," could play only with that hand, having lost the other in an accident. I arranged a long routine in which each of the contestants got to show off a bit, singly and in pairs, including a stride section for the Left Hand Of God. Of course, I allowed Joplin to win the cutting contest. I recorded all the parts myself, successively, using two studio pianos tuned slightly apart in order to accentuate the stylistic differences among the players. The scene was shot to my pre-recording. The film, however, was then cut in the way most advantageous for visual effects, so that we subsequently had to adjust the music track by splicing it here and there to fit the film. It was an effective scene, even so, but for the phonograph record version, Hank Jones and I did the music over again on two pianos. Not having to follow precisely the dramatic requirements of the scene allowed us to improve its musical content.

Through ghosting such scenes as these I have been able to realize my fantasies of playing in other exotic venues. But one situation I would never have thought of myself takes place in the Woody Allen film *Stardust Memories*. While the actors are talking animatedly in the foreground of what appears to be a rehearsal of a musical show, we see in the distance a group of nuns who are practicing a tap-dancing routine to the tune of "Sweet Georgia Brown." It fell to me to produce the sound of a rehearsal pianist in this context, and certain difficulties led to an interesting hour and a half or so in the recording studio.

The brief scene had been shot with a rehearsal pianist (not me) actually playing under the dialog in order to guide the dancers. However, someone forgot to put a microphone in the piano, and the result of this goof was that while the dialog was clear and the tapping properly distant, there was almost no piano sound. The goal in the studio was to re-record the piano. The problem was that the tapping was very imprecise, as a group of tap-dancers is liable to be, and when I played along with the scene I could not hear the very faint original piano. Consequently, I could not find the beat.

It occurred to me, however, that I could construct a guide track by listening to the original playing at a very high level and recording only the bass notes. The single tones did not cover up the sound of the original track which I was straining to hear, as my full performance of the piece did. Nevertheless, I still could not find the beginning of the chorus. Eventually I worked out a bass note guide track which started several beats after the beginning of the chorus. We then back-timed so that we could calculate where the beginning beat was. Then I recorded a dummy introduction for myself which was spliced onto the beginning of the guide track. The final job was simply to play "Sweet Georgia Brown" in full along with the guide track. The guide track was then removed, and it all worked out pretty well.

In this context, though, I think of a remark by Boomie Richman, whose career as a studio reed player did not afford quite enough opportunity to display his great gifts as a jazz tenor saxophonist. Boomie, a man known for his biting wit, had just taken part in a radio commercial recording session of the sort where the orchestra would underscore a cigarette commercial. The announcer did his spiel, while the conductor waved the orchestra down to an ever fainter pianissimo. When the session was over, another player remarked to Boomie that the residual payments promised to be very worthwhile. Boomie responded, "Yeah, but how come somebody's always talking when I'm playing?"

CHOPSTICKS AND OTHER FUN ON THE IVORIES

When I was growing up and had already gained a certain reputation in my gang as a piano player, I was annoyed one day at being pushed aside by two assertive little girls who took over the keyboard in tandem and rendered a four-hand arrangement of "Chopsticks":

Having dazzled everybody but me with this classic, the more aggressive of the pair went on to a solo performance of "I Love Coffee, I Love Tea," even managing to get through the flashy second part, which involves crossed hands. (See Example A.)

Her colleague then rose to the competition by performing an untitled but well-known item played with the knuckles of the right hand, the fingers being retracted into a fist:

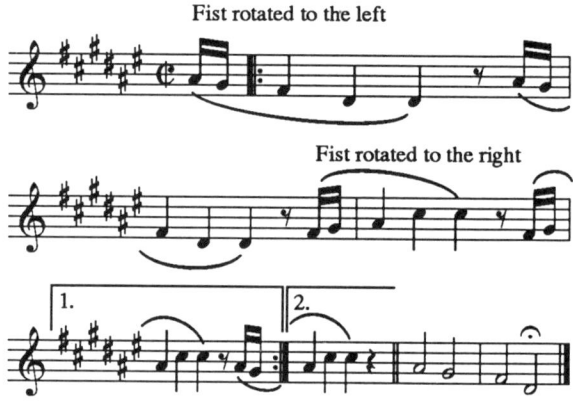

For their flag-waver, the little girls brought down the house with a multi-handed arrangement of either "Heart And Soul" or "Blue Moon." I don't remember which tune it was, because in this kind of playing the melodies are interchangeable, the accompaniment for both being the identical Eddy Duchin pattern. The performers bowed out in the sixteenth bar rather than tackle the harmonic problems of the bridge. Even so, their rendition was received with such huzzahs that one would have thought Rubinstein and Horowitz themselves had gotten together for a jam session. (See Example B.)

At that time I had been taking piano lessons for several years. I was also into Benny Goodman and boogie-woogie, and I was doing my level best to grow up hip. Jealousy is not an uncommon component of the artistic temperament, and I admit that these little girls got to me. It took me some years to put them into a context in which I no longer felt bugged by their triumph, but in time I realized that what the two of them were innocently playing at that traumatic musicale was a sort of keyboard folk music. Entirely outside the realm of formal training, this repertoire was passed along like hopscotch or jacks. Nor was it limited to girls, by any means. Substantially the same pieces were heard during leisure hours in our armed forces in recent wars, where such playing was sometimes known as "U.S.O. piano."

Still, there does seem to have been a little girl connection at work in the dissemination of "Chopsticks." According to Fuld's *Book of World-Famous Music*, the work, originally entitled "The Celebrated Chop Waltz," was published in London in 1877. It was composed by a sixteen-year-old girl, Euphemia Allen, under the pseudonym Arthur de Lulli. The publication included the instruction that the *primo* part of the duet should be played by the two forefingers in a chopping manner. The alteration of the title came about later, possibly because of the notion that the double-note melody might be played by a pair of chopsticks rather than a pair of forefingers.

Coincidentally, it was also in 1877 that the daughter of Alexander Borodin intrigued her father with the same musical material. Borodin composed variations on it under the title "Cottleton Polka" ("Cutlet Polka"), apparently taking the wrong translation of the word "chop." Further variations were added by composers Rimsky-Korsakov, Cui, and Liadov. The entire set was published the following year in St. Petersburg under the title "Paraphrases." Subsequently Franz Liszt wrote still another variation.

The beginnings of "I Love Coffee, I Love Tea (I Love The Boys And The Boys Love Me)" are apparently even more ancient. The lyrics date at least to 1842, when similar words were included in "The Nursery Rhymes Of Song." My limited research has not revealed the origin of the melody, but there is little doubt that it has a folk basis of comparable antiquity. The song's greatest popularity was achieved in 1940 under the title "Java Jive," an adaptation by Ben Oakland and Milton Drake which produced a best-selling record by the Ink Spots, a vocal group of the day. Other adaptations and recordings appeared as well; I remember a Fats Waller record called "Nero" which used the melody

with lyrics. At any rate, the *Book Of World-Famous Music* remarks that the piece, including the crossed-hand section, has been played "for decades."

What is curious is that the piano arrangement is always played in *Gb*. This fascination with the black keys is odd, considering that Western music generally has a strong bias in favor of the diatonic scale epitomized by the white keys. The other black-key piece in this folk repertoire, the one played with the knuckles, is completely pentatonic. What self-tutored technician first used the knuckle technique will probably always remain a mystery, but as to the tune itself, I would speculate that it might have been a part of the piano repertoire for accompanying silent movies. Perhaps its exotic character was suitable for Oriental or American Indian scenes.

On the other hand, the other two selections in that famous folk piano concert were completely white-key pieces. "Chopsticks" is absolutely C-diatonic, and so are both "Heart and Soul" and "Blue Moon." The former is a composition by Hoagy Carmichael (music) and Frank Loesser (words) dating from 1938. "Blue Moon," by Richard Rodgers (music) and Larry Hart (words), was written earlier and had a confusing history before becoming a hit. Composed for a 1933 film called *Hollywood Revue*, its original lyrics were different from those we know now. Its title was "Prayer." It was not a success, and was not even included in the film for which it had been written. With a new lyric, the song became "The Bad In Every Man" in a 1934 film entitled *Manhattan Melodrama*, again with little distinction. However, later that year, when the melody was published with its final set of lyrics, "Blue Moon" became a standard song which has since been a part of the scores of no less than six films. Countless recordings have been made of it as well, and I am fairly sure that one of them was an Eddy Duchin piano version which set the predominant style. Duchin was a melodic player whose influence was pervasive in the '30s. Although his emotive style was as far from jazz as that of Liberace, Duchin remained an important pop pianist until his death in the following decade.

At one time a piano could be found in almost every American parlor. This seems less true today, and I wonder if boys and girls have as much opportunity to teach each other these little musical games which constitute the piano's folk repertoire. Is this tiny ripple in the great sea of music still in motion? Is "Chopsticks" on the way out? Most likely, unless the rappers discover it.

THE TREASURE CHEST OF PIANO NOVELTIES

For years I've had in my files a 1937 collection of special material with which an entertaining pianist of that era might dazzle a fairly unsophisticated audience. Some of its suggestions are still interesting, and many of them bring a smile. However, *The Treasure Chest Of Piano Tricks, Imitations, And Novelties* is clearly of its time, and that time is long gone.

The opening pages present a system for playing "Cathedral Chimes" on your piano. Bell-like harmonics are convincingly evoked in an effective arrangement of "Adeste Fidelis." We are cautioned to keep the sustain pedal down and to bring out the melody, which is in the upper voice of the left hand. *(See following.)*

An apparently original composition, "Sunday Morning In London," follows, in which we hear the sequences of Big Ben and other London church bells. Sadly, no credit is given to the composer or arranger throughout the entire *Treasure Chest*. We can surmise that some talented person labored for Treasure Chest Publications for a flat fee. Rather audaciously, the anonymous arranger next offers classical piano pieces into which chime effects may be inserted ("Au Matin" by Godard, "Kamenoi Ostrow" by Rubinstein). One thinks of the occasional chime flourishes Art Tatum used in his arrangements, for example the ending of "Willow Weep For Me."

Page 10 brings us to an alleged "Pipe Organ

Imitation" and an arrangement of "Abide With Me" utilizing spread Brahmsian chords in constant tremolando. I do not find this technique as "astounding" as the editor did, but then I haven't tried it out with the audience "in the part of the room where they cannot see the keyboard of the piano. ... This little hint holds good for all the imitations in this book."

A "Bagpipe Imitation" follows, in which the left hand sounds the famous drone in fifths. Although not too convincing on piano, this is still a stock cliche for any dance routine that leans toward the Scottish. We used a bit of it in the orchestration of *Sugar Babies* when Mickey Rooney did a brief highland fling. Next comes the "Fire Bell Imitation," and here we must cope with the tendency of technological advances to put such impressions out of business. Since fire engines no longer sound this sort of alarm, I am afraid that our long-suffering audience, even if they were facing away from the keyboard, would be unmoved, unless they were all senior citizens. Even then, I have doubts. We had better label this one obsolete, although of historical interest.

Music Boxes, on the other hand, are still with us. Frank Mills had a record known as "Music Box Dancer" on the charts in 1979, and its treatment was essentially the same as the *Treasure Chest* example — high register, Alberti left hand, and bell-like sonorities. Music box impressions have been

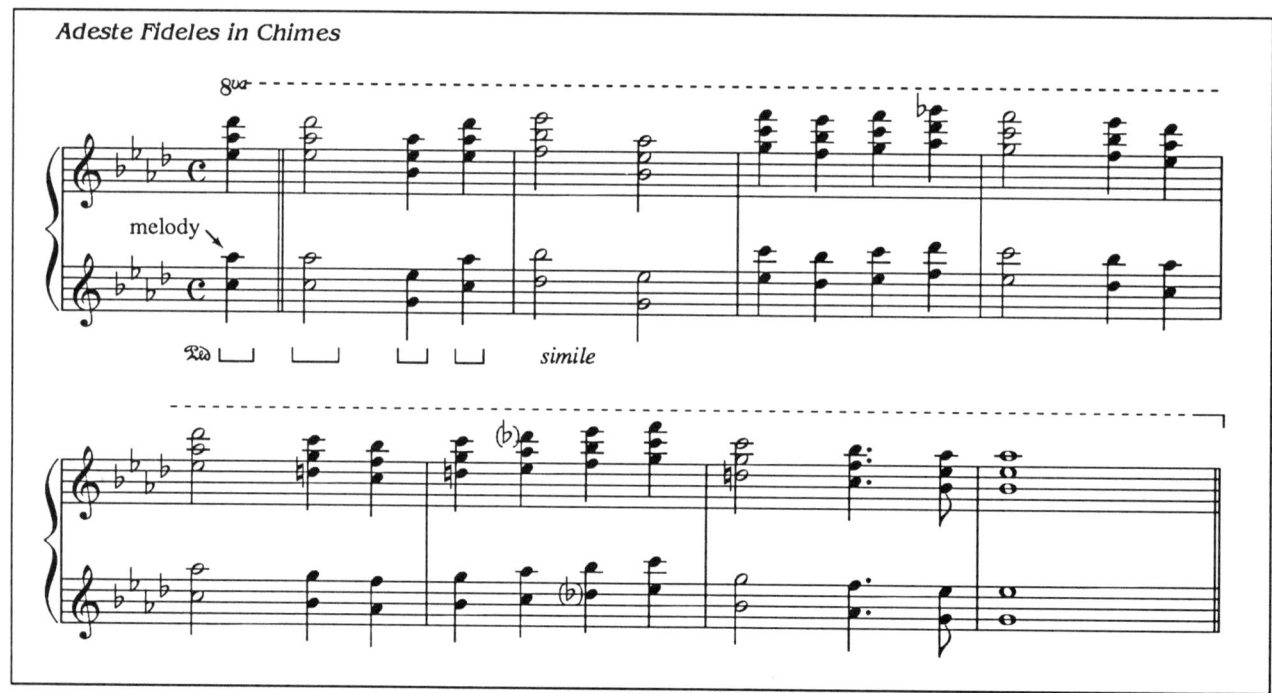

Adeste Fideles in Chimes

melody

simile

The Treasure Chest of Novelties also appeared as *The Magic Pianist*, © 1927 by Bibo, Bloedon & Lang. George Shackley is credited as arranger.

with us throughout piano history. In 1830, according to Grove's *Dictionary Of Music & Musicians*, "a very favorite composition with amateurs of the pianoforte was the 'Snuff-Box Waltz,' the composer of which preserved his anonymity under the initials M.S." It seems that anonymity existed long before Treasure Chest Publications.

Page 16 brings us to "Railroad Train Crossing A Bridge," a short piece illustrated with a line drawing of a steam engine and replete with instructions: "This imitation can be made even more effective by having wooden whistle in mouth and blow (sic) where indicated." It is also suggested that a friend may assist the performance by rubbing sandpaper sections together in order to simulate escaping steam. Did people really entertain each other in this fashion? Train pieces have been frequent, however, in the pop repertoire. In this genre is Scott Joplin's "The Crush Collision March" (1896), which specifies "the noise of the trains running at the rate of sixty miles an hour ... whistle for the crossing ... whistle before the collision ... (and finally, fortissimo) The Collision!" But to my ears the most vivid piano train solo is Meade Lux Lewis' "Honky Tonk Train," recorded several times by the composer and presently published in an abridged version in *Barrelhouse & Boogie Piano* (Oak Publications). The repetitive figures of the boogie-woogie piano style perfectly express the momentum of a train speeding down the tracks.

Back at the *Treasure Chest*, I believe we can pass by the "Bass Drum" (very low) and the "Fife" (very high) and pause at "Tom-Tom, Oriental And Indian," in which the left hand once more uses fifths, but in the rhythm:

In the most striking of several offerings, the melody turns out to be what my generation of snickering little boys knew as "Oh, They Don't Wear Pants In The Southern Part Of France." The lyric must be pure American, but James Fuld's *Book Of World-Famous Music* suggests that the familiar melody is Algerian or Arabian. It has been known in France since 1600, Mr. Fuld avers:

We mustn't overlook the "Steel Guitar Imitation," which calls for the piano's poor substitute for portamento on the Hawaiian song "Aloha Oe":

No one suspected in those days that there would come a time when electronic keyboards would make possible a true keyboard portamento. Now we can really sound like Hawaiian guitars. The question is, are we better off?

What the *Treasure Chest* refers to as "Oh Yeah! Harmony" is what we know as honky-tonk style (see article, "Honky Tonk Piano"). A drawing of a pianist wearing a derby and playing an upright on which rests a mug of beer makes this perfectly clear. The tune is "Frankie And Johnny," and the arrangement suggests an out-of-tune instrument by applying the melody in minor seconds:

In Gershwin's "I Got Rhythm Variations" for piano and orchestra, there is a section in which the composer suggests the non-tempered pitch of a Chinese mode by the same device:

Of the remaining gems in the *Treasure Chest,* the most interesting is the almost forgotten novelty of playing "Dixie" and "Yankee Doodle" contrapuntally. Presumably this idea was developed in the period of reconciliation following the War Between The States, and for all I know there may still be a call for it. In an Irving Berlin program I once presented "White Christmas" and "Easter Parade" in the same fashion. You never know.

The heftiest work in the *Treasure Chest* is a veritable tone poem which includes most of the individual tricks. A synopsis sets the scene in 1918 during the Great World War. "The boys are all excited at going over there to fight. The music starts with fife and drum corps coming down the main street of the hometown. ... A touching scene when the mothers and sweethearts bid them goodbye. The boys, after much similar and musically interpreted detail, arrive in France (play 'La Marseillaise' with cathedral chime effect) just as the Armistice is being signed. They immediately return home across the Big Pond, where 'Home Sweet Home' sounds mighty good to them." Ah, well. All this was before MTV.

LET'S HEAR IT FOR THE PI-ANO PLAYER!

I wrote a melody for a catchy set of lyrics by my friend Mort Goode, who felt that the indispensable cocktail pianist should finally get his or her due in a song of tribute. Mort, who makes the rounds of lounges in New York City, came up with the title, "Let's Hear It For The Pi-ano Player." He begins his obeisance with these lines:

Let's hear it for the pi-ano player,
How can he remember all those tunes?
He's played 'em all a million times,
In a million saloons.

Of course the term "cocktail piano" itself is tricky. In Germany this kind of playing is known as *barmusik,* and in some cases it might be better to use the foreign term rather than risk a punch in the nose from some pugilistically inclined jazzman who doesn't quite see himself as a "cocktail pianist."

In order to promote peace and understanding in a confused aesthetic area where many misunderstood players and writers are doing their best to make a living, I'd like to offer some definitions:

"Cocktail piano" refers to a kind of job or playing situation, rather than to a style of playing. The job takes place in lounges, bars, restaurants, clubs, or private parties, and involves more or less anonymous performing by a skilled soloist who sets the ambience of the room. The cocktail piano repertoire is drawn primarily from a large body of popular songs, with particular emphasis on show tunes, played in a direct and melodic style. The chief task of the cocktail pianist is to use these songs to bring into aural focus the various components of the place — the food, the drinks, the talk. The pianist may get some applause now and then, but in general he or she is invisible. The audience is mainly there for the ambience, not the pianist.

According to my definition, when the pianist steps into a more assertive role and begins to command the full attention of the patrons, he or she abandons the role of the cocktail pianist and becomes a featured performer. After going through this transformation, the player will hopefully begin drawing people who are specifically interested in hearing the music. As their numbers grow, they may become the prevailing element in the audience, and thus succeed in silencing the chatterers who haven't yet gotten the message.

Having received a financial inducement I couldn't afford to refuse, I agreed some time ago to play at a cocktail party in an elegantly appointed Fifth Avenue apartment. Tuxedo-clad, I arrived early, tried out the piano — a grand, nicely in tune, but a bit soft — and passed the time examining the paintings and trying to memorize the decor in order to describe the

details to Julia. The hostess, dressed in a ravishing Parisian outfit, appeared and greeted me. I agreed that it would not be necessary to put up the piano lid, on which an exquisite floral display rested. She vanished into the kitchen. I made small conversation with several gloved waiters, and we all watched for the arrival of the first guests.

As soon as the fashionable throng began to enter, I eased into the traditional Cole Porter opening, "Night And Day," and resigned myself to an evening of anonymity. The room filled, and the conversation level rose accordingly. Within half an hour I was having difficulty hearing my own playing. A little later the decibel count was so high that I was certain no one in the living room could hear the piano.

I began to treat the gig as a practicing session, trying out different fingerings, backing up in mid-tune to experiment with altered harmony. If I was not the Invisible Man, I was surely the inaudible one. After a while I took a break and pushed through the crowd into the kitchen to eat a platter of goodies which the catering people were nice enough to offer me.

Back at the keyboard, I was delighted to find among the guests a friend who is a knowledgeable jazz fan. He convinced me to remove the flowers and open the piano. The sound was somewhat louder — that is, standing by the keyboard, he was just able to make out what I was playing. He listened for a while, remarked that he had known intimately every lady in the room, and then drifted off into the crowd.

I started the countdown to nine o'clock, quitting time, and precisely at that longed-for hour, I found my overcoat and inconspicuously sneaked out, fearful that I might be pressed into overtime.

I offer the above vignette as an example of a cocktail piano job at its most anonymous extreme. In lounges, however, and with the benefit of an audio system, a pianist establishes more of a rapport with the patrons, attracts their attention, answers requests, and develops a sense of playing the sort of music that will get a response according to the prevailing mood. Dinner time in a restaurant calls for quiet pieces. As the evening progresses the tempo generally gets livelier. Peppy show tunes are heard, and perhaps some contemporary items. An experienced player can judge whether at a given point his audience will respond to George Gershwin or a Gay Nineties medley, and there can be considerable give and take with the customers.

The point at which a cocktail pianist becomes a featured performer depends on how assertive the pianist is, how receptive his audience is, and whether the management has a specific policy. Many jobs are cocktail piano by definition, and one would not attempt to dazzle a roomful of boozers into silence in such a no-win situation. But in some places the management is indifferent, and while one pianist might be content to play background music, another will try to get the attention of the room. Both modes are honorable callings, but becoming a featured performer, if that's what your game is, is a bit more hazardous.

Cocktail piano jobs offer a livelihood and a situation for artistic expression to pianists of different stripes. Perhaps further definitions are in order: Many pianists make a distinction among themselves as to whether they are jazz players or "popular" players. The latter term is not universal, but I propose its greater use to distinguish between two traditions of playing which, while having many points in common, are quite distinct. On the one hand there is the tradition of improvised jazz piano, which includes Fats Waller, Art Tatum, Erroll Garner, and Bill Evans. Like all great artists, each of these players had his own individual style, but together they shared a group identity as jazz performers.

On the other hand, there are the collective styles of such pianists as Eddy Duchin, Carmen Cavallero, Liberace, Roger Williams, and Cy Walter. If the jazz tradition springs from ragtime and Afro-American expression, I would say that the various forms of "popular piano" go back to Chopin, Rachmaninoff, and the sort of show-tune piano of the 1920's that George Gershwin exemplified and ultimately transcended.

A list of comparisons, to be debated, modified, particularized, and so on:

Jazz people play in tempo; popular people often play rubato.

Jazz people care more for improvisation than repertoire. Since each performance of a given standard is improvised differently, a jazz player is con-

tent to work with a smaller body of tunes. Popular pianists, in contrast, often have a staggering repertoire covering thousands of pieces. For them, repertoire is the most important element in their presentation.

There is, however, a jazz repertoire, and you would not be likely to hear a popular pianist delve into it for pieces like "'Round Midnight" or "Groovin' High." Even in the realm of familiar pop songs, jazz people have a predilection for old tunes such as "Sugar," "Body And Soul," and the works of Duke Ellington, which popular pianists might not normally get around to. On the other hand, unless a jazz player has done his homework, he or she wouldn't know certain obscure Cole Porter songs or such titles as "Of Thee I Sing" and "Greenup Time."

Jazz people, by definition, are improvisers who often rework tunes in fundamental ways. Popular people, although they may improvise to a degree, are not quite so comfortable with it. Their improvisation may be expressed through altered harmonies, but they stop short of inventing entirely new melodies on the harmonic framework of a given tune. Their goal is more that of the arranger and embellisher. Jazz people, of course, often get rid of the melody as soon as possible, and then settle down to business.

A cocktail piano job for a jazz pianist is not quite as natural as it is for a popular pianist, both because of the repertoire requirement and because of the need to put a damper on one's non-melodic inventiveness. Nevertheless, many jazz people hold such jobs, in which they are able to reach an accommodation with their audiences and their own background, even as pianists from the popular tradition can often play in a creditable jazz style when necessary. In either case, as the song urges us, "Let's Hear It For The Pi-ano Player!"

Let's Hear It For The Pi-ano Player!

WORDS BY MORT GOODE
MUSIC BY DICK HYMAN

Medium steady tempo

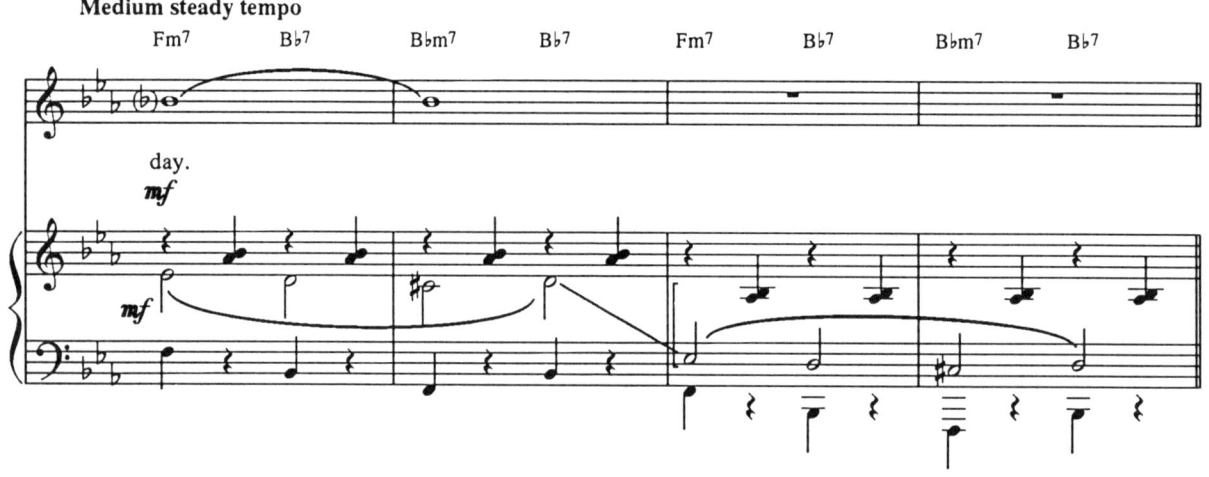

day.

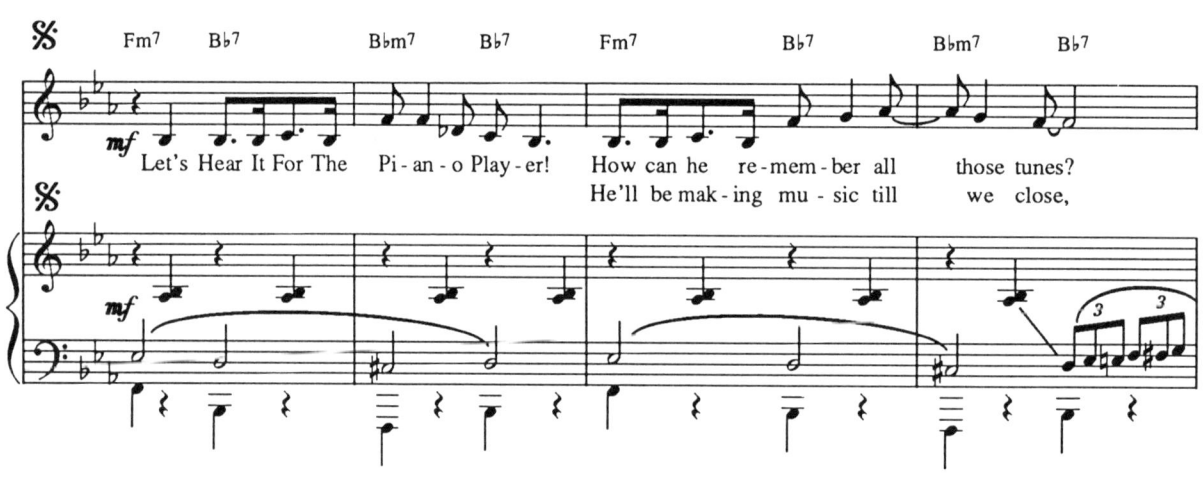

Let's Hear It For The Pi - an - o Play - er! How can he re-mem-ber all those tunes?
He'll be mak-ing mu - sic till we close,

Played 'em all a mil - lion times or more in a mil - lion sa - loons.
Makes you feel that you're a mil - lion - aire, while the Bud - weis - er flows.

Let's Hear It For The Pi - an - o Play - er!
Ask him for your fav - 'rite late   night song,
He's the doc - tor who can cure   your ills,

Ev - en if you get the   ti - tle wrong,   hum a few bars, he'll play a - long.
Makes you hap - pi - er with - out those pills;   and it's for free, he   sends no bills.

He can do Gersh - win and   all the rest.

Those Broad - way   mel - o - dies   are   what   he   does best.

To Coda ⊕

That's the be - gin - ning of "Be - gin the Be - guine."

Let's Hear It For The Pi - an - o Play - er! With spir - it for the pi - an - o play - er!

Hold it down, folks, cut the chat - ter, cut the jokes. Give him a hand now and then! Let's

hear the pi - an - o play - er play it a - gain!

A LONG WAY, BABY!

At its 1901 convention in Denver, the American Federation of Musicians condemned ragtime in a harsh statement delivered by its president. Union musicians were specifically cautioned against playing ragtime, and the Federation's president maintained that "... the musicians know what is good, and if the people don't, we will have to teach them." Clearly, union musicians were a different breed in those days, and the smugness of the A. F. of M. suggests the intensity with which a radical shift in public taste would be debated.

I'm indebted to Neil Leonard, whose 1962 book *Jazz And The White Americans* (University of Chicago Press) documents the opinion above, and the ones that follow, along with much additional insight. I discovered the book in the Lincoln Center Music Library in New York. If you can locate a copy, I think you would find it enlightening reading.

Daniel G. Mason, in the March 1918 issue of the *New Music And Church Review*, admitted that the "jerk and rattle" of ragtime might indeed be the music of the common people, but he had little faith in the people's taste. Ragtime had vitality, he admitted, but it was the vitality of the comic strip, and not a significant example of American culture. Mason's position, interestingly enough, was later attacked by other writers who argued that the comic strip, in particular "Krazy Kat," was indeed a valuable cultural contribution.

Ragtime departed the scene, and jazz arrived. In a 1922 drama entitled *The National Anthem*, which was concerned with the debauchery of modern youth, playwright J. Hartley Manners argued that the new music was a threat to civilization itself, and that jazz was "modern man's Saturnalia." We should recall the social context in which such remarkable anxiety flourished. It was the time of Prohibition, when, as Neil Leonard points out, traditionalists "regarded jazz, along with intemperance and unconventional sexual behavior, as a sign or cause of the advancing degeneration" of society.

"Does Jazz Put The Sin In Syncopation?" asked Anne Shaw Faulkner in a 1921 issue of *The Ladies' Home Journal*. She quoted the opinion of Dr. Henry Van Dyke, a Presbyterian clergyman and professor at Princeton, that jazz "is not music at all." Sigmund Spaeth took the same position in his piece for *Forum* in 1928, which was flatly entitled "Jazz Is Not Music." Mr. Spaeth, who would later become well known as radio's Tune Detective, heard the music of the golden age of early Louis Armstrong, Duke Ellington, Bix Beiderbecke, and the rest as "merely a raucous and inarticulate shouting of hoarse-throated instruments, with each player trying to outdo his fellows, in fantastic cacophony."

The Ladies' Home Journal, apparently obsessed with the matter, printed another article in 1921, "Back To Pre-War Morals." John R. McMahon claimed that "... if Beethoven should return to earth and witness the doings of (a jazz) orchestra, he would thank heaven for his deafness. ... All this music has a droning, jerky incoherence interrupted with a spasmodic 'blah! blah!!' that reminded me of the way that live sheep are turned into mutton." And *The New York Times*, on November 14, 1924, quoted concert pianist Ashley Pettis: "Jazz is nothing more or less than the distortion of every esthetic principle."

Some people were bothered by the bodily movements with which listeners responded to the new music. From *The New York Times* once more, on October 7, 1928: "With music of the old style, even the most moving, the listener was seldom upset from his dignified posture ... the bodily anchor remained intact. The listener behaved as impassively as the radio's microphone. Nothing in his manner indicated either a struggle for self-control or an absence of decorum." For the other side of the picture, we can examine the *Times* for April 14, 1926, in which was printed a charge by New Jersey Supreme Court Justice J.F. Minturn that "... in response to (jazz's) call there ensues a series of snake-like gyrations and weird contortions of seemingly agonized bodies and limbs, resembling an Asiatic *pot pourri*, which ... is called a dance."

And still earlier, in 1921, Fenton T. Bott, head of the National Association of Masters of Dancing, warned that "those moaning saxophones and the rest of the instruments with their broken, jerky rhythm make a purely sensual appeal. They call out the low and rowdy instincts. All of us dancing teachers know this to be a fact. ... Jazz is the very foundation and essence of salacious dancing."

The manner of the musicians themselves troubled H.O. Osgood, an editor of the *Musical Courier* and author of the 1926 book *So This Is Jazz*. Mr. Osgood described the players of the Ted Lewis band as "jolting up and down and writhing about in simulated ecstasy, in the manner of Negroes at a Southern camp-meeting afflicted with religious frenzy." Ted Lewis made some good hot records that featured Fats Waller and Benny Goodman, but his vaudeville performing group was probably putting the audience on, when the author witnessed the simulated ecstasy. What is significant in the writer's concern is the racial element. In many quotations of the period, Black performers and their music were seen as threatening.

In a 1922 interview, the actress Laurette Taylor, who played a lead in the already mentioned *National Anthem*, stated that "... jazz, the impulse for wildness that has undoubtedly come over many things besides the music of this country, is traceable to the

Negro influence." Ms. Faulkner, whom we met earlier in *The Ladies' Home Journal,* opined that "... jazz originally was the accompaniment of the voodoo dancer, stimulating the half-crazed barbarian to the vilest deeds."

Writer H.E. Krehbiel, in *The Literary Digest* of 1920, associated jazz with "the Negro brothels of the South" and feared that ever more music and dance would emanate therefrom. The legend of jazz has by now assimilated the viewpoint that the bordello was in fact one of a number of probable sources; but what is seen today as quaint and even romantic history was then perceived by Dr. John R. Straton, a Baptist clergyman in New York, as a tendency "endangering our civilization in its general revolt against authority and established order." *(New York Times,* May 26, 1927)

Improvisation itself was condemned. An editor of *The Musical Courier* named Fran Patterson, in "Jazz — The National Anthem?" (1922), reported that his colleagues agreed "that the 'ad libbing' or 'jazzing' of a piece is thoroughly objectionable, and several of them advanced the opinion that this Bolshevistic smashing of the rules and tenets of decorous music, this excessive freedom of interpretation, tended to a similar letting down on the part of the dancers, a similar disregard for the self-contained and self-restrained attitude that has been described by the makers of the rules of dignified social intercourse."

In one case, the headline itself tells the story: "Cornetist to Queen Victoria Falls Dead on Hearing Coney Island Jazz Band." *(New York Times,* June 14, 1926)

In this day of rapping and Madonna, it is difficult to grasp the fears of the authorities in the 1920's. Jazz went on to become an art music, society did not disintegrate, civilization is still with us. So what was all the shouting about? Change — change and the inevitable resistance to it. "Jazz," however it was defined, had an important symbolic role in the '20s, but to credit it as the driving force behind all the social changes we have been through would be to exaggerate its importance.

ACOUSTIC THOUGHTS WHILE HEARING BRENDEL PLAY

We would have spent the evening differently, had it not been for an old friend who offered two tickets to a special Carnegie Hall concert. And we would have missed a great event. On the bill was the Y Chamber Symphony, a prestigious group conducted by Gerard Schwarz, and Alfred Brendel, one of the great pianists of this era, and a distinguished Beethoven specialist.

Julia and I found ourselves in fourth row orchestra seats on the keyboard side, no more than 20 feet from the performers. The all-Beethoven program opened with the Fifth Symphony, a work which has survived its association with the V-for-victory slogan of World War II (the rhythm of the opening theme is the same as that of the Morse Code letter "V"), and has even continued to be heard in its original form despite the success of Walter Murphy's 1976 disco adaptation "A Fifth Of Beethoven" and a similarly mechanistic treatment in "Hooked On Classics." It is difficult to be convincing when presenting an overly familiar piece, but Mr. Schwarz conducted a dramatic performance.

During the intermission, Mr. Brendel's Steinway was moved center stage. When the orchestra was again in place, the artist himself appeared, took his seat, and, after a moment's eye contact with Mr. Schwarz, began the solo opening phrase of the "Fourth Concerto." At the time this concerto was written, it was normal for the orchestra to state the entire exposition of the first-movement themes before the solo instrument made its entrance, but Beethoven's remarkable game plan has the piano begin the movement by itself, proposing a relatively brief theme to which the orchestra responds at surprising length. During this response, Brendel adjusted his seat and sat poised patiently. (From my own more commercial background a fantasy floated through my mind: The soloist, trapped in overtime on another gig, arrives onstage in a panic several minutes late and sneaks onto his seat hoping that no one has noticed his arrival. In this concerto he would have missed only the short piano intro, and the conductor, equally panicked, might have begun without him. . . . I guiltily put aside such speculation to concentrate on the performance.)

The piano re-entered, and a dialogue between soloist and orchestra built a symbiosis in which the orchestra might at one moment support the soloist, at another go its own way, at still another subside altogether while the piano played unaccompanied. Brendel was a marvel of expressivity and clarity. Every tone, every phrase was exactly right in relation to the whole. In the first movement Beethoven used sonata form like a wordless novel. The listener was introduced to a protagonist and a host of secondary characters and allowed to follow them through plot complications, conflict, reconciliation, and denouement, all in the abstract.

In the slow second movement there was a moment which made me feel as if I were watching an incredible trapeze artist, worried that he might plunge to the ground. Brendel had neared the end of a sensitive phrase during which each tone had become softer than the last in coordination with a graceful *ritardando*. At the next to last note, one feared that he could not possibly settle on the final one with the ultimate delicacy demanded by the line. He sustained the penultimate note until it had all but died away, then concluded at last with a tone even softer. In the row ahead of me, my neighbor turned to his companion and smiled in marveling awe.

While one side of my brain followed Beethoven's inexorable logic and Brendel's exquisite playing, the other side was entertaining quite different thoughts. I myself have been on the august stage of Carnegie Hall a fair number of times, and have wondered on each occasion whether we ought to be performing with natural sound, as at this concert, taking advantage of the hall's magnificent acoustics. Pragmatically, however, in every situation I can recall we have used some form of audio amplification. This is not to say that I cannot imagine an acoustic jazz concert at Carnegie. Solo piano obviously works fine. The trouble begins when bass is added. An unamplified bass simply doesn't project satisfactorily, at least not with the presence to which we have grown accustomed. The acoustic problem grows worse when we add the drum set. Even if the drummer limits himself to playing with brushes on the snare and cymbals, this tends to distract from the sound of the piano, and as soon as our man picks up his sticks, the game is up. At that point one is forced to acknowledge that, as far as the role of the acoustic piano is concerned, a jazz combo is inherently unbalanced in volume; a jazz band of any size is even worse.

Amplification leads to more amplification. From the point of view of the bass player, it is understandable for him to want to keep turning the knob to the right. Not only does his tone gain in presence, his agility is greater since he can play with less force. Having turned up, however, he is liable to be carried away by the excitement of the song and may well play just as hard as he would have at the lower volume setting. The raised level of the bass, in turn, requires that the drummer play louder. There is no way that the poor pianist can match the pair acoustically except by playing more forcefully than he ought to, which may lead to a hard tone and less than facile technique. Even then, he will probably be overwhelmed. Add an electric guitar to the group, and it is easy to see how tempting it is for the pianist to switch to an electric keyboard altogether.

The answer, and it is not a perfect one, is to convince the bass player that we know he is there, even if we do not hear the tramping of dinosaurs, to beg the drummer to percuss in a more moderate fashion, and to apply a microphone to the piano. The piano mike does not have to be very loud, merely sufficient for the player to hear himself while others are playing.

Our acoustic problem is also related to the requirements of singers. Since pop-jazz singers do not project in the manner of opera singers, they must be amplified. Pop singing since Bing Crosby has depended on the use of the microphone, and an entire idiom has come about because of the discovery in the '20s of microphone technique. This is well and good, but the corollary is that the accompanying instruments, at least the piano, must also be amplified to match the voice.

Stage monitor speakers, in my opinion, are a cure for acoustical problems which is worse than the disease. While their ostensible function is to keep scattered sections of the orchestra in touch with one another, my experience is that they often add to the general muddle of sound, so that the players get progressively louder in an effort to project their individual parts. I certainly didn't see any monitors onstage during the Beethoven concert, and there were 40-odd musicians up there, frequently all playing at the same time — and very nicely, too. A full-

sized symphony orchestra, which the Y Chamber Symphony is not, may consist of up to 100 people, none of them screaming to stagehands to get them a monitor.

One more point needs to be made: Pianists like Alfred Brendel are trained to play with a full dynamic range, from very soft to very loud. Jazz pianists generally play within a more circumscribed range. When Brendel plays softly, however, it is not necessarily the pianissimo the audience assumes it to be. He is able to play tenderly and delicately and still cause his sound to sing out. Many of us, on the other hand, have come to depend largely on amplification and have not thought enough about projection.

On the positive side, a new idiom has been created with an esthetic based on the technology of amplified sound. Without even thinking about synthesizers, we should consider the variety of guitar styles, the enriched possibilities of tone control and agility for brass instruments played directly into a microphone, the use of an amplified flute, the dazzling technique of amplified bass players. My plea, therefore, is not to do away with all amplification. Rather, it is to use it only as needed for balance in halls such as Carnegie. And perhaps, for chamber jazz, we might attempt now and then to get by with none at all, everyone playing more softly than usual.

REMEMBERING JOHNNY GUARNIERI (1917-1985)

I have played too many memorial services for old friends at St. Peter's Lutheran Church. This modern, yet warm, wooden structure on Manhattan's East Side is where John Gensel ministers to those he has termed "the jazz community." Duke Ellington's memorial service was held there, as was that of Thelonious Monk. In addition to these widely publicized events, Pastor Gensel has conducted informal and loving tributes to musicians less well known, always including musical performances as an integral part of his services. The St. Peter's congregation is by no means limited to jazz people, but these constitute the bulk of John Gensel's particular and often interdenominational flock.

In the autumn of 1984 I played the organ, and Ruby Braff played cornet at a service for trombonist Vic Dickenson. Several months later, I was at the piano for a packed service in honor of Zoot Sims. Following that sad occasion I joined other friends of Bob Bach, a television producer and great jazz buff, playing and singing songs he would have liked.

Too soon after that, I played at a memorial tribute to Johnny Guarnieri, whose piano artistry set a standard for me as a teenager. In the 1940's Guarnieri recorded extensively in a swing style in which he neatly merged the influences of Fats Waller, Count Basie, and Teddy Wilson. Those records still sound good to me.

Johnny sailed through the big-band era playing at various times with Jimmy Dorsey, Benny Goodman, and Artie Shaw. He is often remembered as the harpsichordist in Shaw's Gramercy Five, an instrumentally innovative recording group. He recorded a great deal in the '40s, often with Slam Stewart on bass and Cozy Cole on drums, a rhythm section which floated from date to date. His always apt accompaniments can be heard on classic recordings by saxophonists Lester Young and Coleman Hawkins, among many others.

At times he played on 52nd Street at night while undertaking studio work in the daylight hours. As a college student, I saw him in one of the little clubs on what became known as Swing Street. I was awestruck by his technique as he raced through a cut-

time stride arrangement of Chopin's "Minute Waltz," which he played in thirds. I have a hunch now that he did it in C with a couple of fingering slides, rather than in Db. But no matter — it was still a prodigious feat.

Early in his career, Johnny had been unfairly criticized for sounding too much like Waller, Basie, and Wilson, but in his later years, when he was working primarily as a soloist, his playing developed in two original and unique ways. His left-hand technique had always been fast, full, and accurate in stride playing, but he now perfected this technique to a point where he was able to perform complete selections with the left hand alone. In addition, he took to playing his entire repertoire in 5/4 time, introducing into familiar tunes an eccentric element which sounded quite puzzling until you got the hang of it.

I always admired Johnny's technical command, his touch, and his time, and I felt remarkably honored when, several years ago, he dedicated a piece to me. It was this piece, "The Virtuoso Rag," that I played at St. Peter's. Interestingly, Johnny later composed "The Virtuoso Rag II," a work meant to be performed in counterpoint with the original as a duo-piano vehicle. Although we played in duet at the Sacramento, California, Jazz Festival in 1985, we hadn't had time to rehearse "The Virtuosi," so I have never actually heard how they fit together, but it appears to be a neat contrapuntal job.

The tempo in "The Virtuoso Rag" should be steady throughout. The piece benefits from a light, legato approach to the right-hand eighth-notes. The stride bass ought to be light but firm, and softer than the right hand. However, in the section in Bb, the virtuosic two-bar breaks in the left hand should be louder, though still legato. When Johnny recorded this piece for the Pianocorder reproducing piano system, he made small variations in the chord voicings and bass notes on each repeat. In addition, two of the breaks were completely different in performance from what he had notated. Almost all jazz pianists vary their performances to some degree in this fashion, and an original composition is no less subject to improvisation than another person's piece.

The Virtuoso Rag

JOHNNY GUARNIERI

GEORGE GERSHWIN: RE-EVALUATING HIS LEGACY IN JAZZ

The fiftieth anniversary of George Gershwin's death took place in 1987. Since that time we have been reconsidering the remarkable works of a true American phenomenon, a composer/pianist who died at the age of 39. As far back as the World War I years, his songs began to reach the public. In the 1920's his Broadway scores established him as a leading composer of musical comedies, while in concert appearances he performed two major works for orchestra and piano, his "Rhapsody In Blue" and "Concerto In F." In the following decade he composed more concert pieces, scores for film musicals, and what many consider his greatest triumph, the opera *Porgy and Bess*. Dozens of his individual songs figure in the basic repertoire of singers. The standard jazz library would be significantly poorer without such titles as "I Got Rhythm," "Oh, Lady Be Good!", "The Man I Love," "Liza," "Embraceable You," "A Foggy Day," "S'Wonderful," "I've Got A Crush On You," "Strike Up The Band," "But Not For Me," "Somebody Loves Me," and "Summertime."

To have succeeded in so many venues is something no other American composer has achieved. Yet Gershwin's tremendous output has not been free of criticism, either during his brief lifetime or thereafter. In his anniversary year, at any rate, superlatives abounded. Gershwin was at last seen as a figure who transcended each of the categories into which his work falls, his disparate accomplishments constituting a grand unity. Even the New York Metropolitan Opera finally accepted *Porgy and Bess*, although its probationary period lasted 51 years. If the "serious music" critics have now embraced Gershwin, there still seems to be some unfinished business among the jazz cognoscenti. In his *Encyclopedia Of Jazz*, the esteemed jazz critic Leonard Feather states that "Gershwin's symphonic works made only superficial use of jazz devices and are now not generally considered to be an important part of jazz history." On the other hand, the writers of the 1920's constantly cited "Rhapsody In Blue" as their primary reference in a critical furor over the merit of jazz as the new American music. How can we account for this discrepancy? Perhaps some historical notes will aid us.

When Paul Whiteman commissioned Gershwin to compose a jazz concerto, which would become the "Rhapsody," he had good reason to trust in the composer's ability to undertake such a fusionist project. An impressive pianist-around-town, Gershwin had come to Whiteman's attention two years earlier as the composer of the brief opera *Blue Monday*, an interpolation, soon dropped, in a Broadway musical revue. It was a juvenile work, yet it had fascinating intimations of what he would one day achieve with *Porgy and Bess*. At the time Gershwin had had one important hit song with "Swanee," which was introduced by Al Jolson, and numerous others had been heard in various Broadway productions. He had studied piano, theory, and orchestration in his teens. At 15, he had dropped out of high school to work as a song-plugger's accompanist in a leading publishing company.

The job involved constant playing, the young Gershwin demonstrating the latest output of Tin Pan Alley for vaudevillians seeking fresh material. With a weekly salary of $15, it was an apprenticeship in which the keyboard tickler learned to pay his dues. He then became a vocal accompanist, a rehearsal pianist, and a performer, under his own name as well as various pseudonyms, of numerous piano rolls. Judging from his later phonograph recordings, it is fair to say that the prevailing player-piano style shaped him as much as he shaped it. His approach was busy and full, with an active left hand and frequent octaves in the right. Syncopated attention-getting devices place him with Zez Confrey's influential school of novelty piano. There is a tendency to think of Gershwin's piano playing as *sui generis*, but the relationship is particularly clear once one hears Confrey's piano rolls, some of them on Gershwin tunes.

Additional linking can be made between Gershwin and other pianists of his time such as Frank Signorelli and Lennie Hayton, who played on recordings of Bix Beiderbecke. And we might add to the list Rube Bloom and Arthur Schutt, whose work is on numerous contemporaneous recordings.

Gershwin's playing resembled that of other pianists of his day in another fundamental way: it was without the "classical" nuances which would later be brought to his concert works by others. Even, for example, in his own recording of the lyrical "Second Prelude", the playing is without the romantic shadings of tone color that we have come to expect from other performers. In a preface to one of his publications he advised that staccato effects were more appropriate for American popular music than excessive use of the sostenuto pedal. His experience as a "piano pounder" had profoundly influenced his approach to the keyboard.

"Rhapsody In Blue" was commissioned by the popular bandleader Paul Whiteman to be the finale of a concert in New York's Aeolian Hall. Billed as "An Experiment In Modern Music," Whiteman's stated goal was to demonstate how a crude ethnic music could be refined into concert material worthy of a discerning audience. For the sake of contrast — to present jazz as it had been prior to Whiteman's purifying ministrations — the evening began with a group from his band recreating the raucous "Livery Stable Blues" as it had been played six years previously by the Original Dixieland Jazz Band, the first self-proclaimed jazz group to record. Filled with barnyard hokum — the cornet neighs like a horse, the trombone imitates a lowing cow, the clarinet produces a rooster cackle — the piece was described in the program notes as jazz in its "true, naked form."

Whiteman then illustrated the evolution of the genre through increasingly elegant arrangements by Ferde Grofé, novelty piano solos by Zez Confrey (whose presence, rather than Gershwin's, was intended to add star quality), a commissioned suite by Victor Herbert, and finally, the '"Rhapsody." Gilbert Seldes' program notes are to the point: he writes that Gershwin "has built his 'Rhapsody' out of materials known to him, the rhythms of popular American music, the harmonies produced by . American jazz bands." As the concert has been recreated in recent years by Maurice Peress (this writer taking the role of Zez Confrey), it is clear that Gershwin's work was directly related to the rest of the program.* In fact, it was exactly as Seldes described it — a construction of American music. Seldes' reference to jazz bands, on the other hand, is problematic: According to the current definition of a jazz band, Whiteman did not have one. The semantic trap was thus sprung, and we are still trying to extricate ourselves.

The basic problem, one which has stayed with us till the present, is that in 1924 there was no agreement on the meaning of the word *jazz*. Although we have hardly reached unanimity, at least a certain concensus exists; back then, all was semantic chaos. To some, jazz meant the songs of Irving Berlin; to others, anything having to do with saxophones.

The critical reaction to the premiere of "Rhapsody In Blue" was mixed. One writer hailed the composer's "extraordinary talent"; another could "only weep at the lifelessness of the melodies, so derivative, so stale, and so inexpressive." Note that there were no jazz critics at this time. Those reviewers who attended Aeolian Hall, necessarily the classical crowd, made no connection with the music of Duke Ellington and Fletcher Henderson, whose earliest orchestras were playing nightly only a few blocks away. Musicologists had not probed the world of dance halls and cabarets, let alone the New Orleans bordellos from which issued much of the ragtime aspect of Gershwin's keyboard approach. It was not until the 1930's that knowledgeable writers on jazz would emerge.

Despite the critical debate, the "Rhapsody" became a giant success with the public, while jazz musicians of the time, fascinated by it, emulated the work in their own compositions. James P. Johnson's "Yamekraw," subtitled by its publisher both "Negro Rhapsody" and "Rhapsody In Black," was performed at Carnegie Hall in 1928 with Fats Waller as soloist.** Ellington's "Creole Rhapsody," recorded in 1931, also bears some relationship. Yet these pieces, each essentially a series of tunes strung together with simple piano connectives, are not comparable with their source of inspiration.

With the arrival of the jazz writers some six years

following the dazzling premiere of the "Rhapsody In Blue", a different sort of criticism was heard. It was an anti-Gershwin attitude that has prevailed to the present time. With a mission to codify the new music in the face of what they saw as profound public misconception, writers such as Charles Edward Smith and Hughes Panassié seized on negative aspects of the work, the better to clarify their emerging definition of jazz.

Underlying the harshness of their revisionist viewpoint, it seems, was the very success of the piece. Because the work conformed to the non-improvisatory conventions of concert music, it froze the superficial practices of 1924 as though Aeolian Hall had witnessed a solution for all time rather than an experiment, and as though the subsequent phenomenal evolution of the music had never taken place. The critics particularly resented what had appeared to be the concert's main implication, that jazz had merit only when fused with classical music. A subtext of their anger was that the true heroes of jazz, who at the time were mostly Blacks, had been neglected. And they were basically correct: The earlier authorities had dealt with the Black roots of jazz with the casual contempt that was prevalent among racial attitudes of the time. (A later jazz writer would exercise similarly poor taste by noting that Gershwin's sponsor, ironically, was named White Man!) The critics' greatest complaint was that the price paid by jazz, in the process of its becoming a lady, was the loss of its rhythmic component. The "Rhapsody" didn't swing; its shifting tempi didn't settle down long enough to get a toe tapping.

History has mellowed these accusations. Whatever Whiteman and Gershwin believed they were doing, the "Rhapsody" is a towering monument to its period, and, more than that, a work of genuine originality and drama. It is no longer necessary to derogate it and its composer for fear of misrepresenting the concept of jazz, as it has now come to be defined.

Throughout his career, Whiteman attempted to discover another "Rhapsody In Blue." He introduced works by Ferde Grofé, John Alden Carpenter, Dana Suesse, William Grant Still, and others in eight successive "Experiments In Modern Music." Grofé's *Grand Canyon Suite*, a striking orchestral piece with no jazz content, has come closest in stature, but none of Whiteman's presentations had the magic of the "Rhapsody."

Gershwin's second work for piano and orchestra, however, did. The "Concerto In F" was commissioned by Walter Damrosch and the New York Symphony Society, and in 1925 received its Carnegie Hall debut. It seems that in writing this piece, Gershwin took to heart at least one criticism of the "Rhapsody" — that it was undisciplined in form, a puzzling criticism, since a rhapsody, by definition, has an irregular form. Although not precisely

* See Recreating Paul Whiteman's 1924 Concert (page 38)
**See Recreating W.C. Handy's 1928 Concert (page 34)

a master of concerto form — this was his first attempt at a structured large work — Gershwin followed the rules fairly closely in each of his concerto's neatly crafted movements. The first is in classic sonata form. Its motivic use of the early '20s dance rhythm of the Charleston (in 4/4 time, a dotted quarter followed by an eighth-note and a half-rest) offers a reminder of Gershwin's pop background. The second movement is bluesy, and takes an expanded song form. The third is a sort of rondo, with themes from the first movement being reintroduced.

No longer bound by the instrumentation of Whiteman's dance band, Gershwin orchestrated the concerto with a confident, symphonic approach. If his use of jazz elements is even more rarified than in the "Rhapsody," the whole nevertheless reflects his jazz background, however fused with the ideals of a Romantic concerto.

Considering Gershwin's jazz roots, is it possible that Gershwin and Duke Ellington influenced each other? As an exercise in speculation, one might play a little game: Consider, for example, the great lyrical theme of the first movement of "Concerto in F," a series of gorgeously harmonized phrases played *rubato* and *expressivo*.

Now suppose that Ellington were playing the same section, slightly rearranged and in strict tempo, in his own fashion, harder and less romantic.

The kinship is clear, although inexplicable unless we credit Gershwin for being more conscious of the jazz currents of his time than his critics have allowed. It is known that he liked to hear Ellington play at a restaurant in midtown Manhattan called the Kentucky Club. On the other hand, Ellington had not recorded anything quite this subtle as early as 1925, so we can speculate that the Duke could have been the one who was influenced. Of course, such a scenario is pure fantasy. The great advantage of our being so far removed from those times, though, is that we can entertain ourselves with such a speculation without fear of contradiction.

The writer thanks Ed Jablonski, whose many works on George Gershwin constitute basic source material.

MAKING A BALLET

In its dependence on music, ballet has something in common with film: Both are visual arts, but neither can exist for long without musical support. Film, obviously, is the more independent and can of itself command the attention of a viewer with little or no accompaniment, but it is indisputable that it is usually enhanced by a musical score. On the other hand, ballet is basically the visual expression of music in terms of movement of the human form, and while there are rare experiments in dance without music or to organized sound of a non-instrumental nature, such abstract movement invariably illustrates in a negative way how interrelated the two arts are.

I had had some experience with the Twyla Tharp Dance Company, conducting, playing, and arranging several dances, and I'd done similar service with the Cleveland Ballet. What I had not yet done, however, was to compose a dance piece. Dennis Nahat and the late Ian Horvath of the Cleveland company gave me the opportunity. They proposed a piece in a pop or jazz vein for solo piano with me as the soloist. Following their all-important phone call (Sammy Cahn likes to say that the phone call comes first, before either the words or the music), I sent Nahat and Horvath a cassette of a set of original pieces which had just been published, my *Etudes For Jazz Piano.* The two choreographers responded positively to my idea of using these short works as the basis for the dance, and we agreed to meet as soon as it was convenient.

I was in Cleveland soon afterward to play another engagement. Dennis, Ernie, and I met to clarify our direction. Playing the *Etudes* in sequence amounts to a history of jazz piano from Scott Joplin up to Bill Evans, but Ernie, who was to be the choreographer and principal dancer of the new piece, did not have in mind such a literal treatment. We began to group the *Etudes* into segments, so that the sequence would be dramatically and choreographically effective as well as logical in a musical and historical sense. It was clear that even if we used all of the *Etudes,* and this was not certain, additional material would be required. The running time of all 15 pieces was only 15 minutes. We wanted the dance to last between 20 and 25 minutes.

Choreographers work in a world of abstract movements. They can recall and execute patterns of movement the way we musicians refer to chords, rhythm patterns, and melodic phrases. They have a mental catalog of all this material, and, they can both execute their ideas and teach others to do them. I don't pretend fully to understand the cre-

ative process of choreography, but my impression is that it is analogous to music composition. A germ of an idea in terms of movement or attitude suggests a chain of development. A second and then a third element is introduced, relationships are established among them, and gradually an increasingly complex structure of movement is built. The choreographer, in addition to preparing his ideas in advance, works them out directly with the dancers, as a pianist tries things out on the keyboard. The original ideas will become modified in the grueling rehearsals which take place over the course of several months.

This is a complex process, not nearly so easily realized as the playing of a score by an orchestra. Each dancer in the company of 16 (excluding Horvath, who himself danced the principal role) had to learn his or her movements from the choreographer on a one-to-one basis without the help of a written part. This struck me as something like the way some jazz or rock groups work, but with less individual input and correspondingly greater dependence on the ideas of the person in charge.

Ernie and Dennis made two trips to New York, and we gradually structured 14 of the 15 *Etudes* into a continuity which included considerable new material and extensions of the original pieces. I wrote an important new theme which functions as a prologue and as a connective device between the different segments. A bit like Aaron Copland crossed with Duke Ellington, it ties the whole work together, expressing remembrance, and meditation. I added entirely new sections of blues and gospel and did my best to oblige Ernie when he would request "another minute of the same thing" or would ask, "Can you give me a slow, bluesy part right here?" At these moments I would improvise something which might or might not be right on the first try.

When we had agreed on all the adjustments, I took some time off and made the first draft on the piece we were then calling "Piano Men." I made photocopies of the *Etudes* and cut and pasted them into their new sequence, interspersing them with the new material until I had a part which I could actually put on the piano rack and play through. I then went into a small recording studio and made a demo cassette. "Piano Men" was at this point 20 minutes long, and it didn't seem to want to get any longer.

Ernie played the cassette on his Walkman for a few days and then called me. The dance was becoming clearer in his mind. He said that we needed an entirely new section, contemporary, with a strong rhythmic drive and a powerful ending. I decided to write something in the style of McCoy Tyner, and managed to develop several minutes of material using a propulsive left-hand figure in fourths along with characteristic single-note pentatonic patterns in the right hand. This was built up to a series of explosive stabs played with the palms on the keyboard in the manner of Cecil Taylor. A final crash, sustained with the sostenuto pedal for twelve seconds, gave Ernie the climax he had been looking for.

Some time passed during which each of us was involved in other things, and then I began the lengthy process of writing out the final version of the piece. I made many small improvements along the way, correcting various shortcomings. Finally we met again at the same recording studio, Seltzer Sound at the edge of Chinatown. I would perform the piece exactly in tempo for use as a rehearsal tape.

We recorded each section separately, getting precisely the right tempo and the best execution possible. The new length turned out to be 30 minutes. After a demanding evening, we celebrated with a Chinese dinner nearby. The following day I returned and worked with Carl Seltzer on the splicing as well as the interpolation of blank leader tape to cover points where applause or non-musical stage movement was expected. The dancers would be guided by this tape in every detail.

Several months before, I had spoken to Steven Harlos, a pianist who was a recent graduate of Indiana University and had begun to teach at North Texas State. A classically trained pianist with a jazz background, he would replace me during the run of what we had now named "Piano Man." I sent him the tape and the music at the beginning of August. After that I had nothing to do with the rehearsals of "Piano Man" except to feel a sense of pleasurable anticipation for the performances, which would take place starting on October 15.

The week before the premiere I flew to Cleveland to rehearse with the dancers. Everything had been going well, I was told, except that the evolution of the choreography now required a particular section to be played much more slowly than it was on the tape. Stanley Sussman had been augmenting the rehearsal tape with his live keyboard services, moonlighting from his position as one of the conductors of the Ballet orchestra.

Seeing the dance for the first time I began to grasp what Ernie had imagined all this time. Much of it was in classic ballet style, and the idea of so treating Fats Waller and Art Tatum was as successful as it was daring. There was a story line involving Ernie himself as a sort of Chaplinesque character who always fails to get the girl, and the four segments were entitled "The Concert," "The Club," "Jammin'" and "Gospel And Goodbyes."

I returned to Cleveland the following week for the final rehearsals on stage and in costume. Dramatic lighting enhanced a bare-bones set in which the piano acted as a focal point. In the mornings Steven Harlos and I practiced and got to know each other both musically and socially. He had agreed to be my page-turner during the first four performances, which I would play. He would take over after that as soloist for the remaining seven. My already considerable respect for his musicianship rose even higher when he remarked that he had memorized the score and thus would not have the page-turning problem I did. When I heard him perform my music, it was uncanny how he replicated my own playing.

Friday arrived, the night of the performance. As the Piano Man himself, I donned my costume, a black suit with grey shirt, white cuffs and collar, and a string tie, a sort of Old Professor-playing-in-the-bordello look. The piano microphone was tested for the final time. I sat at the piano, Steven at my left, inhaled deeply for a minute or so (it helps the inevitable pounding of the heart), and waited to begin. The curtain rolled up with a *whish*, we could hear the audience murmuring, the dimmed onstage lights brightened, and I began the first dissonant notes of the prologue.

"Piano Man" has been performed for several seasons since its premiere, with Stephen Harlos as pianist. Ernie Horvath has passed on, another victim of AIDS.

FAKING IT

Webster defines it as "composing and rendering music, poetry, and the like extemporaneously." As musicians practice it, improvisation is a sort of instant composition. The results are less rigorously constructed than the product of formal composition, although it is said that Bach, Beethoven, Mozart, and Mendelssohn, great keyboardists all, could have blown us jazz ad-libbers right off the bandstand at The Blue Note with improvised four-part fugues and whole extemporaneous sonatas. Still, when a composer has the opportunity to revise, insert cross-references, develop counterpoint, and make internal links, the work will certainly have a more complex structure.

Even within a less ambitious form, there is magic in the sudden surfacing in performance of a successful improvisatory idea; for the player as well as the listener there is the immediate joy of discovery. For me, the most moving performances of classical repertoire are those by pianists who can convince me, for the moment, that they too are making it up. Rationally I know otherwise, but I love to experience that illusion. In fact, a top-drawer classical pianist brings to a memorized piece a subtle sort of improvisation in of-the-moment reinterpretation of the details of tempo, phrasing, pedalling, dynamics, and other means of expression, if not the notes themselves.

The jazz viewpoint with which I am burdened is at odds with the conventional limitation on a classical performer's interpretive license. Chopin waltzes, for example, have suitable embellishments built into them, but we can sense that at these moments Chopin is more the improvising pianist than the note-transcribing composer. Would it not be possible for a pianist today to invent his or her own embellishments, even spontaneously? I am not urging that anyone tamper with a monumentally constructed Beethoven sonata, but it seems to me that certain Chopin waltzes are elegantly arranged dance music. A sympathetic improvisation on this material ought not to be considered a mortal sin. I myself have experimented along these lines, and have not yet been struck by lightning. As a jazz pianist, I can get away with it; what I would like to hear is a performance by an expert classical pianist who had the nerve at least to vary some of the embellishments in the score.

There are various motivations for improvisation. One is the boredom that arises when you've played a piece once too often. Another is curiosity. (How would it sound if I tried it *this* way?) Still another is simple whimsy or playfulness. One of the most compelling motivations, on the other hand, is panic.

Your mettle will be tested when, during a film soundtrack recording session, you are handed a cue for some tormented atonal underscoring and quickly arrive at the conviction that you are not going to get the hang of it in the allotted time. Fortunately, such moments do not occur often, but I can recall that at a particular session a certain pianist once had to resort to playing any key on which his fingers happened to fall (although in the proper rhythm). Evidently, the resultant muddle didn't sound significantly different from the way the composer wrote it; at any rate, no objection was raised.

I have heard tales of symphonic performances of contemporary works in which a conductor loses his place, a player misses an entrance, and the whole orchestra in effect vamps till ready until the conductor recovers, calls out a bar number, and gives a strong downbeat. (I should explain that in the days of vaudeville, and still today in musical comedy, the vamp-till-ready, a two- or four-bar figure, repeats indefinitely until the singer has finished some stage business and is ready either to begin or to resume the song.)

When I conducted *Eubie Blake: A Century Of Music*, a television show we staged live at the Kennedy Center, a situation of this sort came about during a number that featured singer Anita Morris. * Miss Morris' remarkable performance displayed seductive movements choreographed so acrobatically that her skirt fell off in mid-performance. She stopped singing and began to adjust her costume, while the delighted audience inundated the stage with waves of laughter and applause. Miss Morris played the situation like a true professional, extracting the greatest possible audience reaction. The orchestra and I waited, poised, until, a minute or so later (and to us it seemed like ten), she finally sang the eighth-note pickup to the continuing phrase. In this instance, our improvisation was merely silence, until the singer had fastened her garment and was ready to move on.

Other moments of panic at this level of show business can take place when a microphone fails, when the music parts blow away in a sudden gale, when a singer comes onstage late or skips a verse, and so forth. At such times an apoplectic conductor may well point at the piano player and scream, "Play something!" In the act of rising to such an occasion, the pianist demonstrates character as well as musical ability.

Not quite improvisation, but certainly great adaptability, is shown by players who cover up the matter when a singer jumps the beat. There is a story

*See Eubie's Final Bow (page 18)

among New York musicians about a society band-leader, not beloved by his orchestra, who had a slightly different problem. His players were marvelously coordinated among themselves, and one night they vindictively and in unison skipped a beat at the end of each four bars of "The Lady Is A Tramp." The leader continued to wave his arms ineffectually as he hissed to his men, "What are you trying to do, ruin me in this business?" It is said that many a formally dressed dancer strained a tendon that evening trying to find the beat, but I for one doubt that they were listening that closely.

Sometimes, when playing piano in a bar or some other request situation, you may get asked persistently and alcoholically for a tune that you don't quite recall. Perhaps you know the first 16 bars but can't for the life of you remember the bridge. Another opportunity for panic improvisation! Make up a bridge! Or borrow one from some other song, such as "Honeysuckle Rose," an all-purpose eight bars. In any case, make a mental note to learn the song correctly later on.

Perhaps, without meaning to sound cynical, we should consider a certain type of incompetence as another powerful motivator for improvisation. Not just any sort of incompetence, of course, but a combination of being unable to read music adequately while at the same time having a superb talent for musical invention, coupled with great instrumental skill. Some people claim that the memorable improvisations in the early days of jazz came about because the players were indifferent readers. If they had been able to read the printed parts, the theory goes, they might not have made great music. This may be as valid a speculation as any as to how jazz

was born, but this is not to say that one necessarily gets to be a great jazz player by not knowing how to read. Far from it.

Surely another motivation for improvisation is the desire to display one's talent. A sympathetic audience is a persuasive inducement to give it all you've got. A performer must learn, however, that in some ways an audience can be too easily pleased. Playing familiar licks, too many fast notes, and overly familiar tunes such as "When The Saints Come Marching In" can win an audience over even when the player is not actually playing up to his real level of ability. Although we players need audiences, their standards are not necessarily ours. We and not they have the responsibility to do what is right for the music, simply because we have a deeper understanding of it. On some level the message does get through to an audience that the performer is doing his damnedest to live up to his own standards, which he would like to share with them. If you can please the crowd with things that *you* honestly like to play, you're doing the right thing.

A word about the highest moments of improvisation: They come, when they come (if they come), when you are in good technical shape so that you can be relaxed and confident; when the piano is good; when your ideas and the receptivity of the audience are on the same level; and when some other impossible-to-define element is present which puts you in touch with your best. At such times everything seems to flow automatically, and you are as much a bemused listener as you are a player. George Gershwin remarked that when he was at his composing peak on particularly good days, tunes flowed from his fingers like water. It is something like that, and you wish it happened all the time.

THE TROUBLE WITH SHEET MUSIC

When you buy a copy of a Mozart sonata, there is little question but that the composition exists exactly as set forth in the printed notes. Nuances of interpretation aside, it is universally accepted that pianists will play the notes in the score without deviation.

Not so with pop music, and even less so with jazz. Players often learn songs from one another by ear, perhaps with a certain amount of inaccuracy, or they pick them up from records. Arrangers embellish and often improve the original harmonic progressions. Jazz improvisers frequently rework songs altogether, adding radically different chords. On the other hand, publishers of lead sheet versions simplify and often omit crucial harmonies. In general it can be said that we have a tradition of using the original piece which is very different from the hands-off manner in which classical music is approached.

With each new generation of players putting its stamp on the older standard songs, modifying them in accordance with prevailing dance rhythms and fashionable harmonic innovations, it is not surprising that some durable songs have undergone drastic revisions during their evolution. It can be a distinct shock to come across the original sheet music of familiar tunes and realize that the way in which a song is presently performed is different from the original concept not only in terms of harmony, but in the rhythmic values or even the notes of the melody. Great songs permit this flexibility; they work in the manner of whatever era they are performed.

Most songs continue to be printed in their original form, but in certain instances publishers have bowed to the prevailing style and have issued editions embodying the contemporary alterations. For example, the original sheet music of Duke Ellington's "Satin Doll" presents a chord sequence in bars 5 and 6 that was apparently found awkward in performance by Ellington himself. According to Brooks Kerr, the noted Ellington expert, the master

never recorded the tune with these changes. Nevertheless, one can occasionally hear performances by players who have learned the song from the original sheet music, which was picked up as well in some lead sheet editions. The majority of musicians have preferred to use the version that Ellington played, not the one he first published. (A newer edition utilizes the more common progression.) *(See Example A.)*

"Lover Man," by Ram Ramirez, Jimmy Davis, and Jimmy Sherman, is another case in which the practical tradition has proved more important than the written example. Billie Holiday altered the melody in her 1944 recording in a manner which is now considered standard. The sheet music, however, has not been corrected, so that present-day performers and arrangers who base their work on the written version sound oddly wrong to those of us who learned the song from the Holiday record. *(See Example B on the following page.)*

"Star Dust," that standard of standards, is still printed in an arrangement derived from Hoagy Carmichael's original 1927 piano solo. (The lyrics were added later.) One of the most recorded songs in history, "Star Dust" has undergone many transformations. Artie Shaw's recording in 1940 established its present harmonic form, and we should be grateful to arranger Jerry Gray for his reharmonization, an improvement, to my ears, over the original. Players particularly liked his use of the *Bb9* in place of the *Fm*, an innovation at the time. On the other hand, the Shaw recording created some confusion as to exactly where this juicy chord was to be placed. At the beginning of the recording it occurs on bar 4; thereafter it falls on either bar 3 or bar 4 or their equivalents. You pays your money and you takes your choice. Personally I opt for bar 3, where the original *Fm* is, since the *E* in the melody completes the chord as a dramatic raised 11th. To add to the

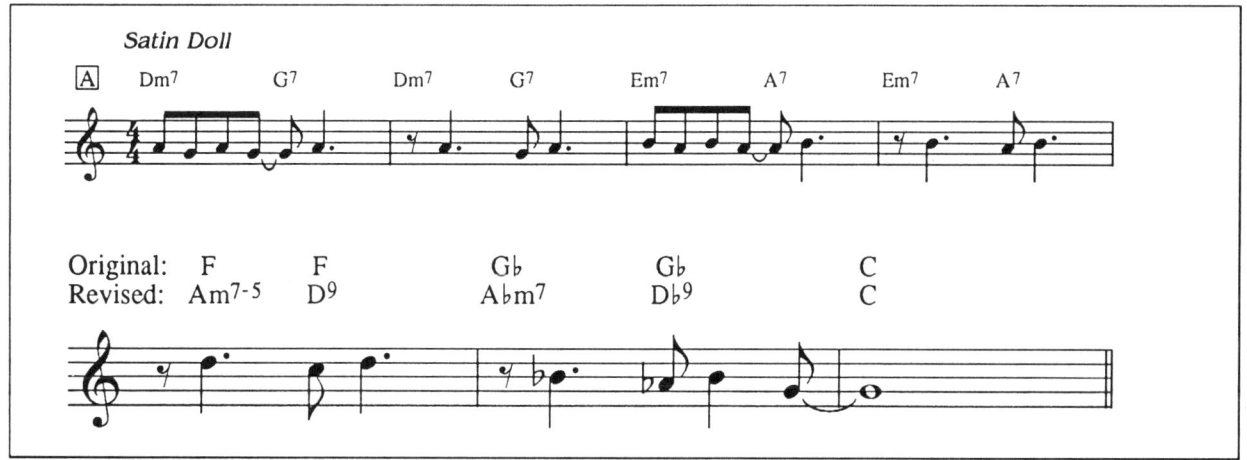

confusion, quite often the first two bars of "Star Dust" are played as *Dm7* rather than *F6*, a difference only of chord inversion. Incidentally, although the song is published in *C,* the common key among professionals is *Db. (See Example C.)*

Of all the songs from the '20s, the Gershwin repertoire seems to me to have the most logical and ingenious harmonic progressions. Even some of these classics have undergone alterations, however, and a pianist and his bass-playing partner had best come to terms with which bass line and chords to

use in the second bar of "Someone To Watch Over Me" as in Example D. The original is Bb 6 (Bb in the bass). The revised manner is as printed here.

There are also some tunes which for jazz purposes have acquired what are known as "blowing changes." These are chord sequences that don't quite go with the melody but are stimulating for improvisers. "I Can't Get Started," Vernon Duke's 1936 show tune, had already gone through a reworking by the players of that generation before Dizzy Gillespie and the other beboppers erected still

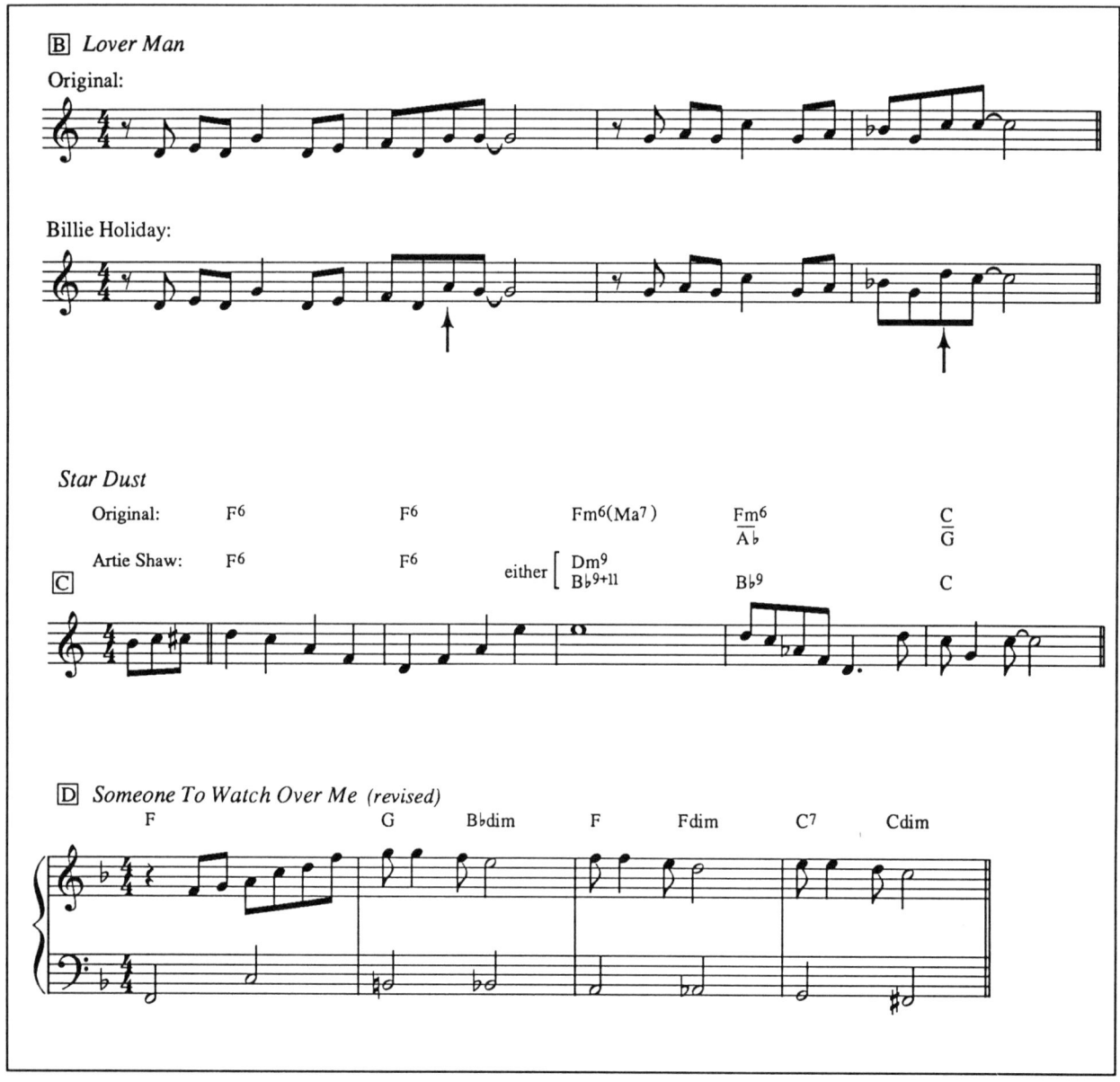

another harmonic variation on it. Not all soloists are comfortable with the bop changes, so the best policy is to talk it over before a performance, if possible, or at least listen carefully during the more conventional first chorus to judge how far out the soloist is likely to want to go. *(See Example E.)*

Of course, with some neutral passing tones, a pianist can cover any uncertainty, and the soloist will be guided in turn by what he hears the pianist doing. In any case, despite all of the above cautions, I don't mean to imply that lightning will strike if there is a momentary discrepancy between piano, guitar, bass, and soloist. Sensitive people will listen to one another and will work out a common ground, at least by the time they get to the next chorus.

The alterations made by performing musicians are sometimes in the direction of simplification and sometimes in the direction of greater complexity. Occasionally the revisions are solutions to harmonic problems that eluded the composer or whoever prepared the original sheet music. Take the old sing-along favorite, "I'm Looking Over A Four Leaf Clover," and consider bars 25-28 of the chorus, as originally published. *(See Example F.)*

Harmonizing the melody in this manner is obviously inept, because the fourth beat of the melody in the second bar clashes with the bass line and the indicated chord. Some arrangers and players insert a rushed *E* diminished chord at this point *(E natural in the bass)*, but a better solution is as follows in Example G.

These first two bars are certainly an improvement, and the second two would most likely follow, although I have a fondness for the old-timey quality of the original progression in the latter two bars. Incidentally, you'll notice that the melody has also been altered rhythmically to a less syncopated form.

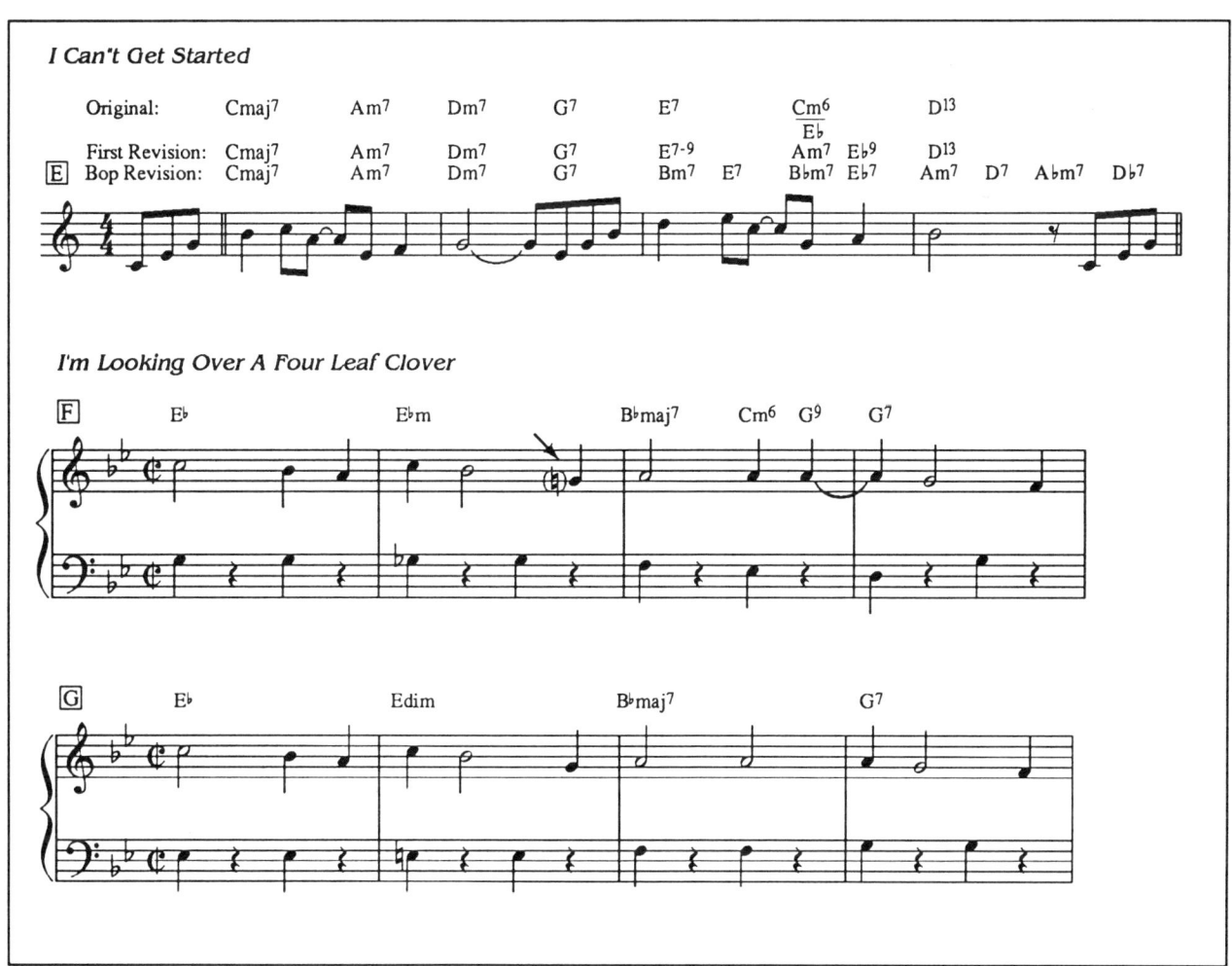

The original melody of "Three Little Words," on
the other hand, has been modified in the opposite
direction, so that it has become more syncopated.
As first published:

Today it is most often played in this manner:

A considerable number of songs are now played
in double time, having been published in slow 4/4.
It is a revelation to discover that "(Back Home Again
In) Indiana," (the actual title) was originally written
like this:

whereas it is now universally played:

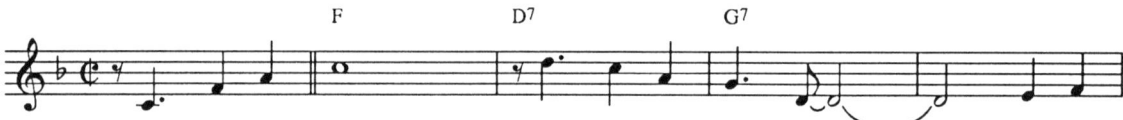

Note the different pickup notes and key as well.
Other songs in which the tempo has been doubled
are "After You've Gone," "There'll Be Some Changes
Made," and "Lover Come Back To Me."

"Everybody Loves My Baby" has a bridge (the third
eight-bar section) which suffers from almost total
confusion. The original, which is perfectly adequate,
went like this:

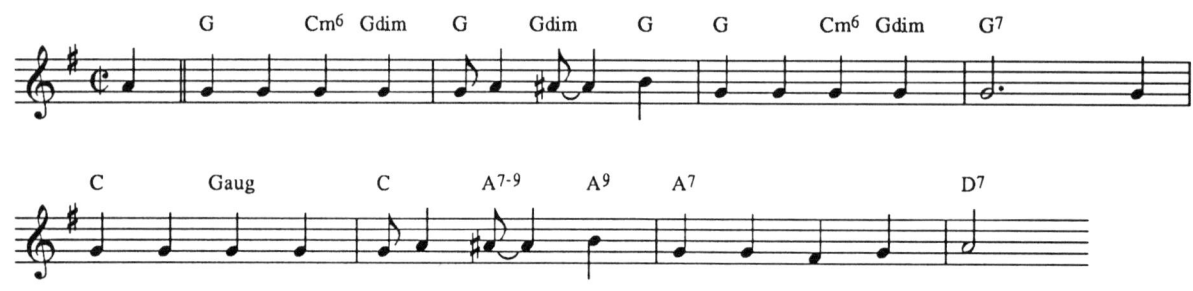

But somewhere along the line, the tune must have
been learned and passed along inaccurately,
because it has evolved to this:

My advice to a piano player would be to assume
that a singer will do it in the original. However, in the
Dixieland setting in which the tune would most likely
be played instrumentally, favor the second way, and
listen closely to the trumpet player.

One final observation on the trouble with sheet
music has to do with changes in lyrics which were
made in the 1950's. Around that time, publishers
began printing new editions of such songs as "When
It's Sleepy Time Down South" and "Mississippi Mud,"
changing the word "darkies" to "people" or "folks."
This was a welcome revision which paralleled the
civil rights movement of that decade. In previous
eras, the lyrics of popular songs sometimes contained terms even more offensive than "darkies."
The history of the so-called "coon songs," which
began in minstrel times, warrants a study in itself.

PART III

HERE'S HOW!...

*"The well-rounded
keyboard player
needs to develop
many musical
skills..."*

IMPROVISATION FOR THE BEGINNER

Improvisation is something mysterious by definition. It is spur-of-the-moment creativity, an expression of an artistic impulse that is not subject either to planned preparation or to revision. People who set out to acquire this skill are often baffled because it does not appear to derive from deliberate, conscious techniques but arises from that other part of the brain which produces non-verbal intuitions. Improvisors, like athletes, live entirely in the moment.

On the other hand, circumstances can be arranged so that a facility with musical improvisation can be practiced and improved. The first step over the hurdle of frustration is to grasp that in the hands of skilled practitioners improvisation is not quite what it appears to be to the listener. It is not pulling ideas out of the air; it is usually not descending into a trance and allowing the spirit of music to speak through one's hands. There are special times when a player may tap the recesses of his subconscious and experience the joy of making music with a minimum of conscious direction, but even on those lucky occasions it must be admitted that even the most inventive improvisation is based on a body of material which the player has learned bit by bit and stored in his memory bank. In improvising, he draws on and reassembles this material in infinitely variable combinations.

There is an analogy here to an old-fashioned kaleidoscope, the optical toy in which the viewer sees an endless variety of reflected patterns, each different, as the bits of colored glass rearrange themselves. Although every new pattern is different, they are all made from the same bank of materials, to which the improvising player from time to time may add new jewels.

As with a spoken language, the vocabulary of jazz is learned through repetition and practice, by listening and unconscious memorizing on the one hand

and by written analysis and directed study on the other. The value of learning aurally cannot be overstressed. Take a record by Oscar Peterson, or by any other improviser whose style appeals to you, and listen to one track fifty times! Do the same the next day and the day after. Then go to the keyboard and try to replicate some of the master's phrases. What has been absorbed by your ears may well trickle down to your fingers after a listening experience of such intensity.

Once you've learned some melodic phrases, you can begin improvising by recombining them in various ways. As an example, let's assume you're going to improvise over this chord progression:

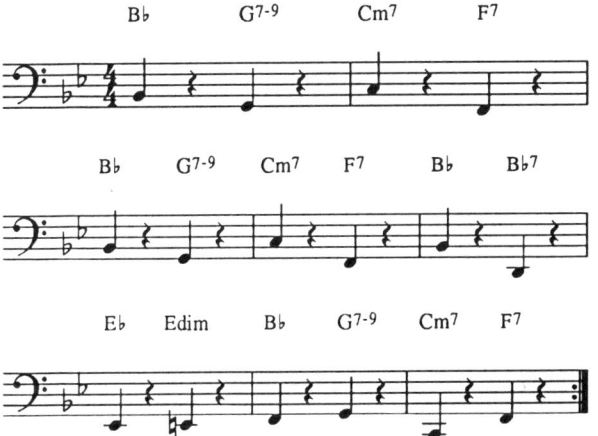

You'll notice that the same two-bar chord pattern is used in bars 1-2, 3-4, and 7-8. So a melodic phrase that works in one place can be used equally well in another. Here are three possibilities:

In playing the eight-bar phrase, you can combine these phrases in any order, which gives rise to six different possible solos. What's more, we can take the first half of one phrase and attach it to the second half of another. Thus we might end up with a solo that sounds like Example A.

Now all we need to do is fill in bars 5 and 6. A couple of phrases that work nicely appear in Examples B and C.

Insert either of these phrases into bars 5 and 6, and behold — a genuine hot solo!

Before you can do much improvising, of course, you'll need more vocabulary than this. Even experi-enced players are constantly adding to their bag of tricks by hearing other players in performance, listening to records, reading transcriptions of solos, and working out ideas of their own at the keyboard. Back in the 1920's, publishers printed collections of phrases under such titles as "Fifty Hot Licks." More contemporary books exist, and the principle has some value. However, it is not merely by memorizing such licks that you produce a good solo. The artistry is in combining, connecting, and reworking phrases so that something new results. Ultimately, the player has to make his own spur-of-the-moment statement, shaking up his personal kaleidoscope.

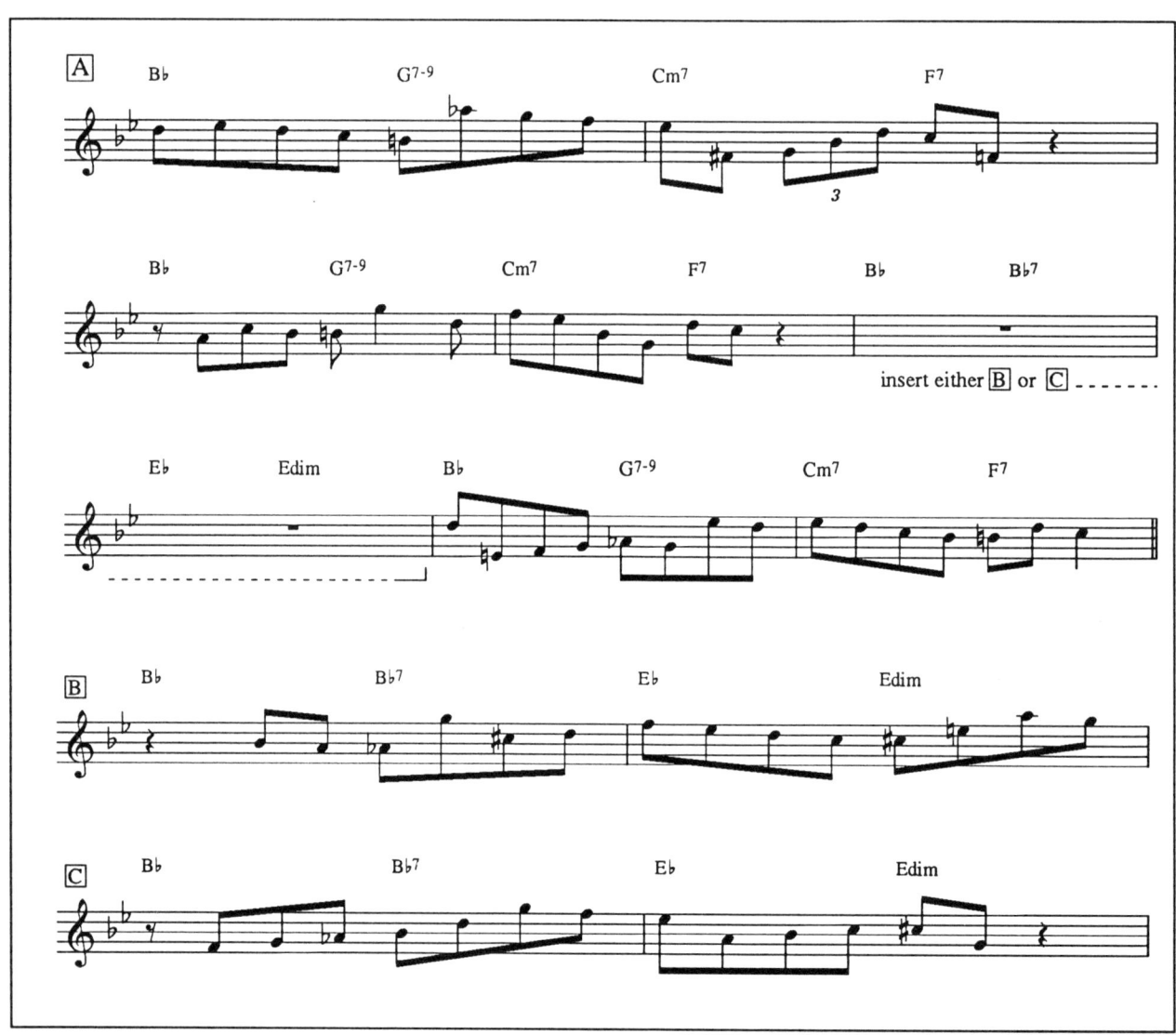

PRACTICING FOR A CONTINUOUS MELODIC LINE

Improvising musicians constantly face the challenge of creating spontaneous melodies. Keeping a melody moving is difficult for the beginner, who may stumble or have to stop entirely to think about what to do next. But it is possible to develop a melodic flow through practice. To begin with, it's easy to see that creating a melodic line is comparable to drawing a visual line from point A to point B. We may proceed straight:

or in a series of arcs:

or with jagged leaps:

or through less regular convolutions:

The improvising player learns how to create musical phrases which suggest these patterns. It helps to have in the mind and under the fingers a catalog of melodic fragments that can be modified according to the game plan of the given harmonies, the rhythmic pulse, and the convenience of fingering. In addition, the dramatic statement the player intends may make the melody direct or oblique, busy or sparse, bravura or meditative. Finally, old-fashioned luck and inspiration cause things to work out better at one time than another. While some people have more of a knack than others, anyone's melodic skill can be improved by practice.

A useful exercise to begin with is to confine yourself to the diatonic mode in C major, and to create a melodic sequence using, at first, only whole notes. When you can keep a flow of whole notes going, proceed to half notes, then quarter notes, and so on. In the following examples we will use a common bass and chord pattern. Practice with a metronome to keep a uniform, moderate tempo. The game plan is this harmonic sequence:

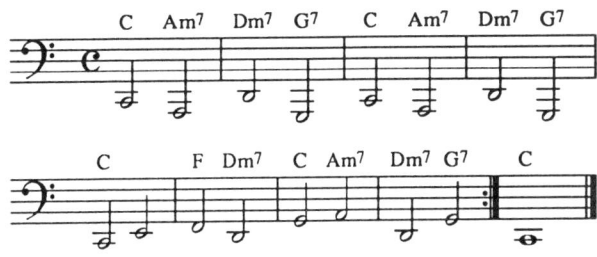

While continuing to play this bass pattern with the left hand, add a right-hand line. You might start with something like this:

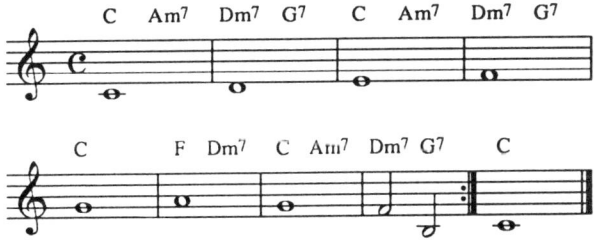

So far, so good. The C scale itself works with these chords. Now try again, using a different melodic pattern — perhaps this one:

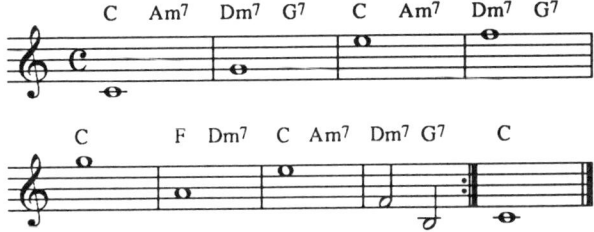

Don't just play only these melodies; run through the chord pattern a number of times while improvising your own lines. When you're ready, go on to half notes while keeping the metronome at the same setting. Here's a sixteen-bar sample:

In quarter notes the melody might take on a graceful, flowing character:

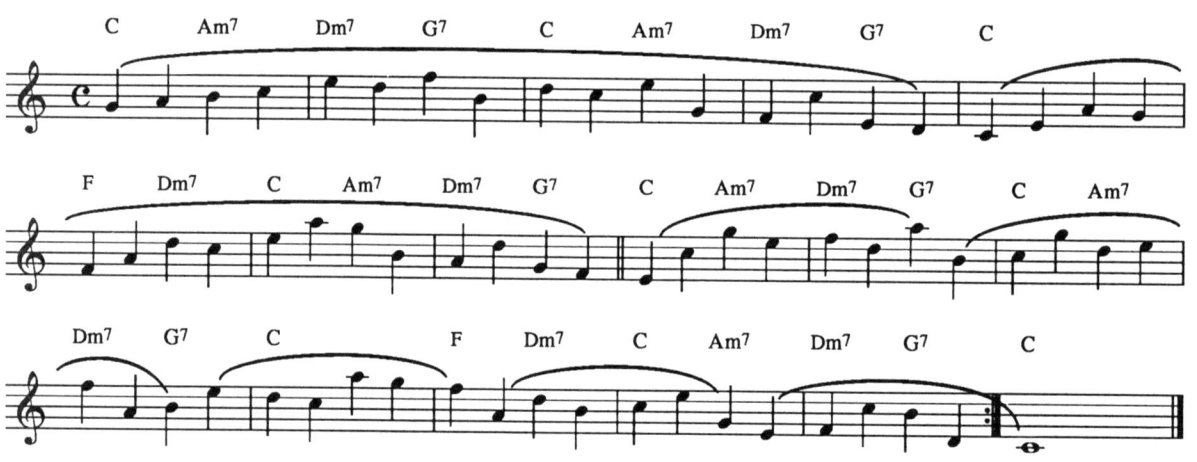

When you've got a flow going with quarter notes, switch to quarter-note triplets.

Working with the larger note values in the forego-
ing examples is more difficult in one way than playing eighth-notes, because you're playing fewer tones
per chord change, and you have to select them with
more care. But thinking about the choice of notes is
good preparation for the eighth-note lines that are
more common in typical playing.

Try the progression again with eighth-notes, using
jazz phrasing and accents.

Practice each of these note-values in a nonstop
series for several minutes. Decide in advance
whether you intend to keep on going no matter
what, or whether you'll stop and analyze the reasons
for the inevitable breakdowns. Both kinds of practice are necessary, but if you mean to continue,
don't stop! Bluff your way out of whatever momentary difficulties arise, if necessary by simply repeating a two-note or three-note figure until your brain
has a chance to get back in gear.

In addition to improving your dexterity, this exercise should help you get the hang of arcing back and
forth in scale and intervallic patterns, as the above
examples demonstrate. The diatonic restriction is a
good discipline. Later on, when you change the
game plan to include chromatics, pauses, and phrases of different lengths, constructing a melody on the
spur of the moment will seem a lot easier.

Now let's move on to chromatics and see how the process develops. We'll use the following common bass and harmonic pattern as our game plan:

Setting the metronome to ♩ = 100, improvise a right-hand melody of your own. Start with a melody in whole notes. When you're comfortable with whole notes at this tempo, move on to half notes. Selecting melodic tones that make musical sense can be tricky when you only have one or two notes per bar to work with. When you can play a half-note melody with no hesitation, move on to quarter notes. Now the line begins to show a more distinct jazz flavor:

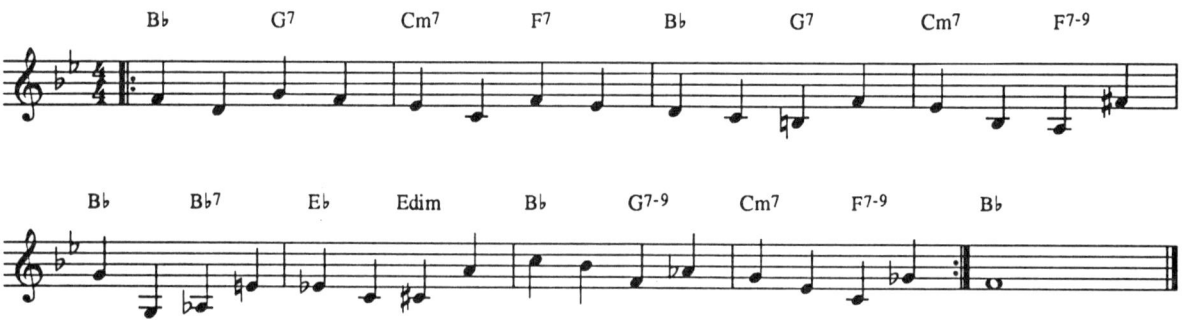

Notice how the 7th chords become flatted 9ths, and how neighboring tones make it easier to get around the harmonic changes. Keeping the same tempo and continuing to use the original bass line and chords, let's improvise a melody in quarter-note triplets. Again, you should play through the progression a number of times while improvising your own melody. The eight bars shown here are just to get you started. Keep repeating the bass line as you invent new melodies with the metronome running.

See how inventive you can be over the course of
several minutes.

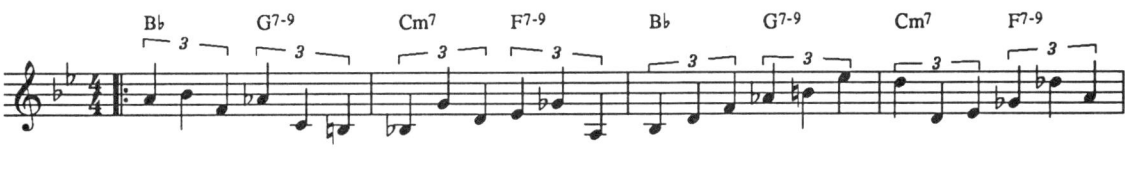

Now take a look at a sixteen-bar run-through of
the same chord sequence with a melody in eighth-
notes. This is the most common manner of jazz
blowing. Note how it is possible and at times desir-
able to go outside the exact harmonies, either with a
sequential series of figures or with something
modal. For now, use these devices sparingly. It's
easy to fall into them, but the point of this sort of
practice is to invent melodies which reflect the
chord changes rather than run counter to them. Play
this example with jazz accents and with a swing
(triplet) feeling.

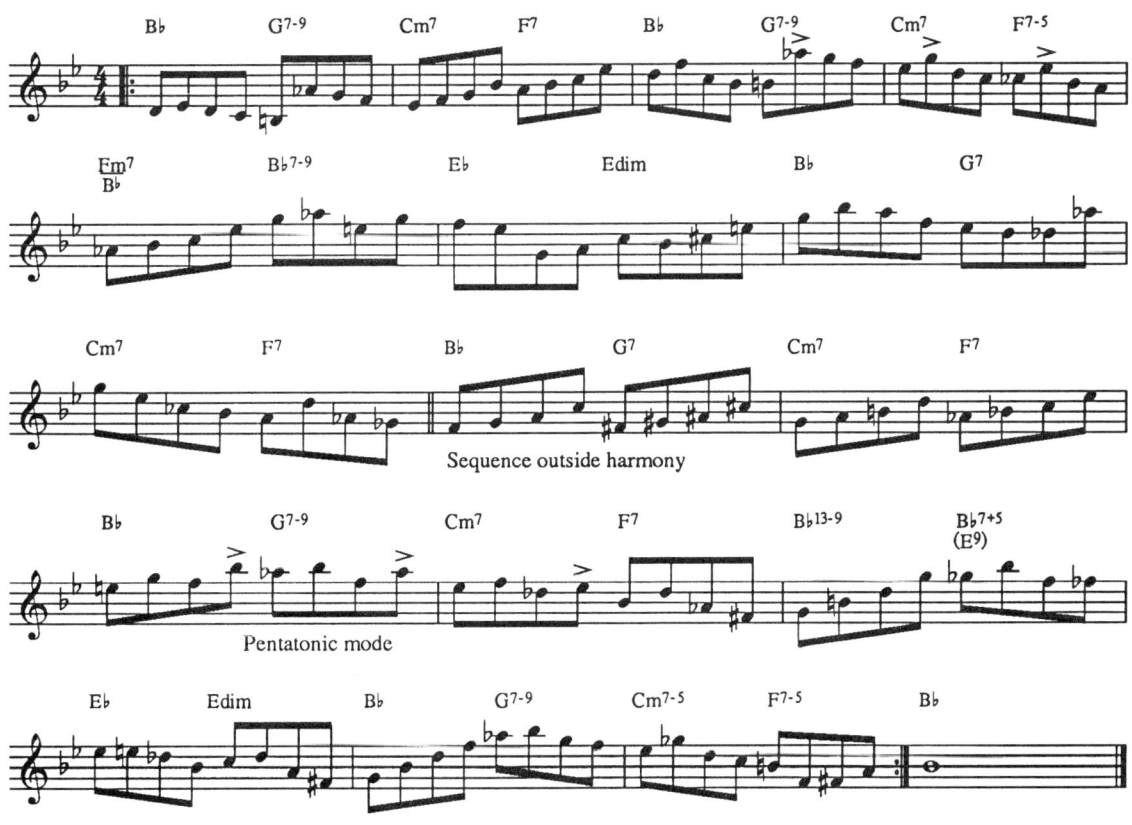

When you're comfortable doing nonstop improvisation at this speed, you can go one step further, with a melody constructed in triplets.

Remember, keep it moving! The value of this type of practice is in teaching yourself not to stop, no matter what. Later on you will want to learn figuratively to take breaths and will want to make the rhythms less regular.

CHORD STUDY

In every musical area that involves improvisation, keyboard players are expected to know the conventional symbols for chords. The four basic triads are *major, minor, augmented,* and *diminished,* and there are many more extended chords based on these. The symbols used to represent these chords appear in various forms, according to the individual taste of the composer or arranger. For example, some people abbreviate *minor as m,* while others prefer *MI* or simply a minus sign (-). *Major* may have no abbreviation at all in some symbols, or may appear as *MA* or *maj. Diminished* might be *dim* or a raised circle (°). *Augmented* is often indicated with a plus sign (+), although you may find it as *aug.* My own preferences, in the example below, are the choices preferred by many musicians and publishers.

I've assembled all the chords I could think of in a little study which demonstrates the relationship of the different chord names. It should be remembered that the notation system we use is not perfect; it breaks down at the edges of tonality. In addition, there may be several ways to name a given chord, depending on one's point of view concerning the bass note and the inversion. Nevertheless, despite its flaws, the system works quite well as the basis for improvisation or embellishment, and unless we go back to the medieval figured bass, it is the only system in general use.

Hearing music is, I think, the best way of learning it. Try this chord etude on your keyboard, and study the terminology as you play each chord. Your ear will make the chord relationship clear in a more direct way than any theoretical discussion could.

Chord Study

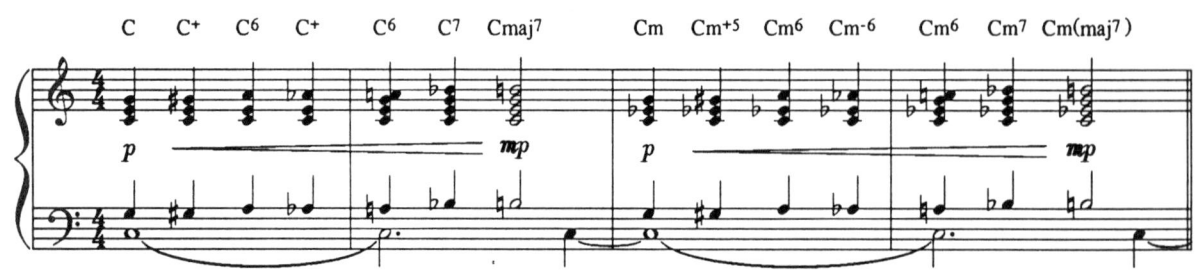

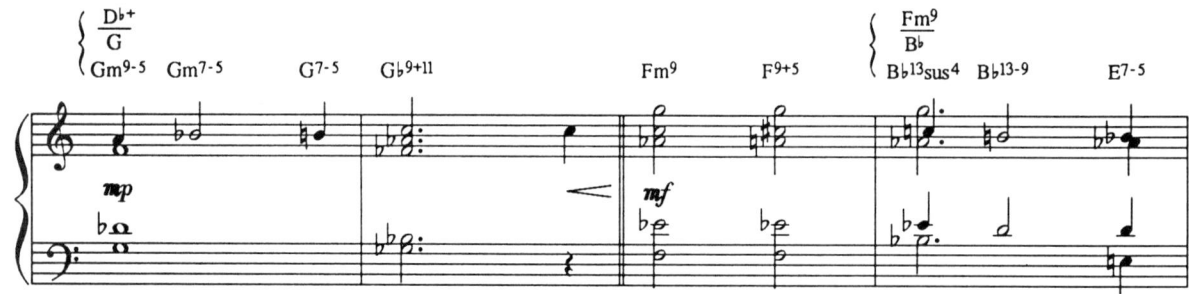

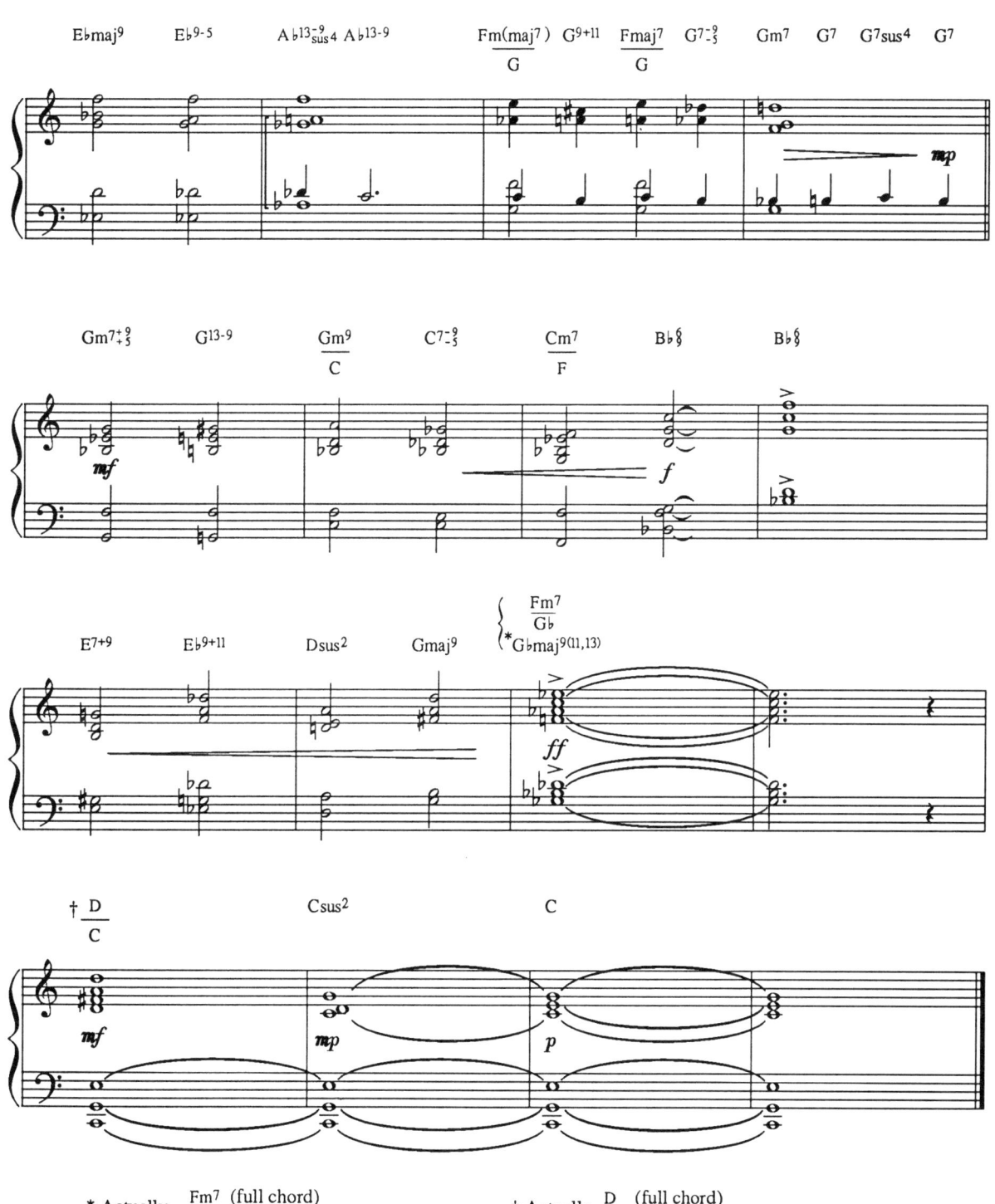

* Actually $\dfrac{Fm^7 \ (\text{full chord})}{Gb \ (\text{full chord})}$

† Actually $\dfrac{D \ (\text{full chord})}{C \ (\text{full chord})}$

PRACTICAL PLAYING POINTERS

The well-rounded keyboard player needs to develop many musical skills in addition to simple finger dexterity. For example, he or she needs to know ways of filling in harmony when reading a lead sheet in addition to simple rhythm comping patterns. One of the most effective of these is block chording. In block chording, both hands shift in parallel with the melody, harmonizing each melody note with its own chord. This can be done with either closed voicing or open voicing.

Here is an example of the use of closed voicing with block chords. The left hand doubles the melody an octave lower, and the entire chord is contained in this octave:

In open block chord voicing, there are wider intervals between the neighboring tones:

Another important point that beginners sometimes have difficulty with concerns the notation of jazz rhythm. In contemporary playing, there are two basic rhythmic styles — *even* eighths (also called *straight* eighths) and *swing* eighths. In rock and Latin music, as in classical music, eighth-notes are played exactly as written. Each quarter-note beat is divided into two equal parts. in swing music, on the other hand, a slightly elastic triplet feeling is used; each

quarter-note beat is divided into two *un*equal parts, or alternatively into three equal parts (a *triplet*).

However, jazz arrangers often notate swing eighths as though they were straight eighths. While it's not technically correct, this type of notation is easier to read, provided that everybody in the band, and particularly everybody in the rhythm section, understands what type of eighths are being used. Swing eighths are also notated on occasion as dotted eighths followed by sixteenths, which preserves but exaggerates the long-short character of the rhythm as it is played. Here are some examples of swing rhythms as they would be written and as they would be played:

Since swing rhythm is difficult to notate, the best way to grasp it is by listening to recordings, especially those made by swing era musicians such as Count Basie and Duke Ellington.

Material adapted from It's Time For Some Piano Changes, *by Dick Hyman and Clem DeRosa.* © 1980 Kendor Music (Main and Grove Sts., Delevan, NY 14042).

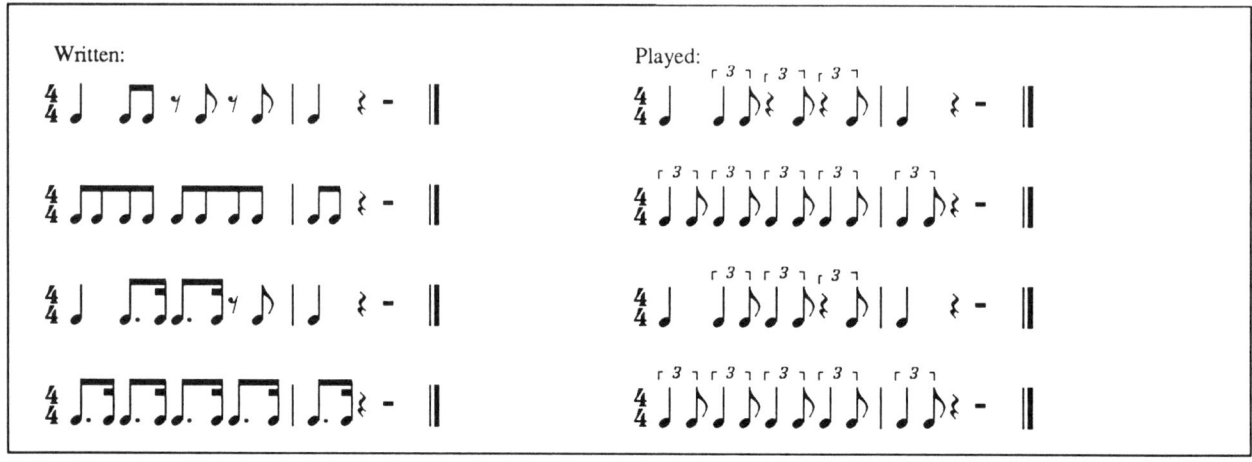

STUDIO KEYBOARD PARTS: TO PLAY OR NOT TO PLAY?

Since the beginnings of Western musical history, when harpsichordists routinely faked their part from a figured bass and organists like J.S. Bach extemporized variations on familiar hymns, the keyboard musician has been a special kind of player. The keyboard itself has always been a flexible unit, and its player the sort of musician who, when the occasion demanded, could fill in for missing instruments or even substitute for an entire orchestra, embellish an ensemble, modulate from one piece to another, deal most easily with vocal accompaniment, and generally be an all-around helpful fellow.

For many musicians these skills are still in demand, and particularly in studio work the keyboard player has developed into a hybrid player who does double duty: He or she must be able to read a fully-written part at sight, but be able to alter it immediately or perhaps invent a new one altogether. What is called studio work is that area where music is made for television, films, commercials, and recordings, and it is because of the many types of music used for these media that versatility on the part of the player is a valuable asset.

In the past, each radio and television network, many independent stations, and the major film companies kept staffs of musicians on call. These staffs have now disappeared, and the business has become entirely freelance. The competition is, therefore, even higher, and the musician who can play all kinds of music will tend to be more active than even the most expert specialist.

What is required of a keyboard player has changed greatly, of course, since the advent of synthesizers. Ever greater versatility is demanded in order to stay on top of new technology in this field, so much so that an entire specialty in synthesizers has developed, much of it practiced in isolation. The thrust of this article is less toward such solo work, but is concerned rather with the pianist, perhaps doubling on another keyboard, who needs to relate to a conductor, an ensemble, and the music in front of him. Such a player ought to be able to perform exactly what is on the paper but at the same time be able to grasp what the arranger might be looking for, even if the arranger (usually the conductor as well) wasn't quite sure of that himself. With experience and the exercise of some tact, the pianist in such a group judges what to play and what not to play.

In a typical situation, the first and most important judgment a player must make is this: Should I play this part as written, or is it meant to be a guide to improvisation? In general the presence or absence of chord symbols will determine the decision. If they are not there, the part is to be read normally, but with tasteful interpretation and common-sense adjustments. The player will want to listen carefully to the rest of the orchestra and add the dynamics, phrasing, and accents which may have been left out

in a typically rushed arranging assignment. Also, after the first reading the keyboardist will follow the other musicians' questions about wrong notes and the subsequent alterations which may be taking place in other sections of the orchestra, since these changes may affect the keyboard part. For example, a conductor will appreciate not having to tell the pianist what to do if the guitarist has already questioned a note and had it corrected.

Most music the studio player encounters is new; it hasn't been played before, and there are liable to be errors in the parts. In the interest of speed, an efficient player will fix his part if possible without raising the issue with the conductor. However, it is the player's responsibility to clarify any questionable notes, and in the case of any uncertainty he ought to consult the conductor. Although musicians at a recording date can often be helpful to each other in a discreet way, it is inadvisable even if the conductor is a close personal friend to call across the studio to the trombonist and ask, "Hey, Sam, what have you got in bar 46?" Conductors can get testy when several of these exchanges are going on at once.

At times keyboard players may judge that some adjustment of their part is called for, even if no chord symbols are indicated. The business of bringing this up requires some tact, and common courtesy should be exercised in asking the conductor's permission to make any alteration. For example, a pianist might suggest that a passage would cut through better if it were played in octaves rather than single notes. Possibly an arpeggiated figure might sound fuller in harmonization:

becomes:

In a certain type of solo, the player might be able to add a left-hand element:

such as this:

Generally, music in the pop vein is more susceptible to this sort of alteration, and music of a classical or dramatic nature is not. The player should bear in mind, furthermore, that the arranger may have given a great deal of thought to a completely written-out part, and the player's ideas for improving it may therefore be altogether wrong. On the other hand, quite often the arranger will be grateful for the player's keyboard expertise. There is a fine line between being helpful to a conductor and being a pain in the neck, and experience is the only way to learn where that line is.

If the part contains chord symbols, the arranger is signaling that the keyboardist is expected to use his powers of invention within the idiom. It should be understood that piano parts of this type are often automatic copy jobs which simply reproduce the guitar part for the right hand and the bass part for the left hand. The pianist is not necessarily expected to duplicate the notes of these other instruments, although at times he may play the bass notes in unison with the bass and supply the indicated chord after the beat. If the tempo is bright and in cut time, the chances are that a traditional musical comedy style is indicated:

becomes:

In the above example, the left hand might better play octaves in fortissimo passages. Also, the register of the bass notes must often be adjusted, since bass players read their music an octave higher than their tones actually sound, and the copyist may not have written the piano part an octave lower, where it should be played. The same sort of problem often occurs with celeste parts, since the tones of this instrument sound an octave higher than they are written. The keyboard player should remember that the lowest note on a celeste is usually a middle C, and that this tone would be written one octave lower, in the bass clef. If, as sometimes happens, a part goes out of the instrument's range, the player would naturally make an octave adjustment.

If the bass line is in 4/4, the tempo medium, and the style big band swing, the bass part would not be played at all. Some Basie fills might be a good idea, or some kind of comping.

Unwritten orchestra part:

becomes:

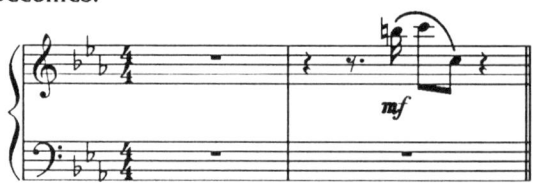

or:

But if such a part is written out in some detail along with chord symbols, the symbols are probably a kind of backup reference for possible alterations later on. Play it as written to begin with. It is also possible that the arranger is merely being considerate of the player's reading ability and has added symbols to facilitate the keyboardist's quick grasp of the part.

Sometimes an arranger will merely write the name of the style he or she wants, along with the bass and chords. This information can be very helpful. "Nashville," "concerto," etc., are frequently employed, and the player's knowledge of styles and musical clichés, past and present, will guide him. Once upon a time this writer found himself on a date playing with a large orchestra. His piano part consisted only of chord symbols — no bass line, no melody — and the instructions: "75% Beethoven piano concerto, 25% Rolling Stones." Or maybe it was the other way around. He did his best.

Sometimes an arranger will indicate how a part should begin, and then, by writing *simile*, suggest to the player that he or she continue in the same manner.

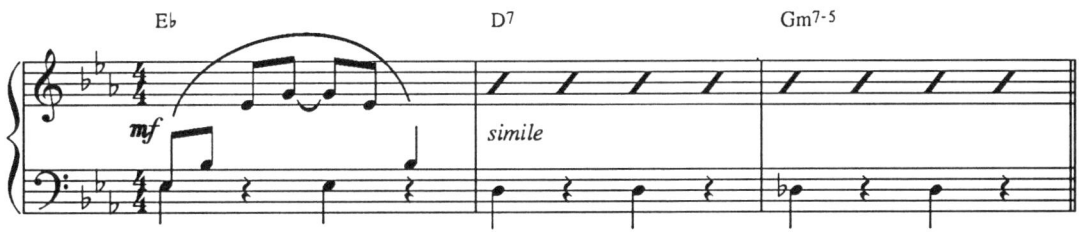

becomes:

If the rhythm is even — in straight eighths — and the arrangement is in a rock character, a part written in this manner:

might be played like this:

or even, depending on what the other people in the rhythm section are getting into, like this:

Listening to the rest of the orchestra while reading a new part is important for keyboard players. Piano music will not usually indicate, for example, that at one point you might be playing a *soli* with the strings, which would suggest a slow attack and great sonority, and at another point you might be in unison with the xylophone, requiring a fast, exact attack and staccato. It helps to watch the other players if at all possible. Unfortunately, the studio setup may make either watching or listening difficult, but the use of earphones usually compensates for this. Earphones are often an asset in playing with precision, and if they are worn half on the ear and half off, the player gets the benefit of hearing the overall sound as well as the sound, say, of the rhythm section as it is being recorded. At the very least, the player should be able to see the conductor while playing, even if this requires moving the piano a bit before the session begins.

All of these points, of course, constitute only a few of those lessons an experienced player will have picked up along the way while working in any style of music. But in a studio situation, such know-how has a greater urgency because the economics of a film, jingle, or album recording session demand a clean performance in a minimum amount of time.

Musicians will typically enter the studio field as specialists in one type of music. They will always be in demand for their specialties, but if they can adapt to other kinds of playing as well, they will be far busier. The jazz and rock players who become good readers and double on synthesizer, the conservatory pianists who learn improvisation — these are the people who become the hybrid artists known as studio musicians.

ART TATUM IN SLOW MOTION

In his day, Art Tatum (1910-1956) was universally recognized as the most technically accomplished of jazz pianists. A generation of players was awestruck by his command of the instrument; it is said that even Vladimir Horowitz was fascinated by his playing. Even today, when a young pianist discovers Tatum's recorded legacy for the first time, the impact is staggering.

Art Tatum's foremost stylistic heir is probably Oscar Peterson, whose great dexterity enables him to replicate much of the master's musical vocabulary (Peterson often plays in several other styles as well, and has combined them into a personal synthesis.) Another virtuosic player whose style owes much to Tatum is the Polish pianist Adam Makowicz; like Peterson, Makowicz also explores non-Tatum terrain. Tatum's influence is apparent not only in the dazzling runs and arpeggios of those pianists with the agility necessary to attempt them, but in the harmonic approach of such players as Hank Jones, Roland Hanna, and George Shearing.

Tatum recorded a great many solo albums during his comparatively brief career. Among the most noteworthy are the series originally put out on Decca 78 rpm discs and now reissued on MCA compact discs, which include such classics as "Tiger Rag" and "Get Happy." The high point of his recorded output is the Pablo *Solo Masterpieces* and *Group Masterpieces* series, a set on which the playing is so consistently on the highest level that pianists of all backgrounds might benefit from hearing the sheer ease of performance.

Jazz players in particular, understanding that the basis of Tatum's playing was improvisation, have always been impressed by his unflagging inventiveness. On the other hand, after he had performed certain pieces many times, and because (as he once noted) his listeners expected it of him, a body of set arrangements evolved. The original improvisations became crystallized into fairly definite forms which were repeated from performance to performance, so that they became more like classical piano pieces — although even these set arrangements were varied much more than a classical pianist would dare to alter, for example, a Chopin waltz. The set arrangements included "Elegy," "Tea For Two," and "Humoresque" as well as the above-mentioned titles.

Once the listener has heard a certain amount of Tatum's playing and is past the state of gasping at his instrumental command, the analytic ear begins to notice a group of devices that are used as a basic vocabulary. In the examples below I have set out some of the more often heard right-hand patterns that constitute a very small portion of the Art Tatum technique.

Much of Tatum's idiom is adapted from the classical repertoire. The runs below are built out of the kinds of turns found in Mozart and Beethoven.

Diatonic patterns in the key of C can be strung
together.

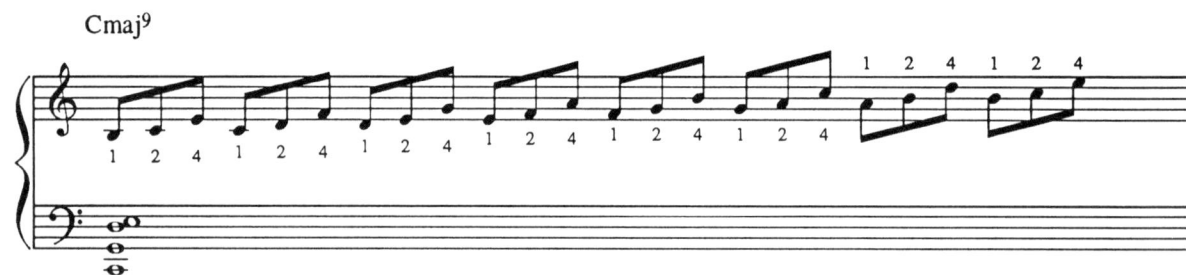

Similar figures can be played in Db using fingerings that keep the thumb on the white keys.

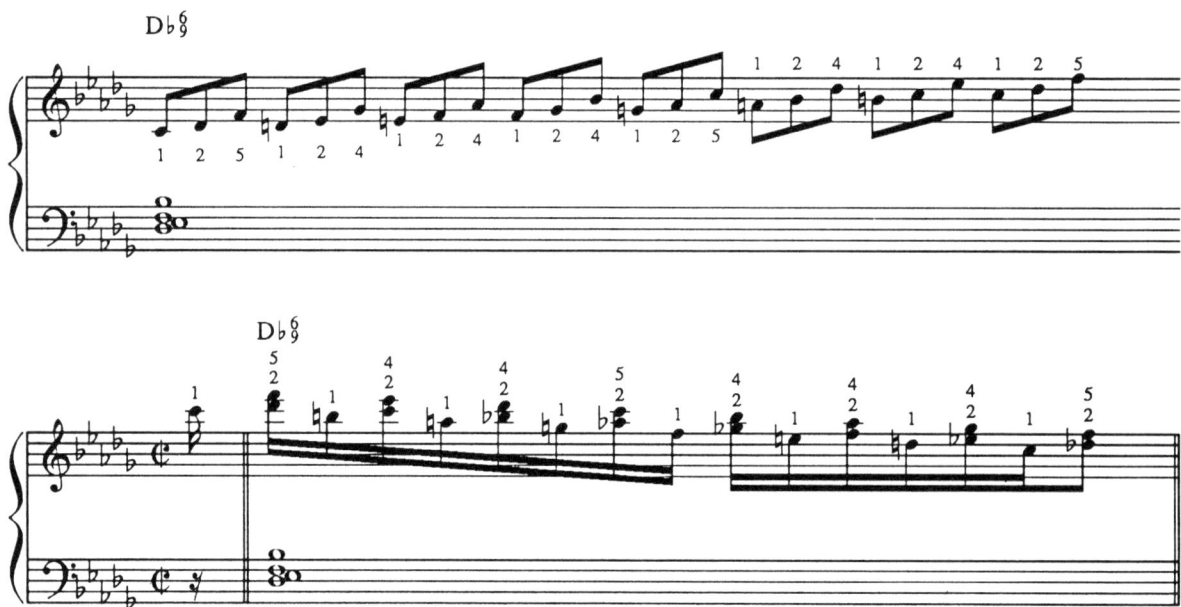

Tatum's playing shared many patterns with that of Teddy Wilson. The following pentatonic run and its harmonic support are an example. It may be played in all keys.

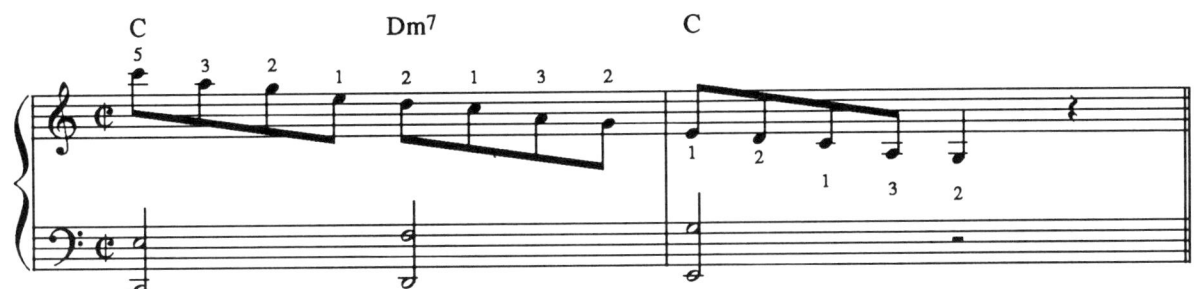

Tatum frequently embellishes the beginning of this run —

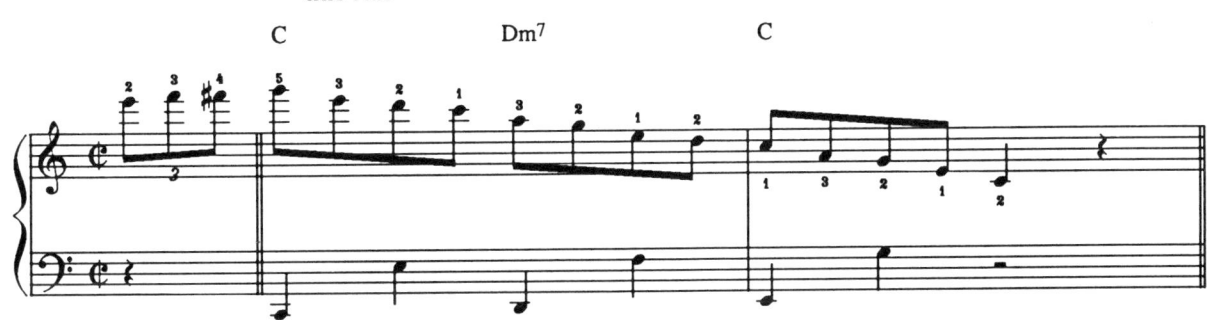

— or converts the pentatonic pattern to a ninth-chord pattern:

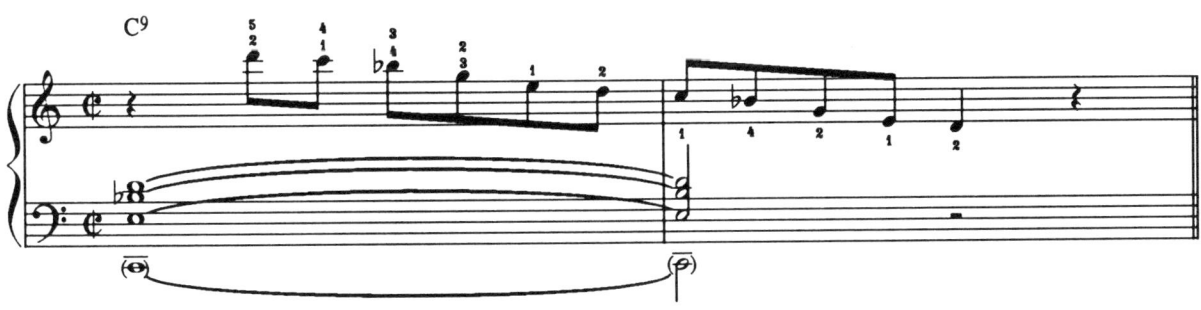

Sextuplets are used in all keys. Here we see a typical pattern over a dominant chord:

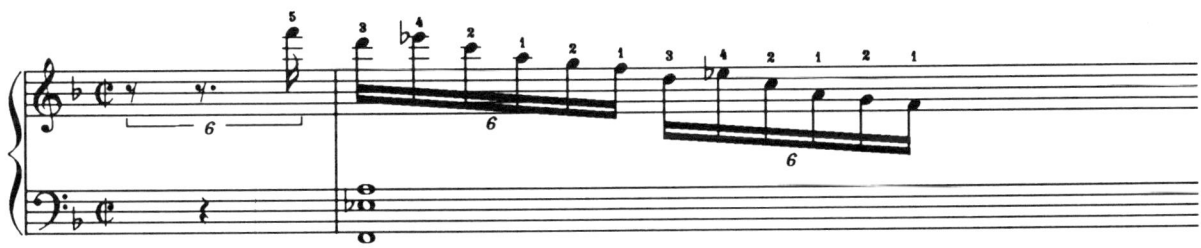

And here the same pattern is adapted for use over
a shifting dominant-subdominant harmony:

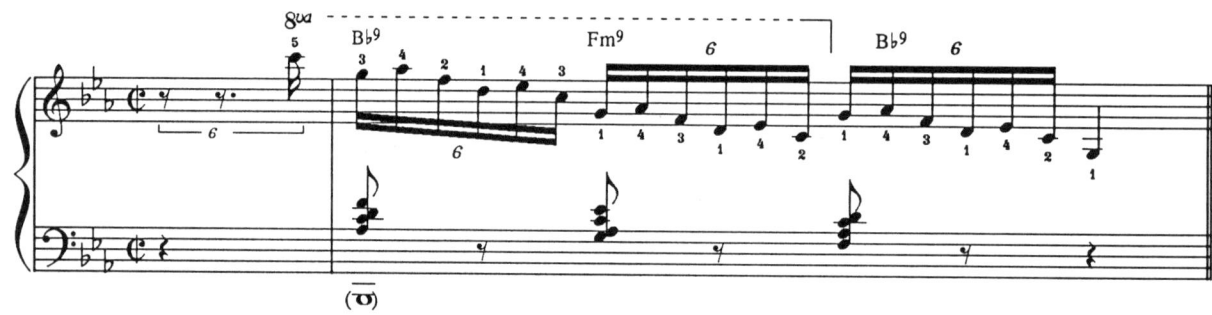

Sextuplets can also be used to run sixth-chords,
or compressed into quintuplets:

The harmonic minor scale can be played in sextuplets to create a flatted ninth chord:

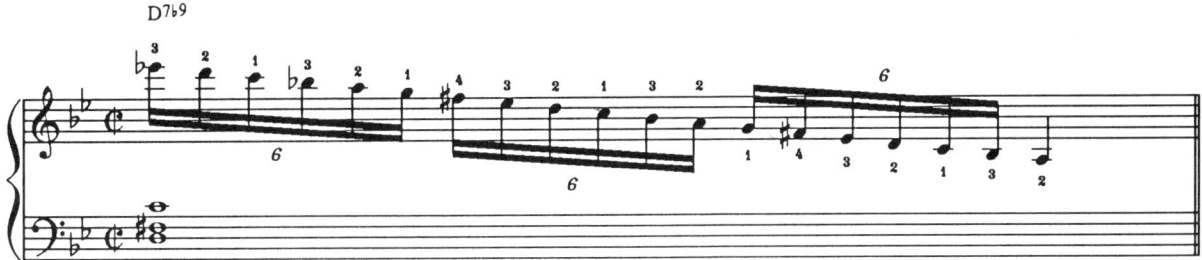

Tatum finds frequent use for this arpeggio —

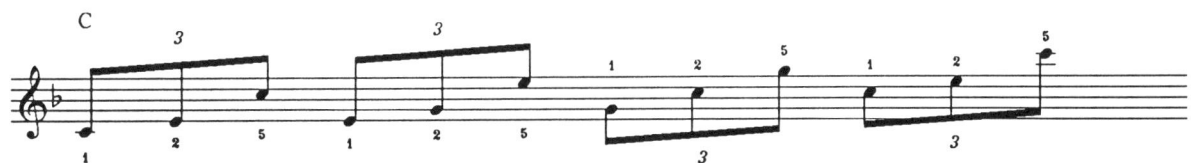

— and he may use it as the upper structure in what appears to be a different chord:

Here is another broken arpeggio, and different uses for it:

It should be understood that while Tatum sometimes uses various patterns in a decorative or embellishing manner, at other times patterns may form an important part of his single-note lines. Furthermore, he puts different patterns together in kaleidoscopically varied combinations:

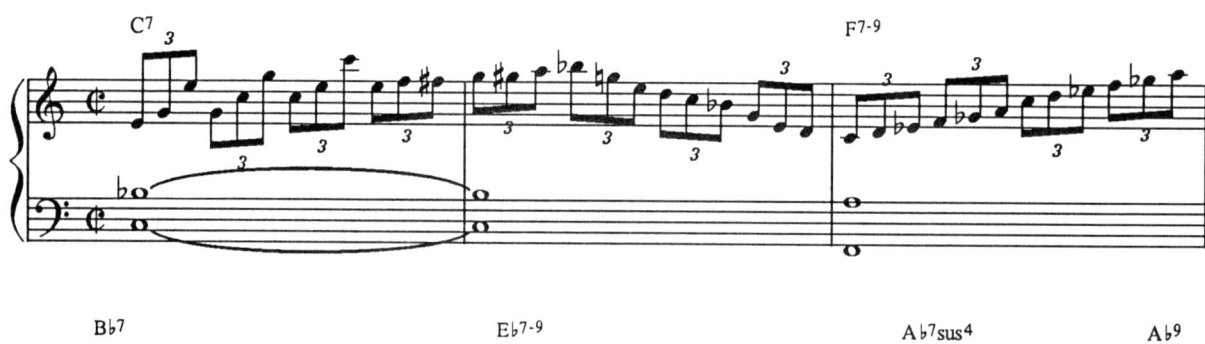

Obviously, a lifetime of work by a major jazz artist cannot be explained fully in a single article, but the basic ideas outlined here should help to gain an understanding and an appreciation of the incomparable contributions to music in general and to jazz piano in particular of Art Tatum.

CHROMATIC PROGRESSIONS

If you've been searching for some new chord progressions for the tunes you write, here's an approach that may give you some ideas. Now, to begin with, an octave is divided into 12 tones. If we assign a major triad to each tone, the series will sound like Example A.

Simply playing these chords in succession makes a pleasant enough sequence. Suppose, however, that we want to make the progression more interesting. Let's place a dominant chord before each triad and adjust the voice-leading for 4-part chords as in Example B.

Okay; very nice, although a little barbershop. Let's fancy it up as in Example C.

Now we're beginning to sound like Richard Wagner, Cesar Franck, George Gershwin, Art Tatum,

and other exponents of chromatic harmony.

You might arrive at a progression like this merely by ear or by trial-and-error finger work, but the numerical theory that underlies it is interesting. There are 12 tones within an octave, and 12 is an unusual number. It can be divided evenly by 1, by 2, by 3, by 4, by 6, and by 12 itself. This means that we can divide the octave into 2, 3, 4, 6, or 12 equal sections. In the example above, what we really did was divide 12 by 1, and by inserting the dominants we made 12 different key centers within the octave.

Let's follow this idea further. Suppose we divide the 12 tones by 2. There will now be 6 key centers in a given octave, occurring every other half-step. By themselves, the 6 centers form a whole-tone scale. Assigning major triads to the notes of a whole-tone scale and inserting a dominant before each of them, we have Example D.

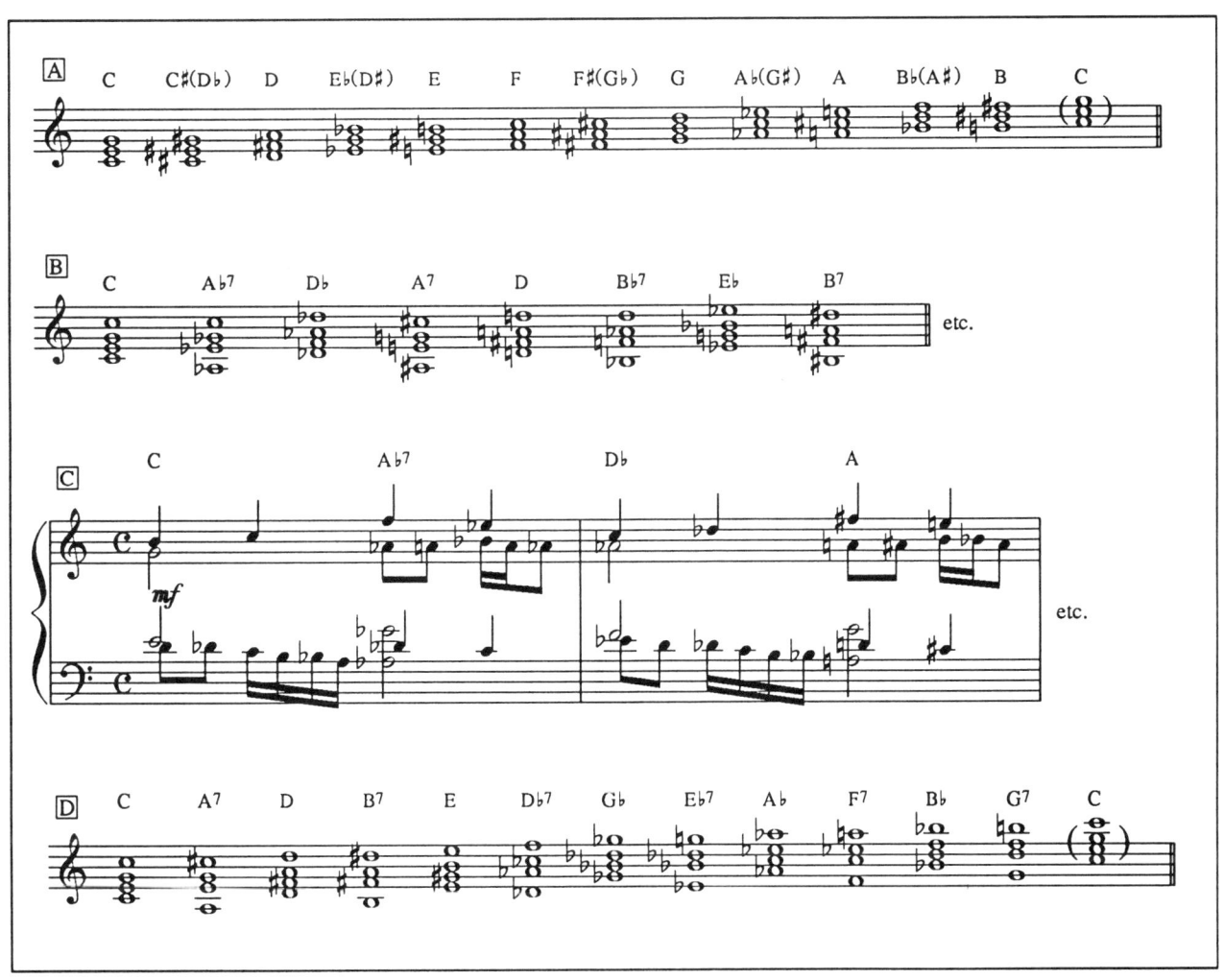

A Gershwin-like application of this progression
might sound something like this:

With all of these progressions, you should continue them all the way up until you arrive back at C.

Dividing by 4 gives us 3 key centers corresponding to the notes of an augmented triad (C, E, Ab, C).
Here's what a progression using these centers might
sound like:

Sound familiar? Play it sort of backwards, and it's
John Coltrane's "Giant Steps":

The same sequence can be found in Richard
Strauss' "Rosenkavalier Waltzes," and you can spot it
as well in the bridge of the Rodgers and Hart standard, "Have You Met Miss Jones?"

Dividing by 3 yields 4 key centers on the notes of a diminished chord. From this sequence we might develop the following:

Dividing by 6, we'll end up with only 2 key centers, a relationship known as a tritone (*C-F#*). Rimsky-Korsakov was fond of using chords a tritone apart. So is everyone who creates flashy endings along these lines:

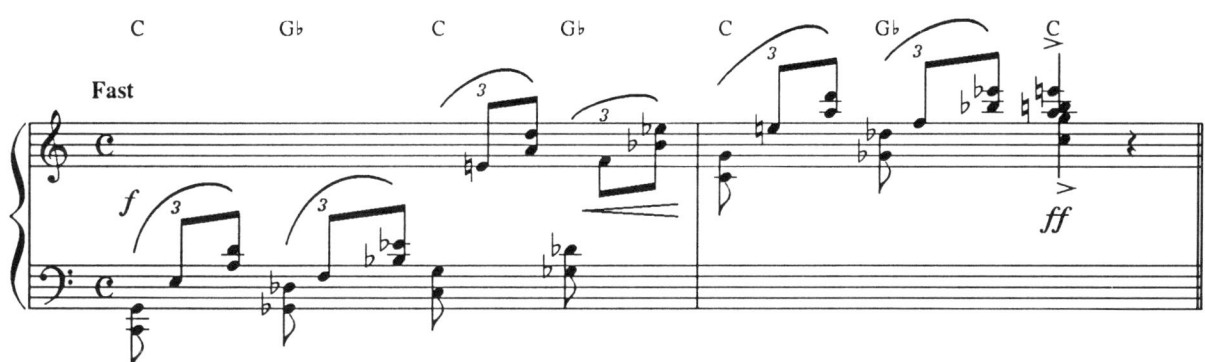

The final division of 12 by 12 is a paradox, since it leads to the relation of *C* to *C*, which is obviously going nowhere!

All the examples above are explorations of ways to extend one's playing, arranging, and composing. While it's true that some musicians get along fine without analyzing what they do in technical terms, it's also true that knowing some theory and applying it imaginatively can often lead to fresh possibilities and areas for further exploration. For a monumental listing of every possibility in harmonic and scale analysis, one should study and be amazed by Nicolas Slonimsky's *Thesaurus Of Scales And Melodic Patterns* (Scribner).

MODES AND MODAL PLAYING

Our modern scales grew from the system developed by the ancient Greeks. The Greek scales were known as *modes,* and the choice of which mode to use in a piece was of primary importance in determining its mood and character, since the Greeks had no harmony as we know it to accompany the melodic lines. Using only the white keys on the piano, we can construct seven of the Greek modes. By playing a scale from *C* to *C,* we get the Ionian mode, which is the same as our major scale. Playing from *D* to *D,* gives us the Dorian mode, which is similar to the minor scale used in many blues and rock settings. Playing from *E* to *E* yields the Phrygian mode, a variation of which is used in much Spanish music. From *F* to *F* is the Lydian mode, whose raised 4th step gives it a different ethnic character. From *G* to *G* is the Mixolydian mode, which corresponds to the major blues scale with its lowered 7th. From *A* to *A* is the Aeolian mode, the natural minor scale of classical music that is often altered by raising the 6th and 7th to create the melodic minor scale. And finally, from *B* to *B* is the Locrian mode, a mode that is close to the blues, provided the *C* and *G* are omitted. All of these modes can be transposed to any of the twelve key centers.

In contemporary modal playing, the emphasis is placed on a key center, around which the harmonic movement is narrowly limited. For example, a typical modal passage might stay in the neighborhood of *D* minor for 16 bars or more using a back-and-forth movement of chords. A typical piano pattern might sound like this:

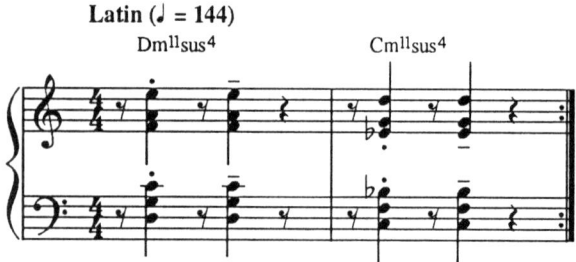

This rhythm is much like the *montuno* of Latin music, and the chords are based on the Dorian mode in two positions — *D* Dorian and *C* Dorian.

Modal playing often involves chords built of stacked fourths. Chords may be placed in a decorative, impressionistic manner in parallel movement above or below the key center. Here is an example in the *E* Phrygian mode:

A very common chord is derived from the Lydian mode:

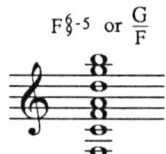

While this can be written as $F^{\S -5}$ or something equally complex, it is more often called simply "*G over F*". The right hand plays the *G* triad while the left plays the *F* triad.

While the harmonic sequence in a modal piece often seems not to "go anywhere," the individual chords may be very full and rich. On the next page is an example of contemporary usage. The mode is *D* Phrygian, with chords moving in a parallel manner toward and away from the tonal center of *D.*

While an entire concert of modal playing might be somewhat limited, the concept is extremely useful in conjunction with other approaches to harmony and is commonly employed in various jazz styles. (*See example on following page.*)

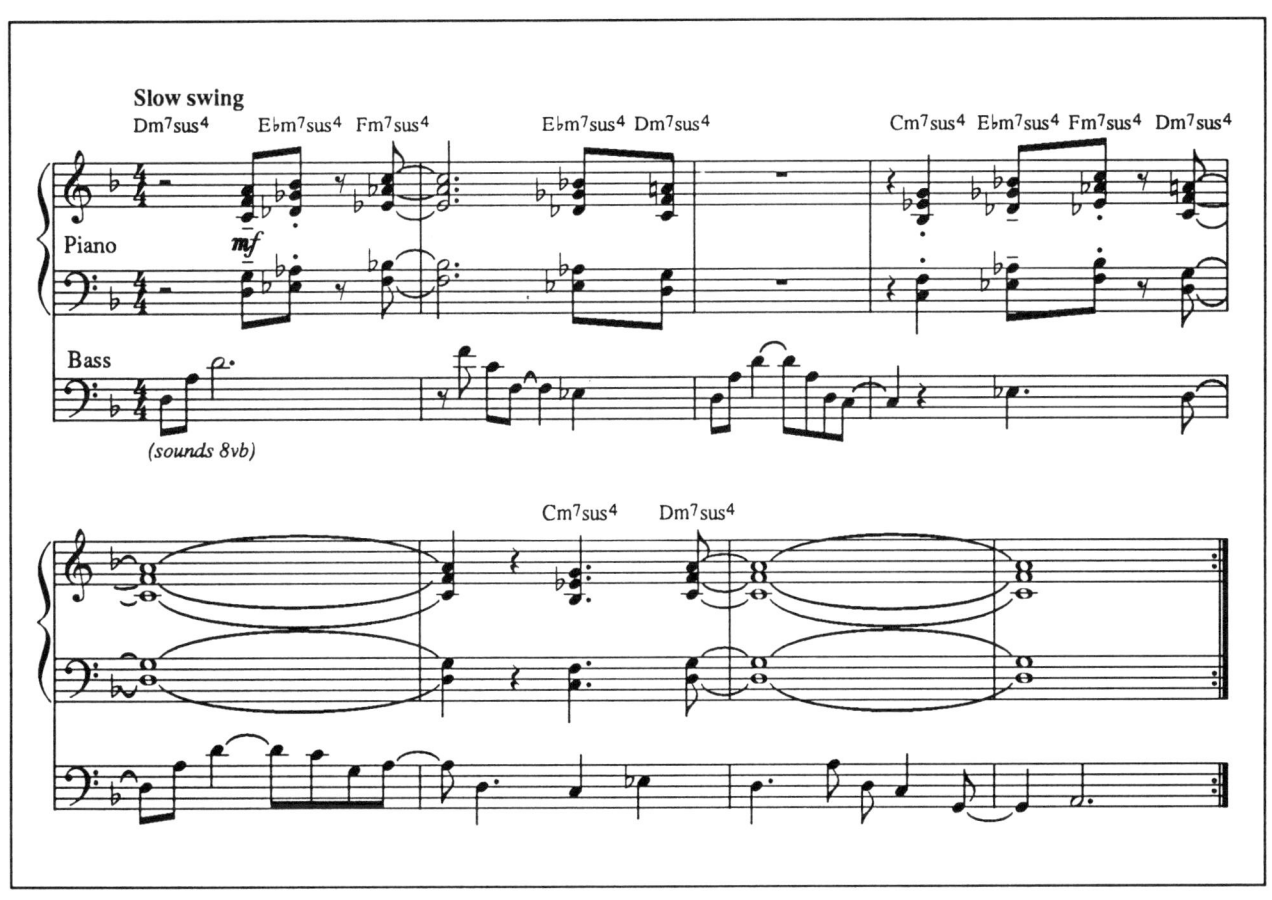

WALKING BASS FOR THE LEFT HAND

The left-hand pattern known as stride, which developed when jazz was first evolving out of ragtime in the '20s, is by definition a pattern that divides a normal 4/4 bar in half, using bass notes on the first and third beats. Piano styles which have arisen in more recent years have usually been based on the four pulses per bar which are provided by a string bass player. Pianists have come to depend on bass players to provide this pulse. That this symbiotic relationship works is undeniable, and the rhythm section with piano has become one of the great staples of jazz.

But what happens if you want to play unaccompanied and still have the feeling that a walking bass gives to a piano solo? One way to do this is to use your left hand to play the sort of lines that bass players favor. With a steady walking bass line, the right hand can be as sparse as Count Basie or as active as desired. Dave McKenna was the original innovator in the use of a walking bass for solo piano, and he has perfected the technique into a marvelously rhythmic and full style, playing both melody and mid-register punctuation chords with his right hand.

In the example below, I've illustrated some of the possibilities for 4/4 walking bass in a casual chorus in *F* minor. Try practicing this for independence of the hands, particularly in terms of touch. As you begin to develop your own storehouse of walking bass patterns, you might listen to any of the great jazz bassists — Milt Hinton or Ray Brown, for example — to see how they construct their lines.

Walking Bass Study

(Dedicated to Dave McKenna)

DICK HYMAN

131

CHORDS AND VOICE LEADING: DON'T BLAME ME

Too often we tend to think of chords in a vertical sense, as if each of them stood alone, a collection of tones complete in itself. A more productive way of thinking harmonically is to look at the horizontal movement of separate voices. In this situation, the harmony results from the convergence of several simultaneous lines moving contrapuntally. To illustrate this idea, I've arranged the old standard "Don't Blame Me" in strict four-part har-mony, with each line moving separately but all of them relating to one another. This arrangement could be played by a string quartet, a saxophone quartet, or any four instruments with the proper ranges. It also sounds fine on the piano, although care must be taken to bring out the melody when it is not in the top voice. I've given the melody and basic chord progression separately so you can see how the arrangement works.

Don't Blame Me

McHugh & Fields
Arranged by Dick Hyman

Legato, not too fast

* Bring out alto melody. ** Bring out tenor melody. *** Bring out bass melody.

Original:

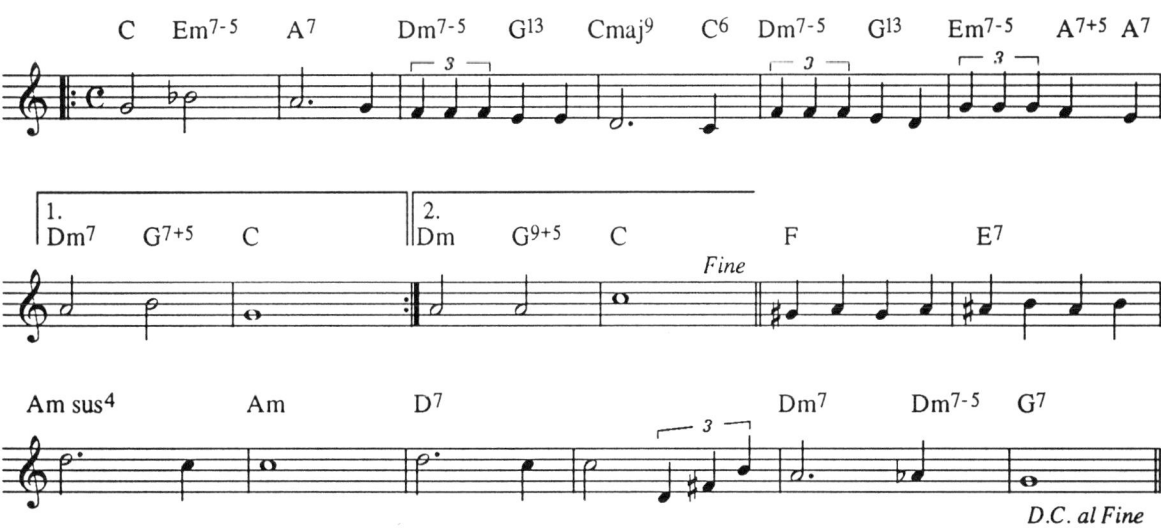

PLAYING HOAGY CARMICHAEL'S GREAT SONGS

oagland Howard Carmichael was born in Bloomington, Indiana, in 1899 and was 82 years old when he passed on. His initial connection with music was as a jazz pianist and composer of the '20s. His admiration for the great "hot" players of that era led him into the elite group of New Yorkers which included cornetists Bix Beiderbecke and Red Nichols, clarinetist Benny Goodman, and violinist Joe Venuti. On occasion Carmichael played piano and recorded with these legendary names, but it was clear that songwriting would be the most important of his numerous achievements.

Successively Carmichael became his own lyricist, a convincing character singer (almost always of his own material), and eventually an actor in nine Hollywood films. His dramatic roles were usually the archetypal barroom piano player, as in *Young Man With A Horn*, but Hoagy's Hoosier twang and mobile physiognomy enabled him to undertake several assignments away from the keyboard. His songs, even when he was not the performer, found their way into the scores of 23 other movies. "In The Cool, Cool, Cool Of The Evening" won him an Academy Award in 1951 when Bing Crosby sang it in *Here Comes The Groom*.

A generous collection of Carmichael's songs is available in a 208-page volume published by CPP/Belwin. His most popular pieces are included, as well as many other worthy items which are known to a smaller circle of musicians and singers. His tunes are staples for pianists who aspire to familiarity with the important standards. The repertoire would be considerably diminished without "Blue Orchids," "Georgia On My Mind," "I Get Along Without You Very Well," "In The Cool, Cool, Cool Of The Evening," "Judy," "Lazy River," "Lazybones," "The Nearness Of You," "Ole Buttermilk Sky," "Skylark," "Smallfry," "Star Dust," "Two Sleepy People," and "Washboard Blues."

Nevertheless, as is the case with many standard songs, pianists may be surprised to encounter printed harmonies in sheet music which are at some variance with those commonly used. As I've described elsewhere, there are frequently discrepancies between the original setting of a song and the harmonic and rhythmic preferences of a later generation.

The chord sequences shown here are intended to dovetail with the familiar Carmichael melodies. They are not elaborately different from the originals, but they are more to my taste and in some degree are more likely to be used by present-day players, particularly of the mainstream jazz variety.

Star Dust

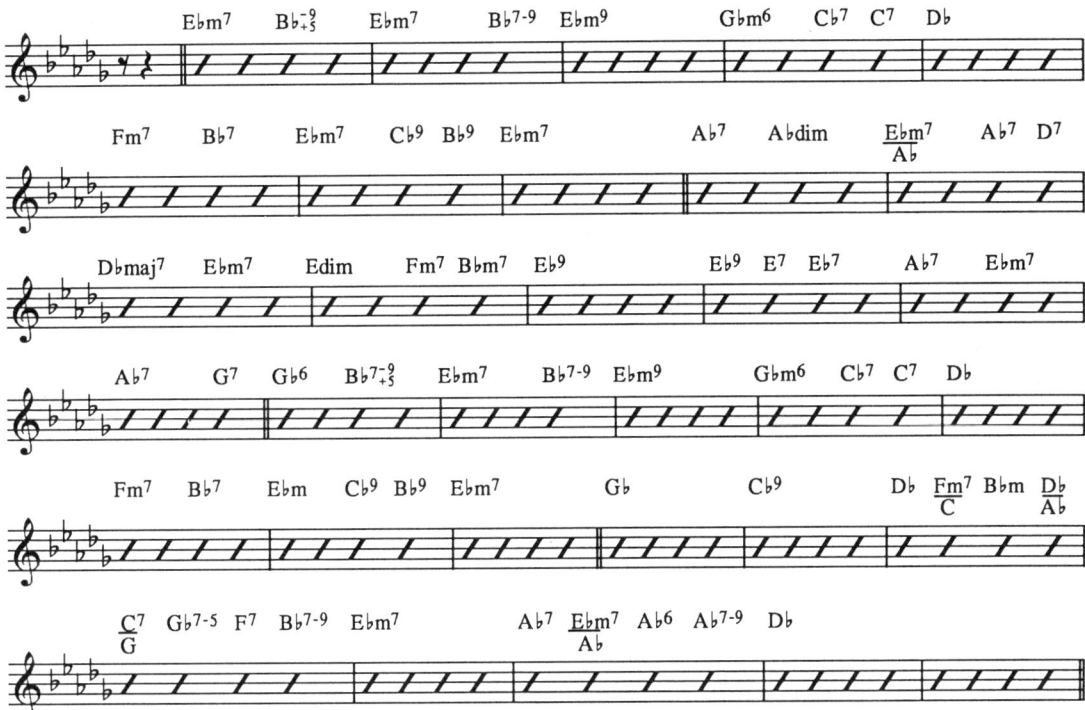

Georgia On My Mind

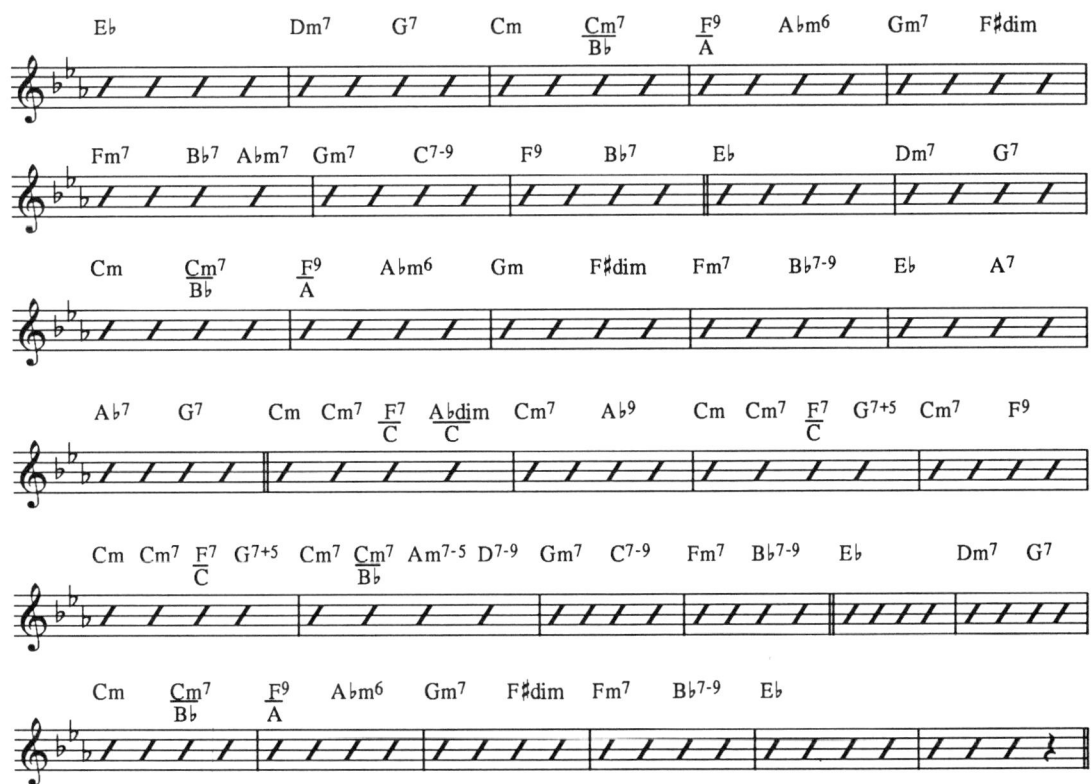

BEYOND 4/4

Walking along 9th Avenue the other day, I heard a noise that made me think I was in the midst of a construction project. With a New Yorker's ingrained sense of caution I looked up to make sure that I was not in danger of being struck by a falling brick. Everything appeared normal above, and as I looked around me I could not account for the regular insistent fortissimo sound as of a saw ripping through plasterboard. Then I spotted the source: an enormous double-speakered tape player hoisted by a teenager who wanted the rest of Manhattan to marvel at his macho. The cassette being played was rap music stripped to the core of meaning — not even the voice, only a rasping sound in regular rhythm.

The power of rhythm has been known to human beings in all cultures through the ages. Its effect on us must have something to do with our physiology — our very heartbeat — and as such, it is probably a more fundamental musical component than melody. Paradoxically, recent technological developments have brought us closer to this primeval basis of music. In addition to the beat box or ghetto blaster that got me thinking about these matters, there are drum machines, click tracks, sequencers, the play-along rhythm units in electronic organs, and undoubtedly other devices that I haven't run into yet, all synced together by a MIDI connection.

It's very exciting stuff, and often dramatically effective. However, I would like to interject an arhythmic word of caution into the incessant pulsation of modern times, by pointing out that there are a lot of other rhythms besides 4/4. Although no current pop record of which I am aware is in three, there used to be something called a waltz, and various forms of ethnic music in South America and Africa are often based on triple rhythms. Greek and East European music is frequently in five- or seven-beat patterns, and the rhythmic system of Indian music is of tremendous complexity.

Contemporary classical music is often written in mixed meters. Music for films may be very irregular, both for dramatic purposes and in order to sync with the action.

All of these instances lead me to my main point, which is that a professional musician ought to expect to encounter bars of odd lengths, changing meters, and peculiar time signatures. This is true despite the fact that a good deal of the equipment presently being manufactured seems to have been designed for people who are unconcerned with rhythmic possibilities beyond 4/4 with an accented afterbeat.

An original duet of mine, easy to play but in mixed meters, suggests some rhythmic situations one might run into. Eighth-notes are of equal value throughout. Following that is a piece from my first Moog synthesizer album, "Evening Thoughts," reworked a bit as a piano solo. The album is long out of print, and the piece has never been published until now.

Duet 16

From Duets in Odd Meters and Far-out Rhythms

DICK HYMAN

Evening Thoughts

DICK HYMAN

Andantino expressivo

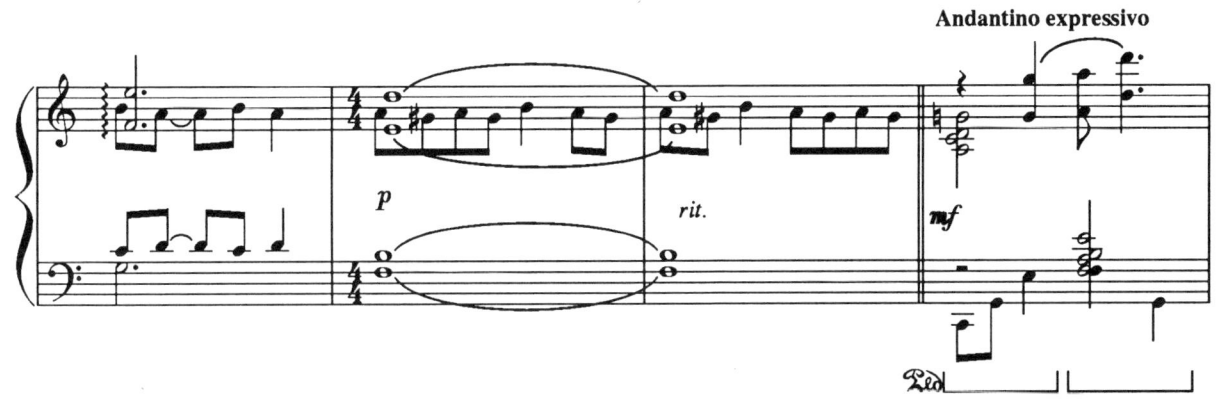

MAKING A RHYTHM SECTION LEAD SHEET

Quite often a pianist who has been rehearsing as accompanist to a singer will be called on to provide parts for several other rhythm section instruments. Singers of standard material are typically accompanied in clubs and cabarets by piano, bass, drums, and possibly guitar. What these players read will most likely be a common part that serves as a guide to some degree of improvisation, rather than individual parts of a more complete arrangement. Although the vocalist may look forward to working with a larger orchestra in the future, the chances are that for the moment he or she will want just enough arranging to get by with a combo. Economics is frequently a shaper of artistic form, and a pianist/arranger will most likely make the best of a limited budget by preparing photocopied common parts for himself and the other instrumentalists.

The first question that arises is how much detail should be expected in this sort of lead-sheet arranging. The decision may vary according to the familiarity of the song, the degree of harmonic sophistication required, whether a specific bass line is required, how competent the faking powers of the players are, and whether the work is to have any permanence or is merely a guide to a particular job.

In any case, strive for legibility. Write larger rather than smaller. Four bars to a line is a good policy, but busy material might benefit from being limited to three bars to a line, or even two. Try to have eight-bar phrases begin at the beginnings of lines, and letter them so that in rehearsal all parties can see where they are. Use ten-line manuscript paper rather than 12-line, so there is room between the staves for additional markings. And make sure that the photocopying doesn't chop off any part of what you've written. (Manuscript paper is often 9-1/2 X 12-1/2 or 9 X 12, while photocopying paper is typically 8-1/2 X 11).

Let's look at some examples of common lead sheet parts. I've chosen an old Dixieland pop tune still used by some singers, "Bill Bailey, Won't You Please Come Home." Ex. 1 is about as bare bones as you can get, and the single chord throughout the first four bars of the tune implies an elementary sort of accompaniment. Note that indications of tempo and style will be a great help to all concerned, including yourself; in the middle of a show, your memory may need some jogging. Also, designations like "Dixieland," "swing," and "even eighths" instantly tell a drummer how to play, and this may be all he has to go by. Bass players are equally grateful to be advised whether they should play two or four beats

per bar.

Actually, for a tune as familiar as this and a treatment so minimal, you hardly need a part at all. Experienced players should be able to fake through a couple of choruses with a big ending merely on the basis of a talk-through. Suppose, however, that you and your singer have worked out a swing version of the old warhorse. At this point a lead sheet like that in Ex. 2 will be a definite asset. Note that in bar 4 an offbeat, which the bass and drums will catch, is indicated with an X under the staff.

Other musical situations may call for other kinds of notation. Suppose you've discovered an appealing bass line that can't easily be represented by chord symbols. (Too many fractionated symbols can be confusing.) You might then write a common part on two staves with the bass line explicitly notated, as shown in Ex. 3. This is very clear for a pianist, but the part will now take up twice as many lines as before, and in a long arrangement the problem of page turns may have been introduced. Bassists, guitarists, and drummers in combos literally have their hands full, and, unlike pianists, have little opportunity to flip pages. Of course this can't always be avoided, but it is a good idea to make their parts no more than three pages long; this is as much as you can spread out on a normal music stand. As a matter of fact, in the layout in Ex. 3 you have given the other instruments more information than they need. Consider making a more concise common part for them, consisting of the bass staff with chords cued above, while you play from the more complete one.

When energy sags and the financial reward seems less than it should be, it may occur to you not even to bother with a full part for yourself; after all, you know how the arrangement goes. True enough, but sometimes memory flees in the face of some panic situation, and it may take an extra moment or two to recall a melody which everyone is waiting for you to count off. Furthermore, another pianist may someday have to use the part you have prepared; on another occasion, *you* might be called to play it again after enough time has gone by so that it is completely out of your head.

There are certain kinds of arrangements which, in the hands of competent players, may not require that a recurrent figure be copied throughout. If you're sure of your players, giving two bars and writing "simile" (Italian for "in a similar manner"), as in Ex. 4, may save you a lot of work, but a singer probably would not want to travel with such a sketchy lead sheet, given the varying competence of the personnel one would find on the road. This approach should be limited to gigs where you can count on your players and on some reasonable rehearsal time.

Playing from common lead-sheet parts requires experienced players, who can fill in a full part from the sketchiest of indications. Performances will be even better if refinements can be worked out verbally in rehearsal. Still, there are times when parts have to be read at sight. The pianist/arranger ought to anticipate such occasions and, without cluttering the part with unnecessary information, supply what is vital.

ADAPTING TO DIFFERENT PIANOS

Once I documented an unusually varied week of freelancing. At this time I encountered such different types of pianos, each with its own playing or tonal characteristics, that I feel envious when I think of all the musicians in the world who perform on their own instruments. It must be great to bring your own axe to a gig and know that you can count on it. Something like a good marriage, I imagine.

We pianists, however, have a different destiny. Much as we may yearn for a stable relationship with some deserving instrument, we must expect only an endless series of quick flings with a motley assortment of partners. We must be prepared for hard or easy action, dull or bright tone, quick or slow response, predominant treble or bass emphasis, fast or slow decay, consistent or uneven action, and any degree or combination of the above. Furthermore, we may have to play on an instrument which is out of tune or which suffers from some mechanical malfunction such as a faulty pedal mechanism or a broken hammer.

As with random romantic partners, we do our best to be polite to those that don't come up to our standards, but even when we luck into the one-and-only, the piano with marvelous tone and perfect action, we can't expect a long-term relationship, let alone a marriage. As fickle as Casanova, when the gig is over we're on our way to the next piano.

There is only one technique I know which is helpful for adapting to the various characteristics of pianos. It is called practicing. Remarkably, all the pianos in town, even the acknowledged dogs, seem to play just fine after you've worked out on scales and exercises for a few hours. Conversely, you are less likely to come to terms easily with a strange instrument if you are not in shape. You need a reserve pool of technique in order to adjust and compensate so that an unfamiliar instrument can be persuaded to work with you.

The process of coming to terms with a new instrument cannot always be verbalized, but as I think about the pianos I played on during the week under consideration, some principles seem to emerge. The first encounter took place on a Tuesday morning, when I was called to play an orchestral session in which dramatic music cues by composer Sid Ramin were recorded for *All Our Children*, a soap opera. I had played the medium-sized piano in that studio often before and knew it to be an adequate instrument with a distinct problem. Literally attached to it is a plexiglass construction designed to isolate the sound of the instrument in order to gain maximum control over the recording process. A transparent cabinet thus replaces the top of the piano, completely enclosing the strings and mechanism. A music rack is attached to the exterior.

The player can see the interior of the instrument, but is able to hear only a faint representation of what he is playing. The engineer's theory is that by wearing a headset the performer can hear what he needs to as the music is being recorded. The headset will also let him hear, at the same time, the rest of the orchestra and the click track (a metronomic beat).

While this system works well enough for most of the radio and TV commercials in which the studio specializes, the pianist may be hampered at times, particularly in solo passages, by not being able to judge the true level at which he is playing or the related tonal quality which is being produced by his touch. In critical sessions in the past in this studio I have removed the plexiglass panel at the front of the piano altogether and have insisted that the engineer solve his isolation problem in some other way. The music at this morning's session was not so demanding, however, so I merely wedged an orange juice container under the panel, keeping it open a few inches, enough to be able to listen to my playing with one open ear while monitoring the recorded sound with an earphone on the other.

As important as it is to hear your instrument as it really sounds, it must be admitted that there are qualities of sound, heard through the headset, which may cause you to modify your playing. For example, you may wish to alter your touch or your phrasing according to the level at which you are being recorded. If the sound man has your instrument at a high level, you don't have to play forcefully in order to project above the rest of the orchestra. You may be able to play quite softly and still be louder than an accompanying brass section, if that is the desired balance. Listening to oneself through earphones can thus be instructive; but as I see it, this technique should be in addition to the player's basic need to hear his own playing realistically.

As a Baldwin artist, I can request that company to provide instruments for important occasions. Tuesday evening was one of these, a performance of two different dances with the Twyla Tharp Dance Company. Baldwin sent over a couple of equally excellent 7' F's for the series. I used one instrument on stage, playing and conducting an orchestra from the piano for the first dance. For the second dance, I played the other piano as a solo, down in the orchestra pit. Each piano was equipped with wide area interior microphones set close to the strings, and the highly amplified sound which filled the venerable Winter Garden Theater on Broadway was quite good during the run of nine performances. I did, however, consult with the sound man once, suggesting that his level had been a bit too high, so that my loud passages caused momentary distortion in the speakers. Sound people sometimes overlook the possibility that your playing may suddenly change from pianissimo to fortissimo.

Thursday evening was devoted to a four-hour recording session with Judy Collins, who sang two songs with a large orchestra. A piano accompaniment was featured on one piece, for which the producer had rented a special instrument. Unfortunately, I was not available to make the selection, and I found that the particular instrument chosen for me, a Steinway B, was not exactly what I might have picked.

The piano was voiced with unusual brightness. A tremendous *forte* was possible with a minimum of effort. Accented chords, as I struck them, seemed to create great white flashes. On the other hand, it was less easy to play softly, or to keep the bass accompaniment figure, as called for in my part, down to the necessary murmur. I would judge that this piano would be well suited to the performance of a concerto, where its ability to be heard above an orchestra would be an asset. I have read, in fact, that this is the sort of instrument on which Horowitz, with his superlative control, achieves his great gradations of color. It took me, on the other hand, a couple of readings to scale down to the desired delicacy, and to a certain extent I obtained the result by rearranging some of the running bass figures and putting them into the less stormy treble.

Friday evening I played a solo concert at Somerset College in Somerville, New Jersey. A new and very agreeable medium Steinway was on hand, and in the small hall it did not need amplification. This was the only situation during the week in which I did not have to deal with microphones, and it felt good simply to play acoustically.

Saturday afternoon there was another performance with the dance company, and Sunday yet another. In between, beginning at 10:00 Saturday night and ending later than I'm accustomed to these days, I subbed with the trio of an old friend, guitarist Joe Puma, at a small Upper East Side club known as Gregory's. The piano here was a Baldwin spinet, amplified and in good condition, but subject to the limitations of its size. My rule for playing a small piano is to accept its tonal range and to play more lightly than otherwise. The danger is to become anxious about the small tone and overcompensate by playing too heavily. The tone is then liable to become percussive and the key response even more sluggish than it is normally. It is better to rely on a microphone in such a situation than to try to force something from the instrument that is not there.*
For grand pianos that have seen better days, I try to follow the same rule by playing lightly and turning up the amplifier. A piano which has lost its resonance may actually sound fairly respectable through a sound system, and the action can seem faster if the performer is able to play lightly.

To sum up, then, pianists need to have great flexibility in dealing with different instruments and audio systems. Listening to one's instrument, judging its capabilities, and working with the sound system are all important. But most important, I think, is to have practiced enough so that unexpected problems can be dealt with as they come up with a minimum of tension.

*See also In the Good Old 1984 Summertime (page 54)

THE SYNERGY OF TWO PIANOS

There is a special sensation that comes to a player in a two-piano team. It must be similar to the sense of wonder symphonic musicians feel when they listen to the instrumental drama going on around them, of which they are one part. It is the sense of synergism, which Webster's defines as "cooperative action of discrete agencies such that the total effect is greater than the sum of the two effects taken independently." To put it more simply, the whole is greater than the sum of its parts. In two-piano playing the individual pianist experiences the synergistic feeling of being part of a mysteriously independent totality; and unlike a violinist awash in a sea of colleagues, a pianist is able to capture the sensation with only one other performer.

Quite apart from the psychological feelings of the players, there are some solid professional reasons for the use of two pianos as an orchestral unit. Technically, almost everything conceivable can be played by twenty fingers. Two pianists can negotiate between them works of the complexity of Stravinsky's Rite Of Spring, and there exists a large repertoire of orchestral works which have been so arranged. There are also many pieces composed specifically for two pianos, by Poulenc, Mozart, Anton Arensky, Liszt, Chopin, and Rachmaninoff, among others. Furthermore, no more economical use of only two musicians has been discovered, and in situations where the tightness of a budget or the limited amount of floor space has made a larger ensemble impossible, a two-piano team may be the only solution.

In the 1920's, two-piano teams such as Arden and Ohman came into vogue as accompanists to Broadway musicals, either by themselves or as the centerpiece of a pit orchestra. This tradition continues into the present era in such shows as Stephen Sondheim's *Side By Side By Sondheim*, *Barnum*, and the revival of *Most Happy Fella*.

In the show tune field, players may be faced with the problem of creating two-piano arrangements from music printed for solo piano. For example, in the production of a low-budget musical comedy, there may be neither the time nor the money to prepare a complete arrangement. Fortunately, there are some elementary formulas for creating instant two-

piano arrangements of typical show tunes. The examples below illustrate two of the basic possibilities. The original piano arrangement is shown in Example A (on the next page). Example B shows a top-and-bottom division. In a typical arrangement of a tune for solo piano, the melody is given mostly to the right hand and the accompaniment to the left. When transferring this arrangement to two pianos, the first player expands the right-hand melody into two or even three octaves, while the second player adds octaves to the downbeat and enlarges the afterbeat chords. An alternative might be called a melody-and-fill-in division. One player stays close to the original solo arrangement in Example A, while the other ad-libs fills, arpeggios, and embellishments like those in Example C.

With some preparation, many effective devices can be worked out in which the combined dexterity of twenty fingers permits effects beyond the technical capabilities of any one player. The dramatic flourish shown in Example D is one of many possibilities.

In two-piano jazz playing, when both players are improvising, each must listen carefully to what the other is doing so that different registers and contrasting functions can be chosen. The danger lies in cluttering up the same area of both keyboards with identical functions. Each player must listen to the other while carrying out his own thoughts, ready to shift into a melodic, embellishing, or supporting role as the synthesis of the two minds develops.

I've played in informal two-piano get-togethers with many other pianists, but in particular I've reached an empathy with three different partners: Roger Kellaway, Derek Smith, and the late Dick Wellstood. Each duo has been a different marriage and suggested different accommodations, but what all three have had in common has been a developing sense of trust in the other man.

With this confidence there can be ad lib key changes, tempo changes, and shifting of the melody back and forth. Each player helps the other. If there seems to be uncertainty with the rhythmic pulse on the part of one man, the other reinforces it. If one man starts a predictable sequence, the other harmonizes with him or gets out of his way. If one man plays the bottom, the other goes to the top. All these things develop, as the song says, with a little bit of luck, and sometimes more successfully than others.

THE PIANO MUSIC OF BIX BEIDERBECKE

The biographical facts are straightforward: He was born in Davenport, Iowa, in 1903, of a well-off German-American family; was largely self-taught on both piano, his first instrument, and cornet, his primary professional instrument; dropped out of high school to work with dance bands around Chicago; played with the Wolverines and the orchestras of, among others, Jean Goldkette and Paul Whiteman; never married; died of pneumonia and alcoholism at the age of 28 in New York City.

Thus, the life of Leon Bismarck ("Bix") Beiderbecke in outline. What cannot be set down in such a sketch is the uncanny inventiveness of his playing on both piano and cornet, the intensity and beauty of his improvised solos on the latter instrument, and the influence he had on other musicians during a professional career that lasted barely ten years.

After his death, both his playing and his tragic life became the stuff of legend. A novel, *Young Man With A Horn* by Dorothy Baker, followed by a film of the same title were loosely based on his brief career. Inevitably, much of the musical point is lost in such biographical vehicles, but Bix's actual playing is amply documented on many recordings, as well as in the four pieces for piano published as *Bix Beiderbecke's Modern Piano Suite* ("In A Mist," "Candlelights," "Flashes," and "In The Dark") and the additional "Davenport Blues."

Bix's recordings number over two hundred, and in collector's editions several different takes of certain titles are available, each with a different improvisation. Although he recorded mostly as a cornetist, it is his piano pieces which interest us here, and it is in his own recording of "In A Mist," the first title in the *Modern Suite,* that we can hear his most extended recorded piano work.

All of Beiderbecke's published works were transcribed by Bill Challis, the arranger for both the Goldkette and Whiteman orchestras during the periods when Beiderbecke was featured with them. Bix's lack of formal musical training frustrated his attempts at composition, but sessions in which Challis notated his improvisations produced a suc-

cessful working relationship. The current availability of these selections as sheet music is problematical; originally published by Robbins, they are now held by CPP/Belwin, Inc. In 1979, all four titles of the *Modern Suite* were included in a mammoth compilation edited by David A. Jasen and published by Big 3 Music, *Ragtime (100 Authentic Rags)*. The title is far off the mark with respect to the Bix pieces; whatever they are, they are distinctly not ragtime.

"In A Mist" has been recorded through the years by various pianists. Perhaps because of Bix's reliance on Challis' notation, there are some hazardous hand positions indicated in the sheet music. The original version is shown in Example A; in Example B, I have shown a more comfortable distribution between the hands. I have also changed some of the enharmonics and reduced the number of accidentals. A bit of a stretch is required for the left-hand tenths, but I find it preferable even to roll these, if necessary, rather than try for the right-hand ninths, which occur in sudden open position. See these and other music examples on the following pages.

There are some other aspects of "In A Mist" which are implied by the printed music, although not explicitly written. I would play the first two bars holding on to some of the notes as in Example C.

Later interpreters have tended to play "In A Mist" more slowly and gracefully, although this tends to pull down the sprightliness of the subsequent jazzy sections. Bix's recording differs significantly from the published version by omitting one lyrical section entirely and substituting some hotter extemporization. We don't know whether Bix's recorded tempo, *vivace* on my metronome (about 166) might not have been due to the relatively short length of the 78 rpm record he was cutting. Perhaps, if he had had more time at his disposal, he would have played more slowly. The fact that Challis marked his transcription *moderato* suggests this possibility. Our conclusion must be that the piece may be performed at various tempos and work in different ways. My own preference is for a slower interpretation than Bix's recording, but not so slow as to turn the dance rhythm into a nocturne.

A   "In A Mist" as published.

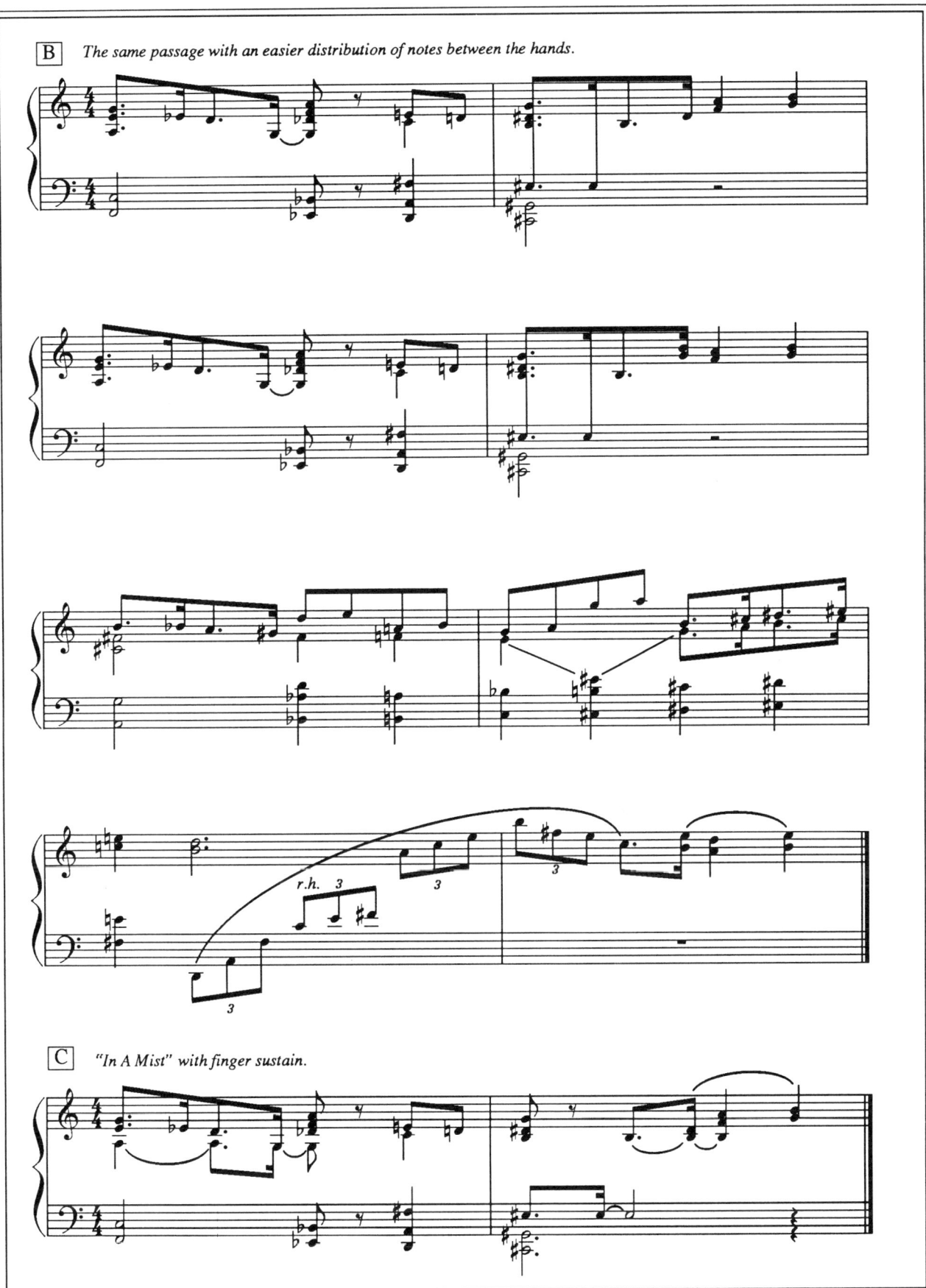

B The same passage with an easier distribution of notes between the hands.

C "In A Mist" with finger sustain.

It was the convention at the time to notate syncopation only in terms of eighth-notes, so measures 27 and 28 as originally published shift from dotted eighths and sixteenths to straight eighths, even though the feeling of swing would have been the same throughout as in Example D.

I would use the dotted notation consistently as in Example E.

However, we're still confronting another old problem in jazz notation. Playing practice then and now has normally been in a triplet feeling. Publishing practice, on the other hand, has been to notate either even eighths or dotted eighths and sixteenths. Both systems are rhythmically inaccurate, but paradoxically they are often easier to read than a syncopation which might turn out in exact notation to look like:

My feeling is that the present-day method of writing eighths but also indicating either "swing eighths" or

at the head of the piece has a lot to recommend it. Of course, when you actually want eighth-notes in such a piece you must designate "even eighths." In any case, it is advisable to be familiar with the conventions of the past and to bear in mind that as far as jazz or jazz-influenced music is concerned, the rhythm of what you play is not necessarily the same as the rhythm on the page.

The second piece in the *Modern Suite* is called "Candlelights." The first four bars are shown in Example F on the next page. (I've adjusted the stems for easier readability.) This impressionistic phrase recalls Debussy and Scriabin, and benefits from a little blurring by the sustain pedal. Pedal once per bar, or even once for each two bars. As with "In A Mist," there are several later passages where the hands might divide the notes more equitably, with the left assuming some of the notes written for the right.

The tempo need not be rigid throughout. "Candlelights" is less a jazz piece than "In A Mist," and in addition to the various *accelerandi* and *ritardandi* which the editor has noted, there are other opportunities for tempo alterations. It seems to me that in this case the eighth-notes should be even, exactly as written, with the infrequent dotted eighths and sixteenths implying slight expressive dips in tempo rather than the feeling of swing. Dynamics

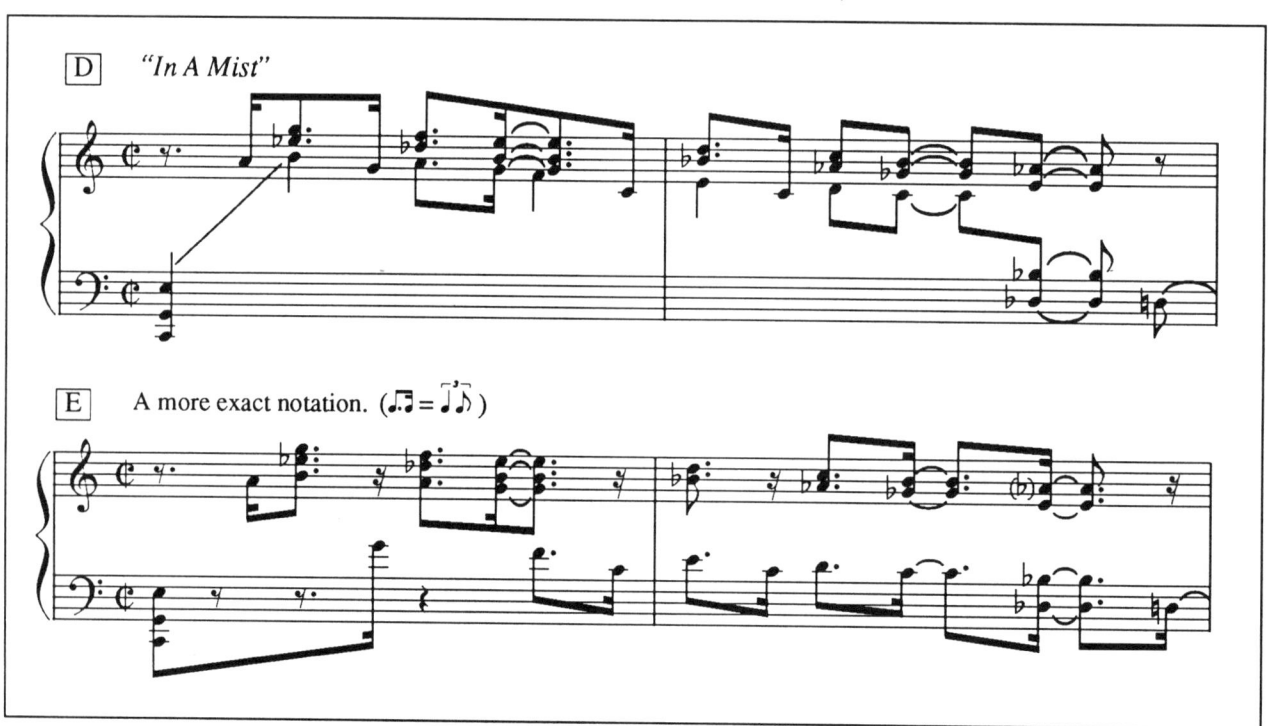

might be considered a degree lower than indicated — that is, *mp* rather than *mf* to begin with. Beiderbecke did not record "Candlelights" nor the two remaining titles in the *Modern Suite,* so we can only use our own judgment as to the interpretation.

"Flashes," which is dated 1931, the year of Bix's death, wants to be in tempo and in even eighths for the most part. An exception would be the little interlude that begins as shown in Example G.

A more exact notation would be as shown in Example H.

"In The Dark" begins with an outstretched right-hand figure (Example I- next page) that requires both the lower half-notes to be played with the thumb on the crack. The reach is awkward, but to redistribute these notes to the left hand would be worse.

The general inspiration for the Beiderbecke piano works would seem to have been the world of Debussy, Ravel, and Delius, with a large admixture of MacDowell. However, Bix was especially influenced by the little-known American composer Eastwood Lane (1879-1951), with whom he became friends in the early '20s. According to Lane's widow, Modena Scovill, a professor of music theory at New York University, Bix was fascinated by the older man's playing and would listen by the hour to Lane's improvisations and performances of his compositions. Bix was particularly fond of Lane's *Adirondack Sketches.* A surviving program indicates that while on a 1926 concert tour with Paul Whiteman's orchestra, Bix left the brass section and was featured as a solo pianist performing, from the *Sketches,* "The Legend Of Lonesome Lake." The relationship of Beiderbecke's music to Lane's can be seen in the opening bars of this piece. See Example J on the following page.

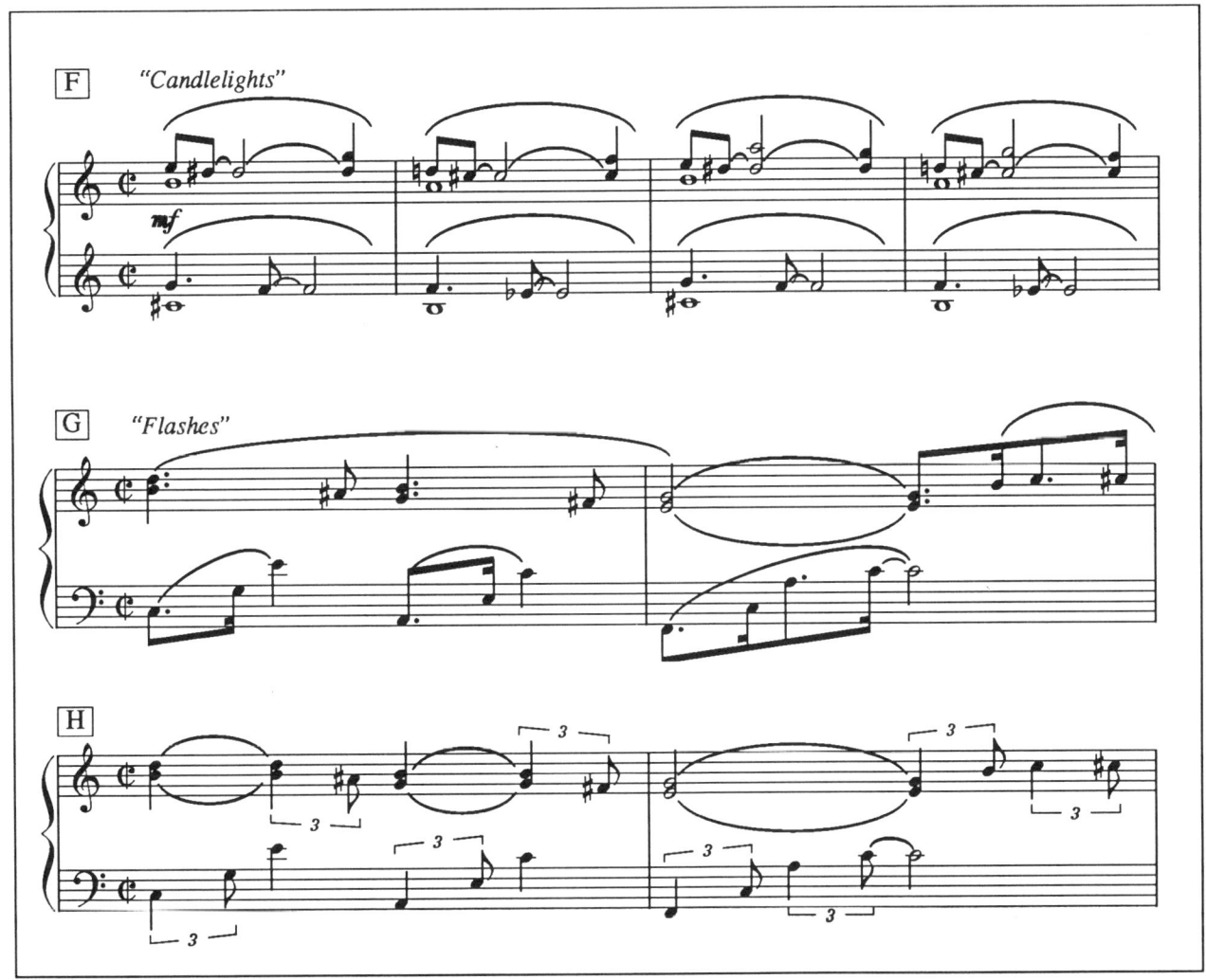

Eastwood Lane wrote numerous programmatic piano pieces in addition to the *Adirondack Sketches*. Such titles as "In Sleepy Hollow," "The Blue-Robed Mandarins," "Sea Burial," "Sold Down The River," and "Fourth Of July" suggest his interests. He recorded some of his works as piano rolls, and some were orchestrated by Ferde Grofé for Whiteman's phonograph recordings. His pieces often appeared in recitals of the 1920's, but they are now entirely out of print although available in some of the larger public libraries. (For information on Eastwood Lane I am indebted to an unpublished monograph by Norman Gentieu.)

One other piece is credited to Beiderbecke, the provocatively titled "For No Reason At All In C," on the recording of which he is listed as co-composer with Frankie Trumbauer. This work, an improvisation on the contemporaneous pop song "I'd Climb The Highest Mountain," remains untranscribed and unpublished. Along with Trumbauer (C-melody saxophone) and Eddie Lang (guitar), Beiderbecke plays piano that is reminiscent of his "In A Mist."

Bix traveled in a circle of professional associates that included members of the Goldkette and Whiteman orchestras as well as numerous New York freelancers. Among the gang of mutually supportive young players was violinist Joe Venuti, whose hot solos enlivened many of the records on which Bix is heard.

At one point Bix shared a hotel room with his fellow cornetist Red Nichols and the latter's upright piano. The place quickly became a social and drinking center for Bix's friends. One euphoric night Joe Venuti, a notorious practical joker, solved in the

most emphatic manner a wager on which he had earlier taken bets.

In dispute was a curious question: What would the predominant tonality of a piano be if all the keys were struck simultaneously? Nichols maintained that C major would prevail. Venuti, perhaps with an insight into Schoenberg's twelve-tone approach, held that all tones would have equal weight. Bix's viewpoint is not known. Soon bets were eagerly placed on one position or the other, and five-dollar bills flowed into Venuti's hands.

As recounted in *Bix, Man & Legend,* by Sudhalter, Evans, and Dean-Myatt, Venuti stage-managed the pragmatic solution to the problem by assembling a number of the more muscular bettors in Nichols' and Beiderbecke's hotel room. They lifted Nichols' piano through the window, and, before the horrified owner could object, dropped it into the alley.

Nichols reported that the piano landed with an enormous crash, but that no tonality whatever could be detected. Since the result of the test was inconclusive, Venuti honorably returned all of the bets, including Nichols' own five dollars. Apparently, the cost of the piano had not been part of Venuti's calculations.

All of the above is by way of qualifying the transcription below. It documents Venuti noodling at the piano during a recording session of mine. To my great delight, Joe had agreed to take part in an album of Jelly Roll Morton pieces that Columbia had commissioned me to arrange. He was then 75 and suffering from certain health problems, but he flew in from Seattle and appeared to enjoy the rehearsal and the session.

At Columbia's 30th Street studio, on December 13, 1975, we recorded "Shreveport Stomp" and "The Perfect Rag" as a trio with Panama Francis playing drums. I also knocked off a piano solo on Jelly Roll's "The Finger Breaker," with Joe sitting by me and offering support.

After a bit, Joe himself sat down at the piano and astonished me by playing what he claimed was an unpublished composition by Bix Beiderbecke. He said it was called "Betcha I Getcha," and added that "Bix liked to fool around with it." I signaled Sam Parkins, the producer, to roll the tape, and Joe's piano playing, itself an oddity, was captured.

Whether what he played is in fact something of Beiderbecke's or merely another of the great Venuti gags cannot be determined. The opening eight bars sound Bixian, without a doubt, but on the other hand Joe was perfectly familiar with Bix's style, and might have been able to replicate it with a theme of his own. What's more, the key of *E* major seems a bit out of the way for Bix, all of whose extant piano pieces are in *C*. Still, giving Joe the benefit of the doubt, we might theorize that when he recalled Bix's playing he automatically transposed it into a more violinistic key. In any case, the middle strain is most likely Joe marking time, and the title sounds like a Venuti invention. Still, the possible validity of the main theme is tantalizing.

The Jelly Roll Morton album containing "Shreveport Stomp", "The Perfect Rag", and "The Finger Breaker" has been reissued as a CD on Sony Classics.

Betcha I Getcha

BIX BEIDERBECKE
JOE VENUTI
TRANSCRIBED BY DICK HYMAN

TUNES EVERYONE SHOULD KNOW

In 1982 two interviews that appeared in the music press got me to thinking. The first was the cover story on saxophonist Phil Woods in *Down Beat;* the second the cover story on keyboardist/composer Bob James in *Keyboard.* Both men, experienced in jazz for several decades, noted that the new crop of players tended in their observations to be deficient in repertoire. Younger musicians didn't seem to know the tunes which were and are still the common currency of players in both jazz and pop music.

Phil Woods held the music publishers responsible for neglecting to reprint traditional material in stage band arrangements. As a result, students in the music schools, the principal training grounds for young players, might not have encountered "Night And Day" until after they had graduated. Since 1982 this deficiency has been remedied to some degree.

Bob James pointed out that modal jazz had created a de-emphasis on the older tunes, as traditional harmony itself had come to seem less important. He saw no harm in this trend and considered it to be the inevitable march of history.

My own point of view was quite to the contrary. Although I agreed that not only jazz but popular music in general could be judged as fleeing from the discipline of chord changes, my belief then and now is that any musician in the jazz or popular field, and in particular a pianist, is gravely under-prepared if he embarks on a career based primarily on the Dorian mode. Sooner or later, it seems to me, someone is going to ask you to play "Star Dust."

I made up a list of 150 tunes that I thought working musicians were likely to encounter at some time. I limited it to those titles which have been vehicles for improvisation by generations of jazz players, excluding more recent instrumental pieces. Then I added another 150 tunes. These lists and the following ones became the basis for *Dick Hyman's Professional Chord Changes And Substitutions For 100 Tunes Every Musician Should Know,* its follow-up, *All The Right Changes, The Best Chord Changes And Substitutions For 100 More Tunes Every Musician Should Know,* and the third volume in the series, *Solo Piano Sketches Of The Great Standards.*

What follows are a compilation of my first lists and a few more songs plus articles presenting specialized categories. Eventually, for publication, we substituted some and winnowed it all down to 200. Still, I believe that the more tunes you know the better prepared you are.

After You've Gone
Ain't Misbehavin'
Ain't She Sweet?
All God's Chillun Got Rhythm
All Of Me
All The Things You Are
Almost Like Being In Love
Alone Together

Am I Blue?
Anything Goes
April In Paris
As Long As I Live
As Time Goes By
Autumn In New York
Autumn Leaves
Avalon
Basin Street Blues
Baubles, Bangles, And Beads
Beautiful Love
Begin The Beguine
Bewitched, Bothered, And Bewildered
The Birth Of The Blues
Black And Blue
Black Orpheus (Theme From)
Blue And Sentimental
Blue Lou
The Blue Room
Blue Skies
Blues In The Night
Bluesette
Body And Soul
Boulevard Of Broken Dreams
The Boy Next Door
But Not For Me
Bye Bye Blues
Can't We Be Friends?
Can't We Talk It Over?
Caravan
Charleston
Cheek To Cheek
Cherokee
Close Your Eyes
Come Rain Or Come Shine
Crazy Rhythm
Dark Eyes
Darn That Dream
Days Of Wine And Roses
Dear Old Southland
Dearly Beloved
'Deed I Do
Deep Purple
Dinah
Do It Again
Do Nothin' Till You Hear From Me
Do You Know What It Means To Miss New Orleans?
Don't Blame Me
Don't Get Around Much Anymore
Don't Worry 'Bout Me
Dream
Dream Dancing
East Of The Sun
Easy Living
Embraceable You
Emily
Everything Happens To Me
Exactly Like You
Fascinating Rhythm
Fine And Dandy
Flamingo
Fly Me To The Moon (In Other Words)
A Foggy Day
Fools Rush In
For All We Know

From This Moment On
Georgia On My Mind
Get Happy
The Girl From Ipanema
God Bless The Child
Gone With The Wind
Good-Bye
Great Day
Green Dolphin Street
Hallelujah
Have You Met Miss Jones?
Here's That Rainy Day
Hindustan
Honeysuckle Rose
How About You?
How Deep Is The Ocean?
How High The Moon
How Insensitive
How Long Has This Been Going On?
I Can't Believe That You're In Love With Me
I Can't Get Started With You
I Can't Give You Anything But Love
I Cover The Waterfront
I Cried For You
I Didn't Know What Time It Was
I Found A New Baby
I Get A Kick Out Of You
I Got It Bad
I Got Rhythm
I Hadn't Anyone Till You
I Hear A Rhapsody
I Hear Music
I Know That You Know
I Let A Song Go Out Of My Heart
I Love You (Weill)
I Love You (Porter)
I May Be Wrong
I Never Knew
I Only Have Eyes For You
I Should Care
I Surrender, Dear
I Thought About You
I Want To Be Happy
I Wished On The Moon
Idaho
If I Could Be With You (One Hour Tonight)
If I Had You
If I Were A Bell
I'll Be Around
I'll Get By
I'll Remember April
I'll See You Again
I'm Beginning To See The Light
I'm Forever Blowing Bubbles
I'm Getting Sentimental Over You
I'm Gonna Sit Right Down And Write Myself A Letter
I'm In The Mood For Love
I'm Old Fashioned
I'm Through With Love
In A Sentimental Mood
In Love In Vain
In My Solitude
Indian Summer
Indiana (Back Home Again In)
Invitation

I've Found A New Baby
I've Got A Crush On You
I've Got My Love To Keep Me Warm
I've Got The World On A String
It's All Right With Me
It's Easy To Remember
It's Only A Paper Moon
It's So Peaceful In The Country
Ja-da
The Japanese Sandman
Jeepers Creepers
Jitterbug Waltz
Jumpin' At The Woodside
Just Friends
Just One Of Those Things
Just Squeeze Me (Ellington)
Just You, Just Me
Keepin' Out Of Mischief
Lady Be Good (Oh, Lady Be Good)
Laura
Lazy River
Let's Fall In Love
Like Someone In Love
Limehouse Blues
Little Girl Blue
Little White Lies
Liza
Long Ago (And Far Away)
Love For Sale
Love Is Here To Stay
Love Is Just Around The Corner
Love Me Or Leave Me
Love Walked In
Lover
Lover, Come Back To Me!
Lover Man
Lullaby Of Birdland
Lullaby Of The Leaves
Lulu's Back In Town
Lush Life
Mack The Knife (Moritat) (Theme from The Three Penny Opera)
Makin' Whoopee
The Man I Love
Manhattan
Mean To Me
Memories Of You
Misty
Mood Indigo
Moon Glow
Moon River
Moonlight In Vermont
The More I See You
More Than You Know
Mountain Greenery
My Blue Heaven
My Favorite Things
My Funny Valentine
My Ideal
My Melancholy Baby
My Old Flame
My One And Only Love
My Romance
My Shining Hour
My Ship

The Nearness Of You
Nevertheless
Nice Work If You Can Get It
Night And Day
Old Devil Moon
Old Fashioned Love
Old Folks
On The Alamo
On The Sunny Side Of The Street
Once In A While
Out Of Nowhere
Over The Rainbow
The Party's Over
Pennies From Heaven
Penthouse Serenade
People Will Say We're In Love
Please Don't Talk About Me When I'm Gone
Poor Butterfly
Prelude To A Kiss
Quiet Nights Of Quiet Stars (Corcovado)
Rose Room
Rosetta
St. Louis Blues
Santa Claus Is Comin' To Town
Satin Doll
Secret Love
September In The Rain
September Song
The Shadow Of Your Smile
The Sheik Of Araby
She's Funny That Way
Should I?
Side By Side
Skylark
Somebody Loves Me
Someday My Prince Will Come
Someone To Watch Over Me
Sometimes I'm Happy
The Song Is You
Sophisticated Lady
Speak Low
S'posin'
Squeeze Me (Waller)
Star Dust
Stars Fell On Alabama
Stella By Starlight
Stompin' At The Savoy
Stormy Weather
Sugar
The Summer Knows
Summertime
Sunday

Sweet And Lovely
Sweet Georgia Brown
Sweet Lorraine
S'Wonderful
Symphony
Take The 'A' Train
The Talk Of The Town
Tea For Two
Tenderly
That Old Black Magic
Them There Eyes
There Is No Greater Love
There Will Never Be Another You
There's A Small Hotel
These Foolish Things
They Can't Take That Away From Me
This Can't Be Love
This Is All I Ask
Thou Swell
Three Little Words
Time After Time
Time On My Hands
Too Marvelous For Words
The Trolley Song
Two Sleepy People
Undecided
The Very Thought Of You
Watch What Happens
Wave
We'll Be Together Again
What Are You Doing The Rest Of Your Life?
What Is There To Say?
What Is This Thing Called Love?
What's New?
When It's Sleepy Time Down South
When Sunny Gets Blue
When Your Lover Has Gone
Where Or When
Whispering
Who Can I Turn To?
Who Cares?
Willow Weep For Me
Without A Song
The World Is Waiting For The Sunrise
Wrap Your Troubles In Dreams
Yesterdays
You Go To My Head
You Stepped Out Of A Dream
You Took Advantage Of Me
You're Driving Me Crazy
Yours Is My Heart Alone
You've Changed

100 SHOW TUNES BY GERSHWIN AND PORTER

Show tunes are an important part of the working repertoire of many musicians and singers. Many feel that the songs that originally graced the Broadway stage from the early 1900's to the present represent the best of American popular music. Certainly until the rock music explosion of the 1960's, musical comedies set the pace for popular music, and even since that time, despite the refocusing of popular taste, Broadway scores continue to pour out of some of our most creative musical intelligences, although in less quantity than when Broadway introduced two dozen new musicals per season.

Composers such as George Gershwin and Cole Porter wrote scores for film as well as for Broadway. Their film scores are usually included in the show tune category, but there is also a sub-category of movie scores by Harry Warren, Jimmy Van Heusen, and others who wrote primarily for Hollywood.

For hard-core show tune buffs, knowledgeable folks who delight in obscurities from the Golden Age of the Broadway musical stage (roughly 1920-1960), the basic repertoire is to a great extent found in the works of George Gershwin, Richard Rodgers, Cole Porter, Jerome Kern, Irving Berlin, Harold Arlen, Vincent Youmans, and their respective collaborators. Within the modest scope of this column we can construct a basic introductory list limited to a hundred of the best-known songs of Gershwin and Porter, each of whom had a total career output that numbered in the thousands.

Show tune people often remember entire productions as well as individual songs, so it is valuable to have some knowledge about the shows in which the songs were introduced. There is endless lore to be discovered in the annals of musical comedy, and for those who like to delve into history, learning the year of production and the names of the original cast can be a matter of great expertise. For many listeners, furthermore, the lyric is at least as important as the melody, and a familiarity with lyrics is an asset to the pianist who accompanies singers, or even to the soloist who wants to make an instrumental performance especially meaningful. In the case of the two composers under discussion, Gershwin composed mostly for the lyrics of his brother Ira, while Porter wrote his own words.

Some of the following titles have already been included in the previous list, since show tunes constitute an important part of the general repertoire.

GEORGE GERSHWIN

Sinbad (1919)
Swanee

The French Doll (1922)
Do It Again

Scandals (1920-24) (a series of annual productions)
Somebody Loves Me
I'll Build A Stairway To Paradise

Lady Be Good (1924)
Oh, Lady Be Good
Fascinating Rhythm
The Man I Love (introduced but deleted from score, later included in **Strike Up the Band**)

Tip Toes (1925)
Looking For A Boy
That Certain Feeling
Sweet And Lowdown

Oh, Kay (1926)
Someone To Watch Over Me
Do, Do, Do
Clap Yo' Hands
Maybe

Funny Face (1927)
S'Wonderful
He Loves And She Loves
My One And Only

Rosalie (1928)
How Long Has This Been Going On?

Treasure Girl (1928)
I've Got A Crush On You (subsequently included in the score of **Strike Up The Band**)

Show Girl (1929)
Liza

Strike Up The Band (1929)
I've Got A Crush On You
The Man I Love
Soon
Strike Up The Band

Girl Crazy (1930)
Embraceable You
I Got Rhythm
But Not For Me
Bidin' My Time

Of Thee I Sing (1931)
Of Thee I Sing
Love Is Sweeping The Country
Who Cares?
Wintergreen For President

Delicious (1931) (film)
Blah, Blah, Blah

Pardon My English (1933)
My Cousin In Milwaukee

Let 'Em Eat Cake (1933)
Mine

Porgy And Bess (1935)
Summertime
I Got Plenty O' Nuttin'
It Ain't Necessarily So
Bess, You Is My Woman Now
There's A Boat That's Leavin' Soon For New York
I Loves You Porgy

Shall We Dance (1936) (film)
They Can't Take That Away From Me
Let's Call The Whole Thing Off
I've Got Beginner's Luck
They All Laughed

Damsel In Distress (1937) (film)
A Foggy Day
Nice Work If You Can Get It

Goldwyn Follies (1938) (film)
Love Walked In
I Was Doing All Right
Love Is Here To Stay

The Shocking Miss Pilgrim (1947) (posthumous film score)
For You, For Me, For Evermore
Changing My Tune

COLE PORTER

Greenwich Village Follies (1924)
I'm In Love Again

Paris (1928)
Let's Do It, Let's Fall In Love

Fifty Million Frenchmen (1929)
You Do Something To Me
You've Got That Thing

Wake Up And Dream (1929)
What Is This Thing Called Love

The New Yorkers (1930)
Love For Sale

The Gay Divorcee (1932)
Night And Day

Nymph Errant (1933)
Experiment
Solomon

Anything Goes (1934)
Anything Goes
I Get A Kick Out Of You
All Through The Night
Blow, Gabriel, Blow

Jubilee (1935)
Begin The Beguine
Just One Of Those Things

Red, Hot, And Blue (1936)
It's Delovely
Ridin' High

Born To Dance (1936) (film)
Easy To Love
I've Got You Under My Skin

Rosalie (1937) (film)
Rosalie
In The Still Of The Night

You Never Know (1938)
At Long Last Love

Leave It To Me (1938)
My Heart Belongs To Daddy
Get Out Of Town

Dubarry Was A Lady (1939)
Friendship

Broadway Melody (1940)
I Concentrate On You

You'll Never Get Rich (1941)
Dream Dancing

Let's Face It (1941)
Ev'rything I Love

Something To Shout About (1943)
You'd Be So Nice To Come Home To

Mexican Hayride (1944)
I Love You

Seven Lively Arts (1944)
Ev'rytime We Say Goodbye

Hollywood Canteen (1944) (film)
Don't Fence Me In

The Pirate (1948) (film)
Be A Clown

Kiss Me Kate (1948)
So In Love
Always True To You In My Fashion (I'm)
Why Can't You Behave?
Wunderbar
Were Thine That Special Face
Another Op'nin', Another Show

Out Of This World (1950)
Use Your Imagination
I Am Loved
Where, Oh Where
From This Moment On

Can-Can (1953)
I Love Paris
C'est Magnifique
It's All Right With Me

Silk Stockings (1955)
All Of You

High Society (1956) (film)
True Love
I Love You, Samantha
You're Sensational

There have been three Gershwin revivals in the past decade: My One And Only, which recycled older material; Oh Kay!, based on the early show but with additional songs from other Gershwin shows; and Crazy For You, based on Girl Crazy, with additional songs from other shows.

There are numerous books on Broadway musicals. A convenient handbook for all categories of songs is known as The Standard Dance Music Guide, published by Ray deVita, 5843 218th St., Bayside, NY 11364.

Throughout my original compilation of Songs Every Professional Musician Should Know, I obtained valuable advice from my bass-playing colleague, Dick Romoff, who knows them all.

JAZZ PARTY TUNES AND OTHER BASIC TENDENCIES

By 1985 things had begun to turn around. Standard tunes have been back in fashion for a while now, to a greater extent than I could foresee. The first big change was when the remarkable sales and airplay of Linda Ronstadt's album *What's New* made a significant impact in what Billboard and the other trade magazines refer to as MOR — middle-of-the-road pop. The tunes Ronstadt sang, in addition to Bob Haggart's title song, were these:

Crazy He Calls Me
A Ghost Of A Chance
Goodbye
I Guess I'll Hang My Tears Out To Dry
I've Got A Crush On You
Lover Man
Someone To Watch Over Me
What'll I Do?

Successful record sales always call for a follow-up, and Linda Ronstadt presently had a second album of standards on the charts. This new bouquet of oldies was arranged once more by Nelson Riddle, who in decades past wrote many of the memorable Frank Sinatra backgrounds. Billy Strayhorn's song "Lush Life" provided the title for the album. The rest of the collection looked like this:

Can't We Be Friends?
Falling In Love Again
I'm A Fool To Want You
It Never Entered My Mind
Mean To Me
My Old Flame
Skylark
Sophisticated Lady
When I Fall In Love
You Took Advantage Of Me

Jazz instrumentalists, too, sensed the change in the wind. In Wynton Marsalis' *Hot House Flowers* we heard, in addition to John Lewis' "Django," the following tried and true oldies:

For All We Know
I'm Confessin' That I Love You
Lazy Afternoon
Star Dust
When You Wish Upon A Star

Later in 1985 I played in the annual jazz festival held in Midland, Texas. In this weekend event the style was mainstream. There was an emphasis on swing-to-bop, and a smaller percentage of traditional Dixieland playing. The musicians were trumpeters Clark Terry, Warren Vache, and Jack Sheldon, saxophonists Scott Hamilton, Jim Galloway, Chris Woods, and Flip Phillips, trombonists Urbie Green, Dan Barrett, and Carl Fontana, clarinetists Phil Bodner and Abe Most, bassists Milt Hinton, Brian Torff, and Jack Lesberg, guitarist Cal Collins, drummers Mousey Alexander, Gus Johnson, and Butch Miles, and pianists Ralph Sutton, Derek Smith, and myself.

I kept track of the tunes performed by groups or soloists I played with, as well as those I heard in other sets. Those listed below are a fair sample of what was required. Following some of the titles I've noted certain standards which have the same chord changes.

There were a few additional untitled bop ensemble lines which the horn players hastily identified for the rhythm section simply as "blues" or "I Got Rhythm." That is, we lay down the well-known changes while they play some special unison melodic line.

The Midland affair was typical of mainstream events which take place frequently throughout the year at various locations. Since my 1985 observations, the repertoire has not changed noticeably. There are also many occasions which favor Dixieland and assume a familiarity with the march-like routines of such warhorses as "That's A-Plenty," "At The Jazz Band Ball," "Jazz Me Blues," and "Muskrat Ramble."

Following are the tunes played at Midland. The list would be about the same for the present time.

After You've Gone
Ain't Misbehavin'
Alexander's Ragtime Band
Always
Autumn Leaves
The Best Thing For You Is Me
Billy's Bounce (blues)
Black And Blue
Black Orpheus (Theme From)
Blue Lou
Blue Skies
Broadway
Cielito Lindo
Come Sunday
Cottage For Sale
Cottontail (I Got Rhythm)
A Day In The Life Of A Fool
Do You Know What It Means To Miss New Orleans?
Don't Get Around Much Anymore
Fine And Dandy
The Flintstones Theme
For All We Know
Georgia On My Mind
Get Happy
God Bless The Child
Groovin' High (Whispering)
I Got It Bad
I Want A Little Girl
I Want To Be Happy
I'm Getting Sentimental Over You
I'm Through With Love
In A Mellow Tone (Rose Room)
It's You Or No One
I've Grown Accustomed To Her Face
Jumpin' At The Woodside (bridge: Honeysuckle Rose)
Jumpin' With Symphony Sid (blues)
Just Friends
Just The Way You Look Tonight
Keepin' Out Of Mischief Now
Lemon Drop (I Got Rhythm)

Lester Leaps In (I Got Rhythm)
Limehouse Blues
Look For The Silver Lining
Love For Sale
Lullaby Of The Leaves
Mood Indigo
Moten Swing (You're Driving Me Crazy)
Nagasaki
Oh! Lady Be Good
Old Fashioned Love
Old Folks
On The Trail
Perdido (bridge: I Got Rhythm)
Robbin's Nest
Rosetta
Royal Garden Blues
St. Thomas
Satin Doll
The Sheik Of Araby
Shine
Smoke Gets In Your Eyes
The Song Is Over
'Sposin'
Stars Fell On Alabama
Stompin' At The Savoy
Sunday
Sweet And Lovely
Sweet Georgia Brown
Sweet Sue
Symphony
Take The 'A' Train
The Theme (blues)
There'll Never Be Another You
These Foolish Things
Time After Time
Time On My Hands
What Kind Of Fool Am I?
When You're Smiling
Where Or When

PART IV

ORIGINALS AND ARRANGEMENTS

Two Little Stride Arrangements

*(in the manner of James P. Johnson, Fats Waller,
Donald Lambert, and Willie The Lion Smith)*

1. Swanee River

STEPHEN FOSTER
ARRANGED BY DICK HYMAN

2. Deck The Halls

TRADITIONAL
ARRANGED BY DICK HYMAN

Baby Boom

Dick Hyman

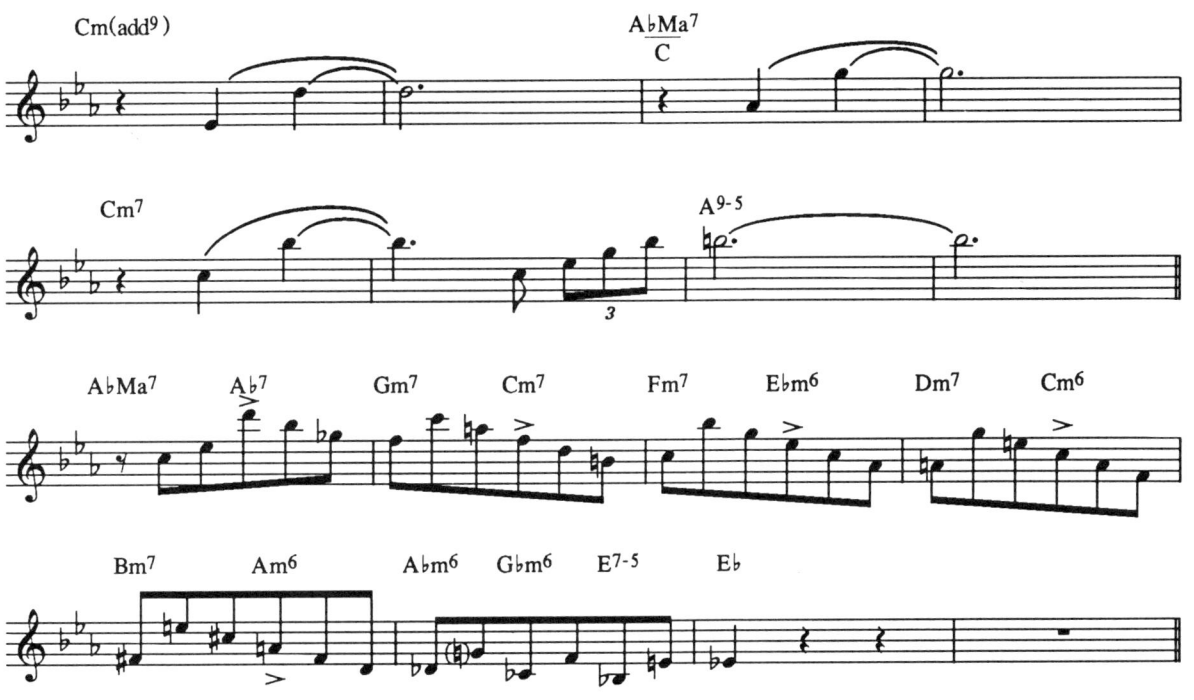

Optional intro and interlude

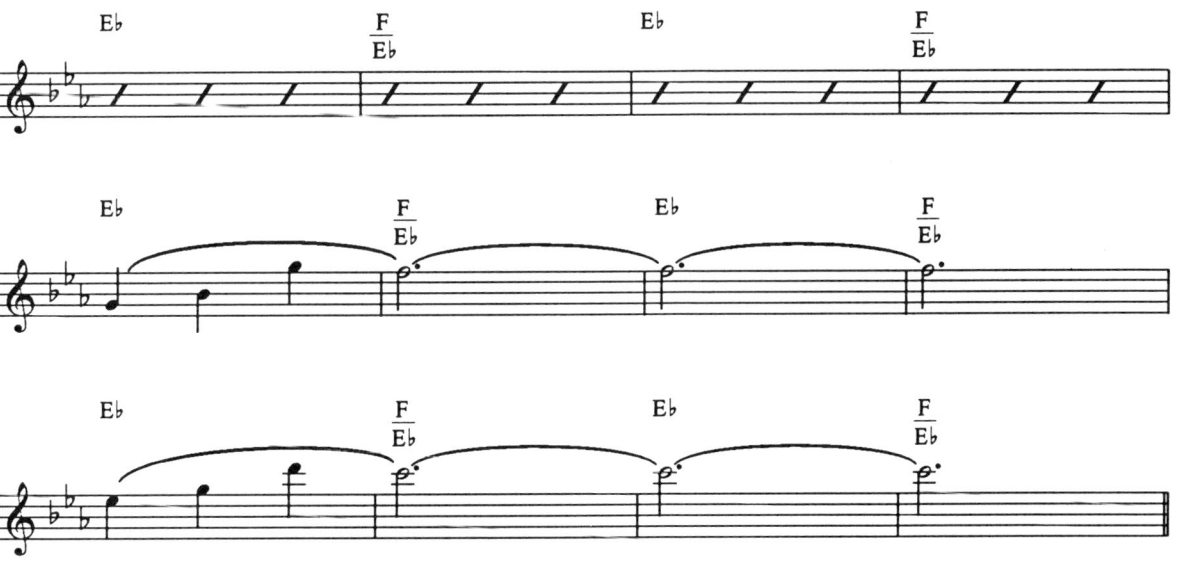

Londonderry Air

(Danny Boy)

TRADITIONAL MELODY
ARRANGED BY DICK HYMAN

Slowly and legato

* Bring out melody

Theme From The Purple Rose Of Cairo

(Cecilia's Theme)

Dick Hyman

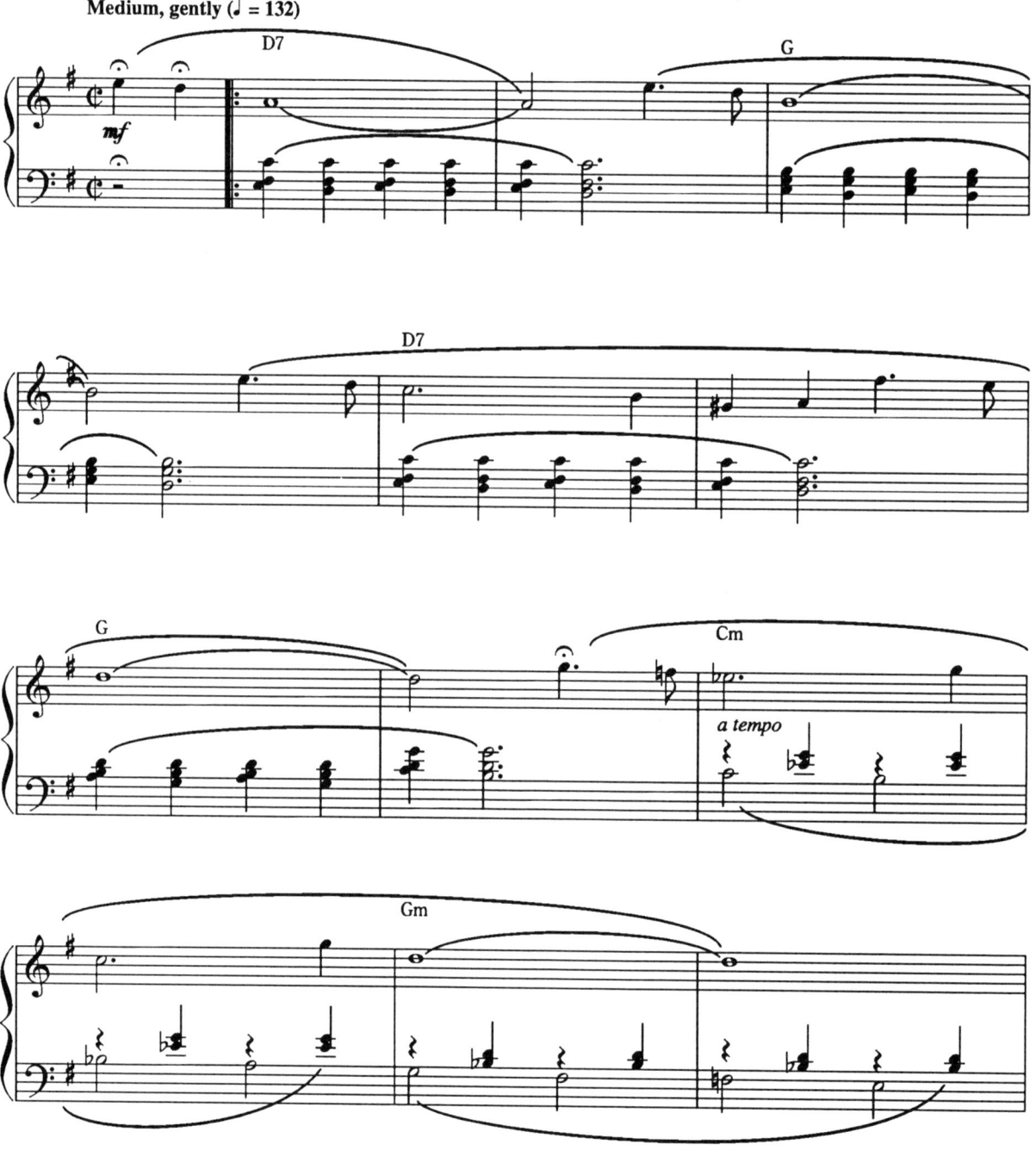

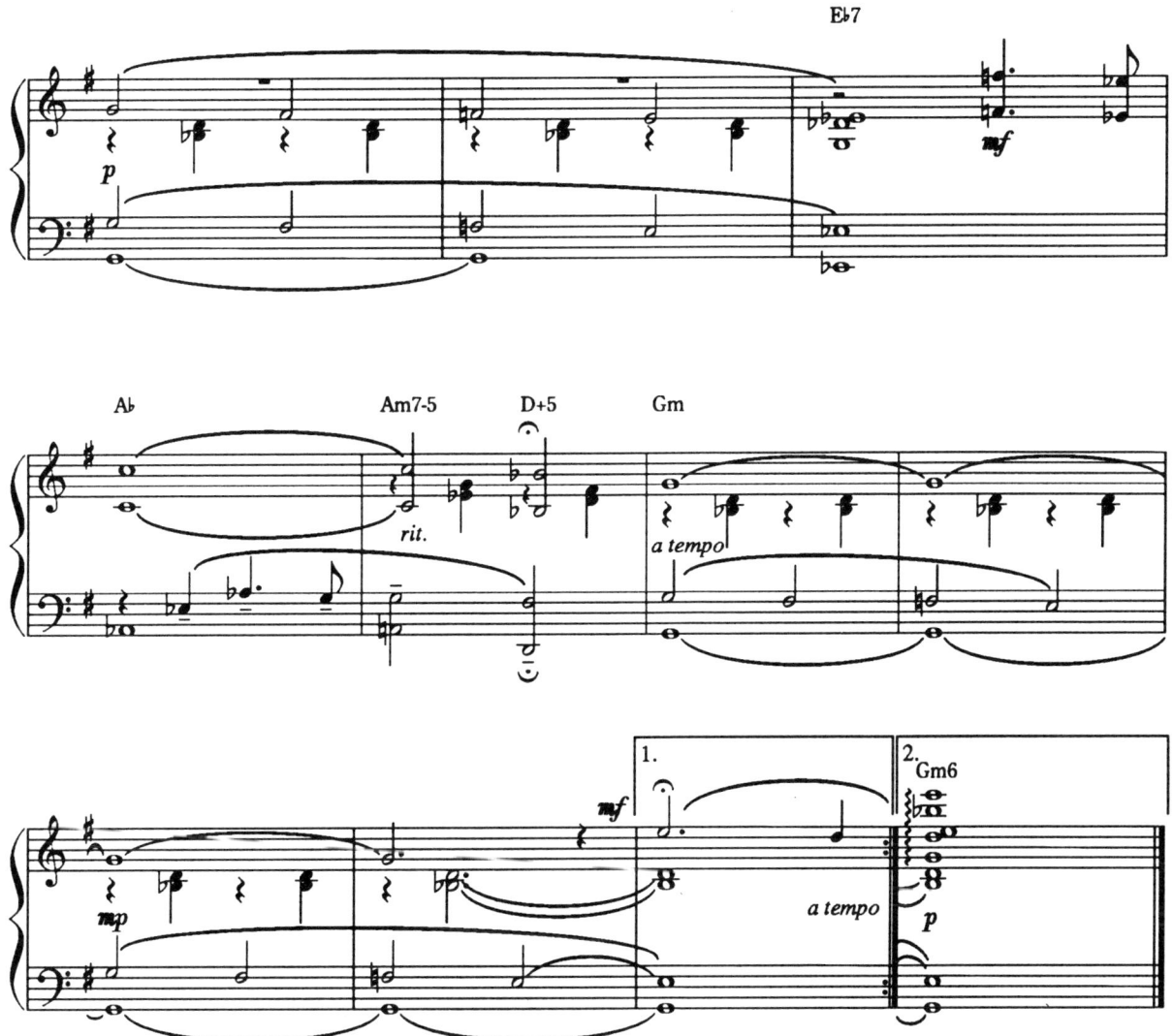

One Day At A Time

from *The Purple Rose Of Cairo*

WORDS AND MUSIC
DICK HYMAN

So let's not speak of love sub - lime, be-cause time brings on a

break - up. There'll be no tears and no e -

mo - tion - al scenes to spoil my make - up.

And when the end comes, I'll take up the slack,

Un - til you call and say you want to come back.

Till then I'm wait - ing, do - mes - ti - cat - ing, ev - 'ry

Sun - day, Mon - day, One Day At A Time!

Let's take it One Day At A Time.

Let's take it One Day At A Time.

Carousel Memories
from The Purple Rose Of Cairo

DICK HYMAN

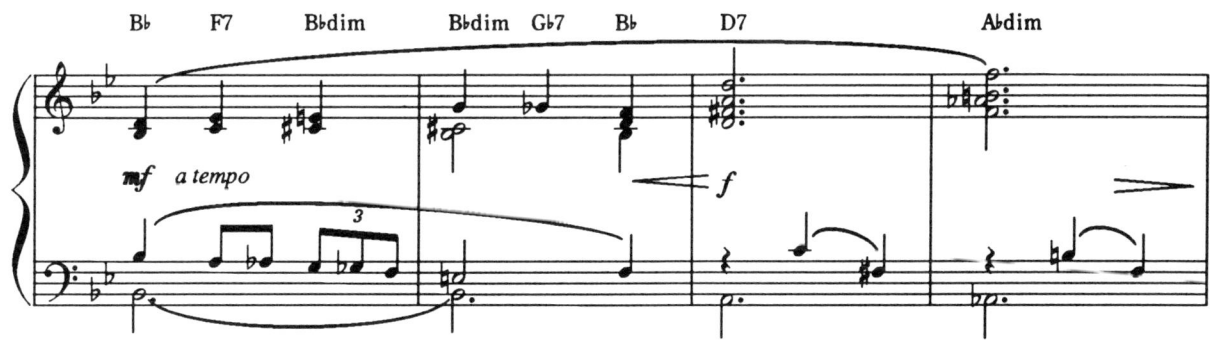

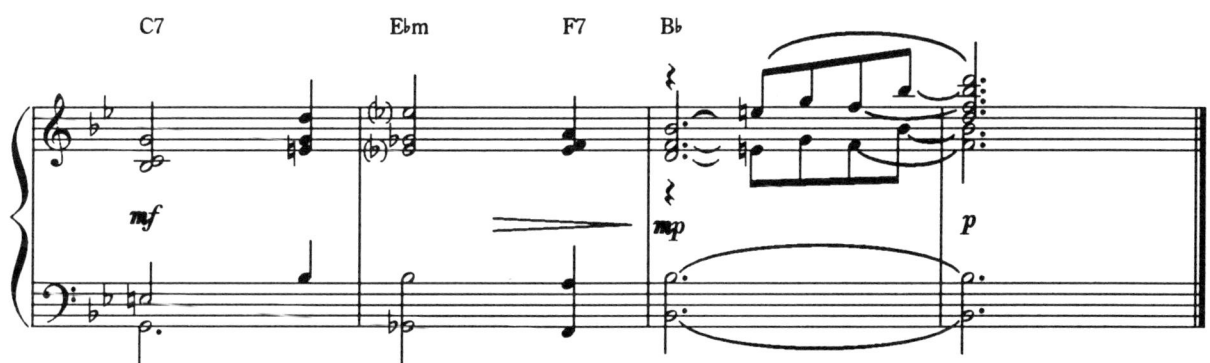

Get Regular With Re-Lax!

from Radio Days

WORDS AND MUSIC
DICK HYMAN

Rainy Day Romance
(Theme From The Lemon Sisters)

DICK HYMAN

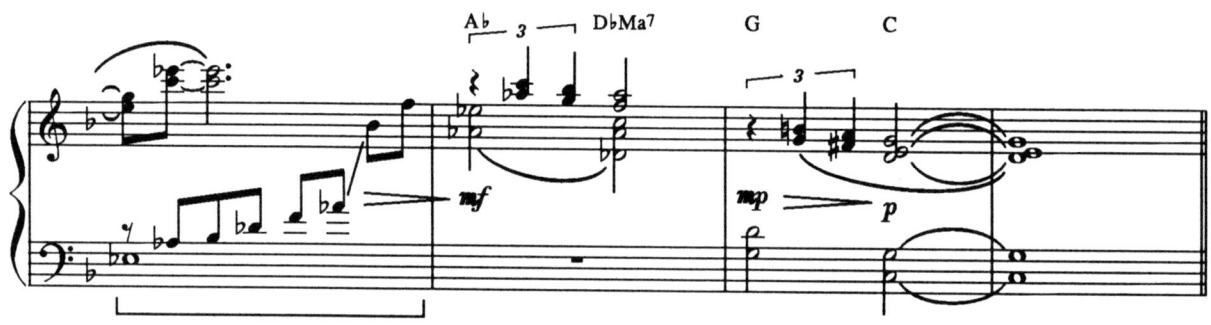

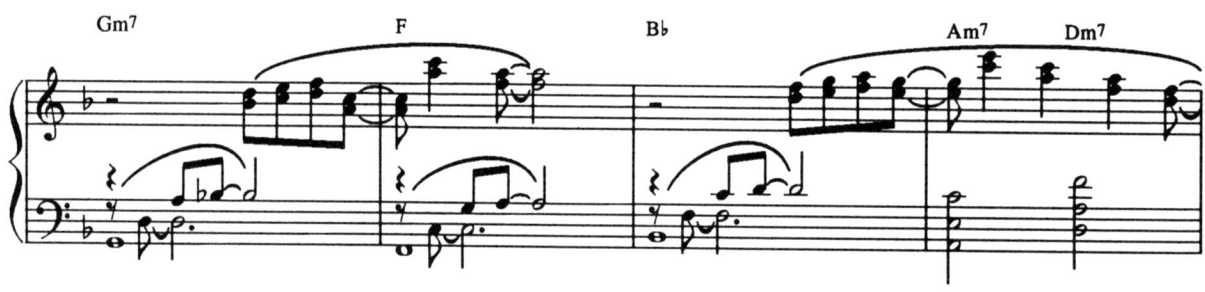

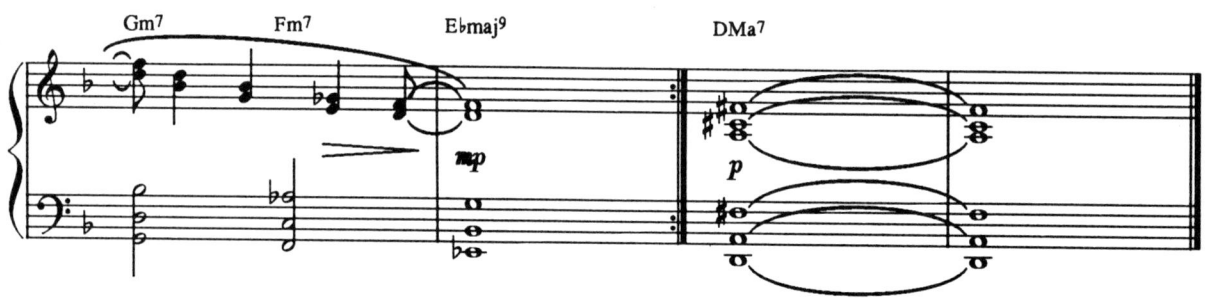

Theme From Alan And Naomi

DICK HYMAN

Also from Dick Hyman . . .

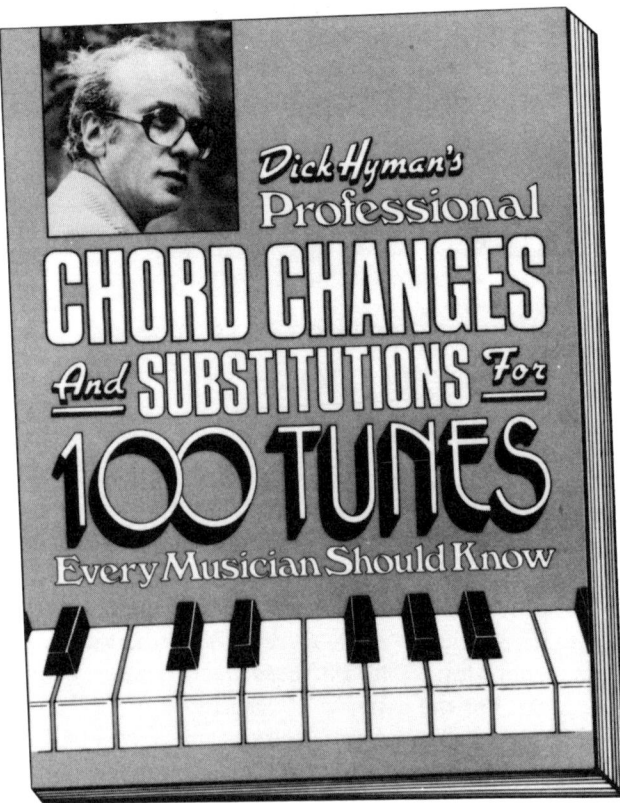